Prosper Up!

To Frankie Boy!
Live long and Prosper!

Your terns friend,

Gary Anderson

Prosper Up!

Learning How to Become Prosperous Today:
An Owner's Manual

FIRST EDITION

Larry Snow

Print information available on the last page.

Rev. date: 05/18/2017

To order additional copies of this book, contact:
Xlibris
1-888-795-4274
www.Xlibris.com
Orders@Xlibris.com
699254

Contents

REPRODUCTION

INTRODUCTION

Many people over the years have urged me to write a book on how I was able to achieve the high level of prodigious prosperity that my wife and I currently enjoy. Many of them told me that I have an obligation to write it. They felt that it was important that I record my personal perspective on the way that it was done, in my own words, that could be possibly used by others to achieve a similar success.

This is not an exhaustive account of my life or career. Instead, I have told the story of many of the life, career, and business opportunities that I took advantage of as well as some of the failures that I experienced along the way on my prosperity journey. It also focuses on the most important part of the story: the process and formula that was used to do it. All the issues are not revealed as the book flows from foundational point to foundational point and not chronologically.

My goals in writing this book are twofold. First, I hope to paint a picture of what it was like to go from virtually nothing (except desire) to a high level of prosperity and through the various stages that were involved in doing being able to achieve the results. There has been a sufficient period now to see how the process effectively worked in many instances and how some of them needed to be adjusted along the way or perhaps even failed to produce the necessary results. My hope is that this book will serve as a resource for anyone studying how to accomplish it and the many methods used in doing so.

Second, I wrote it to give readers a perspective on the necessary aspect of motivation in a highly complex and fast-moving world today that leaves little time for procrastination and penalizes those who do not have the discipline and commitment to follow the process. Many of the prosperity decisions that were made in my life were tough calls, and I had to carefully weigh many of them to make the result something that I was proud of as well as significant. I hope that this will give you, the reader, a better sense of how and why each of the steps in building your own level of prosperity is necessary and be able to clear the way to be able to isolate and identify your own opportunities and challenges that you will face and that it will prove useful as you make your own choices in your prosperity life.

Finally, in the following pages, you will find many of the secrets, strategies, and techniques that many highly prosperous people have used for many years in slowly building their personal prosperity. I have done my best to chronicle the choices that I got right, those that I got wrong, and many of the options to be able to do it differently. Thanks for purchasing it, and I wish you sincerest best wishes in achieving your own high level of prosperity in life.

Larry Snow, Author

A Unique View of Prosperity

True prosperity in life is the virtual tipping point where individuals transition from the receiving (it's all about me attitude) to one of developing and implementing the art of giving—time, talent, energy, and financial resources—to others, which ultimately creates a view and attitude that establishes true joy and happiness within each of us, which demonstrates its effects on others for their benefit.

—L. S.

Prosperity Wisdom

All the words of my mouth are righteous;
There is nothing twisted or crooked in them.
They are all straight to him who understands
And right to those who find knowledge.
Take in my instruction instead of silver,
And knowledge rather than choice gold;
For wisdom is better than jewels,
And all that you may desire cannot compare with her.

—Proverbs 8:8–11

A Sound Prosperity Formula Revealed

When you come to know that you have enough, you will be prosperous.

—L. S.

True Prosperity

*Happy is the man who finds wisdom and the man, who gets
understanding,
For the gain from it is better than gain from silver, and the profits
better than gold.
She is more precious than jewels, and nothing that you desire can
compare with her.
Long life is in her left hand; In her right hand are riches and honor.
Her ways are ways of pleasantness, and all her paths are peace.
She is the tree of life to those who lay hold of her;
Those who hold her fast are called happy.*
—Proverbs 3:13–18

Why This Book Is so Unique

There are lots of self-help books available today in wealth building, yet the majority of those who write these books probably have not achieved much of it in their lives. They may understand the theories and concepts that are needed to do it but may not know or even want to embrace the risk necessary to implement and gain from those principles involved.

There are even a far less number of books that specialize in prosperity building, a term and process perhaps not even heard of by many today. It might even sound *old-fashioned* for some to even consider it. It is for that very reason that this particular book was written because it has been done by the author, who has *been there and done that*. It is not full of just ideas, notions, and mere thoughts but instead contains many of the commonsense, practical, and street-smart techniques for those individuals who desire a hands-on training guide based on someone's real-life experiences and successes on how to do it.

The author, Larry Snow, has encountered and undergone the same questions, challenges, concerns, apprehensions, doubts, emotions, and feelings of inadequacy and insufficiency that many of you deal with when you encounter change yet desire to try something new. This is a manual that provides easy-to-follow, step-by-step, move-by-move instructions for building a high level of personal prosperity in your life. It will serve to build your personal financial confidence and create better decision-making in the future through its many unique and proven prosperity success strategies.

Its approach is unique for many reasons, including the following:

> *It creates each of the necessary planning and preparation elements.*
> *It explains the entire prosperity-building process, one carefully explained detail at a time.*
> *It provides the proven, practical methods and techniques for anyone to be able to accomplish it.*
> *It is presented in a rational, logical, and organized format for anyone to be able to understand it.*
> *The accompanying workbook contains many checklists, to-do lists, and other useful exercises to personalize the learning for each reader.*

Finally, the message contained between the pages of this book is simple yet will require a degree of effort in seeing its eventual results. Don't be discouraged if you don't see results in a week or two. Often, achieving prosperity success in life is similar to priming a pump, which will take you six months to even a year of painstaking effort to begin seeing the eventual results. The phrase "It's always darkest before the dawn" applies to realizing prosperity improvement in your life, career, and personal finances. The results come about slowly yet will eventually compound itself in the future. I know this because I have walked every step of this road.

Guide to the Use of This Book

I strongly recommend a careful reading and study of each section of this prosperity-building manual. It gives a clear understanding and explanation as well as many useful steps that you can take in establishing personal prosperity-building principles that can be used to achieve success. It also shows you how to create, improve, and maintain them in your life and career.

It is an ideal prosperity-building reference work for our present time. It demonstrates the expertise of over thirty years of study and research work as well as the implementation of each of the steps by the author in building his own effective personal template formula. The workbook contains many practical exercises and custom-created activities that are designed to uniquely personalize the element of prosperity creation to each reader.

In the end, the entire process will take time, yet each phase of the prosperity map is revealed for each reader to be able to accomplish it. This is the purpose of this book. Use it to your long-term personal prosperity-building advantage.

How This Book Is Organized

The topical subjects in this book have been carefully studied, researched, prepared, and organized in the following highly useful format:

A. **EXPLAINING THE PROCESS** – This is the section of the book where the entire concept of prosperity building is revealed and discussed and emphasis given on what the specific details are in the process.

B. **PERSONAL PLANNING AND PREPARATION** – Here is where the specific series of steps are outlined and need to be taken by the reader that will lead to significant growth in their long-term process and needs to take place.

C. **LEARNING THE TECHNIQUES** – This is where many of the tips, techniques, and strategies presented are reviewed and explained, which will assist readers in guiding and directing their growth.

D. **CREATING THE NECESSARY CHANGES** – Creating a personal prosperity plan will require a certain number of changes in your thinking as well as in your habits and behaviors. Nothing positive will occur without changes and improvements taking place.

E. **BUILDING ON YOUR EXISTING SUCCESSES** – Each prosperity plan is uniquely different. It is here that you learn to build *success templates* of each of your personal formulas, including the documentation of many of your success stories for your use and your entire prosperity team.

FOREWORD

This book was created and written for several reasons and purposes by the author. Even though there are lots of self-help and self-improvement books currently available today in the areas of job, career, life instruction, and wealth building, there are few that are written concerning the many compelling ways to achieve ultimate personal prosperity in life. There are fewer still that will actually show you the way to do it. This book will show you exactly how to do that.

As you will see by reading it, many of the technique principles involve discipline and commitment, the foundation for many other successful and worthwhile endeavors in life. Without the application of these core principles, most programs will not succeed and cannot be achieved. This book is written in an easy-to-read-and-follow format through a series of carefully chosen impact subjects, topics, and key learning points. They are each designed to help you think about how they affect you and your personal prosperity building. As you will see, many of them involve making several fundamental adjustments in your life and career and describe the reasons for the needed changes. They also illustrate how the needed changes will directly affect you in the pursuit of prosperity achievement.

In the end, prosperity is not a result. It is a process. In this book, I discuss many of the necessary strategies and techniques that have proven to be significant and effectively used by countless people over the years going back to ancient times who have used them to accomplish their own goals and objectives.

This is your personal book. Feel free to make notes in it to underline important areas of interest, to highlight key points, and to make marginal notes so that you can refer to them in the future. By doing this, you will *personalize* it for your future use and be able to use it as your personal instruction manual to keep chipping away and stay on track in your own efforts.

Congratulations for choosing an effective prosperity path and good luck in taking on this important step in building your personal plan!

AUTHOR'S NOTES

The lessons told in this writing, are the result of true stories about the writer/creator/developer and are used to benefit each of the student participants throughout the teaching and training process. The other people that have played a role in this, are drawn from composites that I have known over the years and that I have worked with in the past.

The opinions expressed in this writing are entirely those of the writer/author.

The writing does not address all individual and specific personal finance situations nor is it intended to be used as financial advice. It is intended, instead, to be used as an educational and informational purpose only and specific individual situations should be handled by a qualified professional expert.

It is not the intent of the author/writer to offer tax advice as there are too many specific personal situations that cannot be covered in this writing. A qualified tax advisor or planner should be consulted.

It is likewise not the intent of this author/writer to give estate planning advice since this, also varies with specific individual situations and you are encouraged to seek a professional expert concerning your personal situation.

ACKNOWLEDGMENTS

I acknowledge that it takes more than one person to be able to successfully accomplish the task of writing a book. This project would not have been possible without the active support of the following people:

First, I would like to thank my wife, Kim, for sharing the lengthy prosperity journey with me in our personal and professional lives over the past fifteen years. I appreciate her for expanding my existing knowledge of personal finance, resourcefulness, and ongoing efforts to improve our sense of joy and happiness in our lives together. She has continued to suggest and advise me in many new subjects and areas and is my own best critic, supporter, and advisor. I want to thank her for supporting me through many difficult times in our lives together. Her help, love, and devotion continue to be a source of daily strength and encouragement to me and my work.

I also wish to thank each of my three sons–Andy, Aaron, and Russell– who are pursuing their own prosperity in different areas of the United States now. I also wish to express my appreciation to my father and mother, both now deceased, for their loving efforts to raise a family of five children in rural South Central Michigan during the 1950s and 1960s. I wish to thank all my brothers, sisters, nieces, nephews, and other relatives and friends in the Nashville-Vermontville, Michigan, area who have helped shape and mold my lifelong condition that has enabled me to overcome the obstacles, hurdles, and setbacks that have occurred along the way.

I wish to thank Dr. Ronald Manahan, former president of Grace College in Winona Lake, Indiana, who has encouraged me every step of the way and who has opened many doors for me at The Prosperity Success Institute™ that Kim and I founded in Gold Canyon, Arizona, in 2006, including an active entrepreneurial teaching program known as ECIP (Entrepreneurial Candidate Initiate Program), where students come to our learning center from all parts of the United States to engage in the fundamentals of reality private business building.

I wish to thank all the participants past and present who have attended my classes, courses, workshops, and seminars over the years at the educational entrepreneurial business that I started in 2005 called The Prosperity Success Institute™. They have each personally shared their unique success stories and their struggles, and each has offered their encouragement to me to write this book. Their feedback has greatly assisted me in developing this important and ever-present reality of the relationship of people and their many human personalities, needs, and determinations when it comes to something as personal as their prosperity.

I wish to thank my success coach, business coach, and mentoring clients who have sought my assistance and instruction and who have graciously trusted my advice and guidance in their prosperity and business success over the years.

Finally, I wish to thank our staff for their work and assistance in developing and bringing to press this book you have in your hands. Thank you one and all!

How I Was Able to Become a Prodigious Prosperity Achiever in My Life and How You Can Do It Too!

1. *I developed a solid work ethic and a good understanding of personal finance awareness when I was growing up in rural South Central Michigan.*

2. *I identified my long-term life career work at an early age (early twenties) and chose something that I really enjoyed doing as well as one that produced good annual income in many forms.*

3. *I created a formal life plan and educated myself in my career development to be able to act on it. I worked for several companies in various capacities as an employee to learn and become aware of how they operated both inside and out.*

4. *I took the risk of starting my own logistics business (trucking, warehousing, equipment) at age thirty and never looked back. I became a big fish in a small pond in the Northern Indiana community of Elkhart, which has produced many other prosperous individuals.*

5. *I generated substantial investments in developing the business enterprise and at the same time purchased huge commercial properties and renovated them while leasing them out to other businesses.*

6. *I carefully prepared for an early retirement and a second (encore) career to teach, train, and guide others how to do it too.*

An Overview

We are living today through one of the toughest economic times that the world has witnessed in modern history. The essence of the very future of our hopes, dreams, and aspirations has a lot to do with creating a defined personal prosperity formula that can be used to develop, fine-tune, and implement your individual future prosperity success. In the book *How to Become Prosperous Today*, the author takes the reader through a series of various critical steps needed to achieve a higher level of personal prosperity that includes much more than mere income and wealth building. This book is a study in learning how individuals from many walks of life, ages, and backgrounds can create an unparalleled degree of personal achievement in their job, career, business, and personal life that includes a proportionate balance of joy and happiness as well as personal economics. Education in personal finance is at the very core of this prosperity message, which is something that the author feels is simply not taught in schools today and feels that it's now time to make those corrections.

Learning how to improve oneself requires the age-old process of transformation. This process involves making changes in one's life and personal use and views of money while creating *a conversion from poverty thinking to prosperity thinking*. It also includes discovering one's individual money personality and learning how to create increased value in personal buying decisions. These money decisions affect buying groceries at the market, making the decision to lease or purchase a vehicle, learning the best strategy that can be used in purchasing and mortgaging a house, and discovering how to get starting in long-term retirement planning at a young age by investing a small amount of money on a regular basis over a period of years. The book covers many important aspects that people overlook in designing, or failing to design, their future prosperity plans. It reveals just how important it is to keep an eye on personal indebtedness and to regularly monitor personal credit scores to ensure that you are always getting the very best deals on consumer loans while protecting your personal credit reputation. The book details how to avoid purchasing depreciating assets, such as brand-new vehicles, which lose well over 50 percent of their value in the first twenty-four months, along with many of the methods that can be used in creating and maintaining a monthly spending plan (aka family budget) so that you are always living within your income(s) and expenses.

The reader is guided through many useful quizzes, exercises, and illustrations throughout the book that reveal not only what must be done to improve the direction of their growth but also exactly how to go about creating those needed changes. This is done so that each new step logically builds on the previous one over a period. It demonstrates how the reader can begin to experience significantly improved monetary results via their enhanced discretionary earnings. These new earnings can be utilized to fund increased level of prosperity building within a relatively short period. The book dispels many myths that have been used by various promoters that lure consumers into the "I just gotta have it!" mind-set while carefully identifying many of the practical gauges and measurements that can be used to calculate exactly how much those consumer goods and services actually cost. It also carefully reveals how to distinguish between emotional needs and wants. Chapter after chapter, it helps create many of the needed ratios in areas of personal spending. Finally, it deals specifically with expenses like insurance, investing, and passive income creation in everyday language that anyone can understand and comprehend. Instead of complex theories, theoretical concepts, and abstract thinking, it is based on solid reality that speaks to each reader. *In the end, this book is a guide to a venerable prosperity-building life that can be achieved by following the guidance of someone who has done it himself and is highly motivated to show others how they can do it too with a combination of education, discipline, and commitment.*

BOOKS AND OTHER WRITTEN MATERIALS

LARRY SNOW

<< Each of the Following Are Part of the Unique
Overall Prosperity Success Series >>

BOOK – *Prosper Up!*
<< BUILDING YOUR PERSONAL PROSPERITY
PLAN: An Owner's Manual >>
Key Principles in Building Individual Prosperity in the Twenty-First Century

BOOK – *ENTREPRENEURIAL INGENUITY*
A Primer on How to Successfully Start and Manage a Small Business Enterprise

BOOK – *GETTING STARTED IN LIFE: The Millennium Generation*
Prosperity Building Designed for Late Teens and Twentysomethings

BOOK – *BOOMER GENERATION PROSPERITY*
Finding out Exactly Where You Are and Where You Need to Be in Your Prosperity Plan

SkillUse® GUIDEBOOKS
*A Unique Set of Various Educational Textbooks Dealing with Each Area of
Personal Finance, Entrepreneurism, Job/Career Success, and R. E. Investing*

SkillUse® WORKBOOKS

Custom-Created Books That Accompany and Are Used with SkillUse® Guidebooks

PIQUE® and Other Custom-Created Prosperity Testing and Examinations

A One-of-a-Kind Series of Useful Measurements to Determine Your
Personal Prosperity Knowledge and Areas Needing Improvement

ProsperiScore®
An Original Formula Designed to Estimate and Access
Your Current Level of Prosperity Achievement

ProsperiPlan® - Your Lifetime Prosperity Guide
A Lifelong Plan to Navigate Your Prosperity Vision and Future

THE PROSPERITY MANIFESTO
A Detailed Narrative Discussion of the Challenges
in Creating Personal Prosperity Today

THE PROSPERITY GAZETTE™
A Bimonthly Electronic and Hardcopy Newsletter Covering
All Current Prosperity-Building Issues

ACADEMIC JOURNALS
Specific Articles Covering Many of the Various Aspects of Success Building

Chapter 1

Understanding the Circle of Competence Prosperity Concept

The Circle of Competence© Prosperity Concept is a teaching and training that covers virtually all aspects of personal prosperity growth and development, which include income, savings, and investing. In addition, it also covers much of the personal finance education that is important to know and understand to create, build, maintain, and preserve personal prosperity in your life.

In this chapter, you will learn about the following:

- *Finding What You're Ultimately Looking For*
- *The Founding of Your Personal Prosperity*
- *Many Personal Problems Are Often Really About Finances*
- *Explanation of the Circle of Competence© Prosperity Concept Along with Illustrative Chart*
- *Your Personal "Self-Contained" Prosperity Plan and Practical Exercise*
- *Creating Your Unique Personal Prosperity Plan*

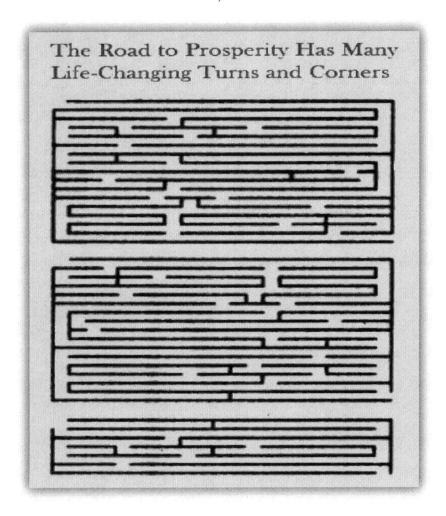

Meeting at the "Corner"

Have you ever looked at your life as a series of corners? The fact is that you don't often pursue life in a straight line. Instead, things often happen that take you in a zigzag pattern and in a completely different course as you turn each corner in your life. Each of you has corners, and they are as different as your individual personality.

When you finish school, you turn a corner. When you get married, you turn another corner. When you become a parent, you turn a big corner. When you change jobs, you turn a corner. Buying a home is a corner, so is moving to a new neighborhood, getting a divorce, and losing a loved one through death. There are lots of these corners in life, and the reality is that you never really know what's waiting for you around the next corner of your growth and development.

Prosperity building has its own unique share of cornering challenges. This list can include such items as income creation, investing, personal debt, retirement planning, building personal assets, and even creating an overall effective prosperity plan and are all corners that need to be navigated through to achieve the most desired results over the long term.

So how do you go about dealing with these "corners" both small and large? What process can you use to overcome each of them and get through them? One of the keys to this process is through the use of preparation and planning achieved with the right type of learning and instruction that can help you to better understand what to do or even what not to do when you reach a certain "corner" of your life.

By having a method of confronting these "corner challenges," you will be able to handle each of them through an effective strategy that will enable you to survive (and maybe even thrive) through each corner in your life.

What Exactly Is the Prosperity Condition?

According to *Merriam-Webster's Dictionary*, prosperity is an advancement or gain in anything that is good or desirable, a successful progress toward, or the attainment of a desired object. It is not, however, the same definition for any two people because of the factor of relevance. It is not in the possession of "things" or "stuff" but in the inexhaustible inventory of all that is desirable in life.

It is the right of everyone to become prosperous. It has a lot to do with your thinking attitude. It has a lot more to do with putting thoughts and ideas into the right relationships that develop what many call a prosperity consciousness, an awareness of the many opportunities that can be selected to achieve it. True prosperity is derived from a combination of creativity, ideas, imagination, hard work, and self-confidence. When combined, they create the necessary environment for prosperity building in each of you.

Those who lack these traits or are unwilling to develop them may come into a level of financial means but will eventually always part from it. It is not a crime to be rich any more than it is a virtue to be poor. The crime is when people don't put their money or capital resources to work for others who may need it.

None of this occurs without effort, however, or without imagining it first in your mind. Once all the elements are combined, it is a relatively easy process to transfer it from your mind to a prosperity document to reality and then to actuality. You can receive these mental pictures from a variety of sources to have all the necessary ingredients as well as an understanding of how to use each of them.

Prosperity is first built from the inside long before there is external substance. There are prosperity opportunities everywhere. You just have to be wise enough to identify and seize them through the necessary preparation and planning. It also comes from not being dependent on others for your prosperity success. It is *your* responsibility because *you* are the one who will eventually benefit from it if you create an effective prosperity formula paradigm to follow.

A Unique Way to Look at Prosperity

One of the most wealthy and financially successful people in the Old Testament was King Solomon, who was the literal personification of prosperity. However, it was not riches that he asked God for; it was wisdom and ideas as written in the Bible. He received the ideas and then gained the wisdom and then developed them himself into prosperity. Because he was so wise, people came to him, seeking his wisdom; and this, in turn, brought him vast wealth in exchange for his wisdom. He is, to this day, the venerable symbol of prosperity in ancient life.

Perhaps for this reason, instead of seeking substance to achieve prosperity in your life, maybe you should seek wisdom, imagination, and ideas so that you can create it yourself. With this, you can build an enduring structure of true prosperity within your life. It is wisdom that ultimately creates the fundamental block of prosperity building and not merely money or wealth. If properly applied, the other material substances of prosperity can be achieved and with less effort than without it.

Wisdom comes from knowledge, which comes from education. If formulated, it looks like this:

EDUCATION   +   KNOWLEDGE   +
WISDOM   =   PROSPERITY

Developing an Accurate Prosperity Algorithm

Definitions of an Algorithm:

1. *Any systematic method of solving a certain kind of mathematical problem*
2. *A set of instructions with a limited number of steps for solving a problem*

Learning to spot potentially successful prosperity achievers in advance can be a combination of both art and science since no two prosperity achievers are exactly alike. It can also be a huge factor in determining the likelihood of accomplishing it by future prosperity seekers. However, to do it successfully requires a two-step process:

1. *Creating a unique prosperity algorithm based on many of the unique prosperity habits and behavior qualifiers that set PAs (prosperity achievers) apart from the general population.*
2. *After creating the formula, fine-tuning it by using the data gathered to identify and assist other prosperity seekers in the methods used in achieving it.*

Many of these traits are included in the ProsperiScore© evaluation criteria; yet some of the other ones include such traits as owning rather than renting or leasing your home and vehicles; investing in real estate property and small business enterprises; maintaining a savings rather than a spending attitude; living within your means instead of a paycheck-to-paycheck existence; effectively, constructively creating long-term yields and cash flow income; choosing good partnership and team members; and many, many others.

These personal traits when utilized together with the ability to spot, recognize, and seize meaningful opportunities will quickly begin to add more credibility and power to the prosperity algorithm. Some characteristics are more neutral than others, such as job or career involvement, marital status, leisure-time hobbies, and personal pastimes and interests.

Some of the negative factors that exist in postponing or even eliminating prosperity opportunities include compulsive or addictive habits and behaviors, illegal activities, extravagant lifestyles, and personal character issues. One of the variables that sharpen the prosperity algorithm is the emotions of *discipline* and *commitment*. These specific factors alone can ultimately give the algorithm formula greater predictive power. Those with these two traits, along with each of the others, have been proven to be a highly intensive factor in achieving personal prosperity than many other markers.

Prosperity Wisdom:
If a man empties his purse into his head,
no man can take it away from him.
Our investment in knowledge always pays the best interest.
—Benjamin Franklin

Key Prosperity Learning Lesson:

The secret to successful investing is to never stop increasing the
level of your prosperity education.
Investment ignorance is perhaps the greatest risk of all.
—L. S.

There Are Two Ways to Learn How to Build Prosperity in Your Life

1. The Hard Way

Through a series of miscues, errors, mistakes, misinformation, blunders, omissions, failures, misjudgments, goofs, misconceptions, delusions, overestimations, exaggerations, illusions, misunderstandings, lapses, slips, underestimations, confusion, botches, bungles, deceptions, and slipups.

2. The Easier Way

Through education, learning, teachings, experiences, explanations, interpretations, certainties, studies, guidance, directions, instructions, skills, schooling, techniques, strategies, reading, preparations, planning, information, and cultivation that all eventually create something referred to as W-I-S-D-O-M.

In the End, Which Way Will <u>YOU</u> Choose?

WISDOM

Many receive advice: only the very wise profit from it.

—Cyrus, Ancient Greek philosopher

Why Prosperity-Building Education and Training Is Often Reserved for those Who Are Older *(and Hopefully)* Wiser

Prosperity-teaching education is often reserved for those who have a deep understanding of how it works, who have actually participated in it, who have even practiced it, and who are now imminently qualified to teach it.

This is one of those educational training situations that are somehow much better experienced firsthand to be able to avoid such things as wild-goose chases, treasure hunts, and gold-pot seeking at the end of the rainbow. While difficult undertakings are usually always challenging the first time they are attempted, they do become easier the second and each subsequent time. Because of the nature of the effect, it is always a wise strategy to learn from those who have accomplished and succeeded in prosperity before they can act as your guide to help you achieve your unique and particular plan.

It must also be remembered that along the way, mistakes are inevitable; and when they do occur, they must first be identified. Errors can even serve as highly useful learning lessons that can continue to direct your individual prosperity building as a source of effective instruction. Without a competent pathfinder, many are destined to a future of trial-and-error, make-do, haphazard wanderings and financial blunders that are the result of omissions, confusions, misinterpretations, and misunderstandings of the long-term prosperity-building process.

Another more pragmatic reason in the choice of older, more senior individuals has to do with the fact that they often have undergone more life experiences, including job, career, spouse, family, business, investing relationships, and even occasional death experiences, and ultimately recognize how finely intertwined prosperity building can be to life itself. The best prosperity trainers also use practical, commonsense, realistic, rational, and sensible approaches rather than emotional, spontaneous, or impulsive ones. After all, it is personal finances that are at stake here, and what could be more important than preserving and increasing your future well-being? Literally, there is no substitute for qualified, competent, skilled, accomplished, well-versed, and savvy prosperity trainers who frequently know many of the right moves to make as well as those that should be avoided at all costs. It is often a consequence of their having learned the best and most accurate methods of achieving the best overall results themselves that make their experience in accomplishing it so compelling and useful.

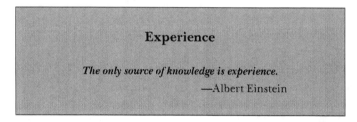

Experience

The only source of knowledge is experience.
—Albert Einstein

Finding What You're Ultimately Looking For

You can usually find what you're looking for if you look in all the right places, don't give up easily, know when and where to look, and especially, if you have a good map and guide to assist you. The same is true with prosperity building. That is why this book was created, to guide you in the process and teach you *exactly* how to do it. Like many good things in life, prosperity doesn't just simply fall in your lap (wouldn't that be nice?!) and does require persistence, determination, discipline, commitment, and desire to get there. With those elements plus a map, compass (this book), and a healthy dose of risk-taking, you are well on your way to creating a formidable personal prosperity-building plan.

This guide will serve as your direction finder in creating and implementing your personal and unique long-term prosperity plan that is like no one else's since no two are exactly alike. Your plan is based on *your* needs and wants, *your* income and expenses, *your* personal dreams and ambitions, and *your* willingness to take the necessary risks to arrive at *your* chosen destination. Many of the important items that we cover in the book could be perceived to be the result of the commonsense, practical, and everyday advice that perhaps was given by our grandparents, parents, former teachers, and others. But how many of us really followed their advice? After leaving home and striking out on our own, how many of us took the time to create such a "prosperity map," much less followed it? Instead, many of us probably followed a trial-and-error, haphazard, and painstaking path of personal financial mistakes, errors, and catastrophes.

As the Familiar Saying Goes: That Was Then . . . This Is Now!

It is now time to create a prosperity plan that can help guide you along your way in life. When people ask me, "Is it difficult?" or "Does it take a lot of money?" or "Will it take a long time to do it?" my answer is always "How large and successful do you want your future prosperity to be?"

It can seem to be complicated at first, just like any new undertaking. It *will* require some initial investment money. **It will** also take a period as well as energy and *will not* be accomplished in just a few weeks or months; yet the end *will always* become a reality that will surprise, amaze, and impress you.

By carefully following each of these steps in the manual, you will achieve a level of personal prosperity that is reserved for only those who are willing to put forth the necessary effort to succeed. In addition, learning and practicing many of the prosperity principles that are detailed, discussed, and explained in the manual will ensure your long-term and continued prosperity in the future.

Is this the only way to develop an effective and useful strategy? Obviously, there are many other methods, yet this is the proven method that has worked successfully for the author, and it was accomplished with a modest amount of capital and a reasonable amount of risk-taking. There are many variations to this template formula too. A greater amount of initial "seed money" can speed the process just like a willingness to take on higher levels of risk (as long as they do not resemble gambling or speculation). However, these are not recommended. Some things in life are meant to be achieved one step at a time or to use another term to be savored. Prosperity building is, in the opinion of the author, one of those types of personal undertakings.

The Founding of Your Personal Prosperity

Here's How it Works . . .

Personal prosperity building is a journey and not an end. You need to understand and remember this concept to succeed in achieving it over the long term. There has been a lot that the author has learned and personally experienced over many years regarding the best way to create prosperity. This is exactly the purpose in writing and developing educational prosperity-building series of instructional materials and this book.

The objective is to teach readers and educational participants the necessary skulls, strategies, and techniques to be able to achieve prosperity successfully themselves. You also must be 100 percent committed to succeed in building and implementing your personal prosperity formula paradigm. The process is not rocket science (although ironically, your prosperity can take off like a rocket ship if closely followed). It doesn't involve calculus, geometry, trigonometry, or other form of higher mathematics. It's not high-level and hard-to-understand global economics. It **is** a practical, commonsense, and everyday disciplined, committed process that virtually anyone can achieve with proper instruction and motivation and for those who are motivated by a personal desire to do better in a job, career, and life.

Personal prosperity *will not* happen by accident. Unless you are willing to make a sincere effort to accomplish it, results will not be achieved. Of this you can be sure. Even if you are among the lucky few who win a lottery, sweepstakes, windfall, or a sizeable inheritance, you may not even be able to hold on to it for very long without learning the necessary skills, strategies, and techniques.

Welcome to founding your personal prosperity building!

Many of Today's Personal Problems Are Often Really All About Finances

Money is how society values things. This is the method that we pay for those things in life that we value and that mean the most to us. We live in a much more complicated world today than what we did twenty-five to thirty years ago. This is especially true when it comes to our personal finances. In prior years, longevity after retirement was a far less period than it is now. Currently, many of us can expect to live for as many years *after retirement* as long as we lived *during* our working years. This alone has completely changed how we look at our long-term financial planning and especially when it's time to begin the necessary process of planning and preparing for retirement.

As a direct result of this, it is important to create a long-term plan for retirement in your post-working life and also for the income that you need to fund it, depending on your lifestyle in future years. In addition, there are many other competing factors and events that will also become increasingly apparent as you reach that period in your life, such as the following:

✓ *Issues with aging parents*
✓ *Education and college funding and also for your children*
✓ *Personal health-care issue and expenses*

✓ *Dependent children that may be living at home*
✓ *Monthly living expenses that arguably might not go down as much as you may think in retirement*

This all boils down to a strong possibility that many people might even have some financial problems that they don't even know about yet, much less have planned for over the years, such as the following:

➢ *Lack of effective long-term financial planning*
➢ *Overcoming bad financial advice and strategies*
➢ *Offsetting ill-suited investments*
➢ *Overcoming improper estimates of needed income production at retirement*
➢ *Creating increasingly higher levels of financial education*
➢ *Rebounding from a bad economic period through no fault of your own*

However, it should also be quickly mentioned that it is not *all* doom and gloom when it comes to repairing and improving your overall personal finances and planning. Often, it is possible to repair damages and to even put together a viable prosperity plan that will achieve good results and even better results over a period. Remember that *you* are the one who is *most affected* by your financial situation, so it makes good sense for *you* to do something to uncover some of the existing problems and issues that affect you.

Unlocking the key to your financial personality is one of the steps that is necessary to do this. This is a compelling exercise that is included in chapter 2 of this book. Another step is to correct any misinformation and misunderstanding that you may currently possess regarding personal finances and prosperity building. Even a modest bit of financial literacy training will serve to help you learn to change your habits and behaviors. This can result in better overall use of each of your money resources. Still, other steps include overcoming previously held beliefs and principles that might be deeply rooted in early childhood through witnessing how your parents handled their money in both positive and negative ways. *There are certain other common problems that are seen today in many people who have desire to build a higher level of personal prosperity that may include the following:*

1. **THOSE WHO DO NOT EASILY UNDERSTAND THE MATH.** Most personal financial mathematics is relatively simple and involves the four basic functions of mathematical arithmetic: addition, subtraction, multiplication, and division. It is, however, made increasingly more difficult as you begin using other financial concepts, such as compounding, ratios, yields, portfolio gains, gross and net earnings, and others. The secret? Taking lots of notes, writing down

personal questions (and the corresponding correct answer), using a preprogrammed software program(s), and/or working with a patient prosperity teacher, advisor, or planner to know and understand how to effectively and efficiently do it. In the end, learn to apply the concepts to your personal finance situation.

2. **THOSE WHO HAVE EXTREME RISK VIEWS.** These extreme views come in two forms: extreme low risk, which often results in minimal rates of return and usually borders on being too conservative or the polar extreme, and high-risk investing, which can be compared to gambling and speculation. Each of these extremes will greatly affect your prosperity results. The optimum is in creating the *balance* that is ultimately needed.

3. **THOSE WHO ARE COMPULSIVE SPENDERS AND HAVE EXCESSIVE DEBT.** This is, sadly, one of the most frequent problems of many people today. It is caused by the abuse of credit cards and consumer loans to fund and supplement personal incomes and is a symptom of a lifestyle that is essentially "living beyond one's means." In some cases, this often becomes a compulsive and addictive behavior and difficult to control.

4. **THOSE WHO HAVE A POVERTY ATTITUDE.** This view is more fully explained in chapter 4. It results in an imposed set of beliefs and values that often are produced by bad economic decisions or poor choices made in the past and a feeling that your personal financial life will never improve or get any better. Furthermore, it is an attitude that your earnings are below your capabilities and are evidenced by frequent struggles with money.

5. **THOSE WHO SQUANDER THEIR WINDFALLS.** Each of us receives windfalls in life. They are not always humongous winnings as the result of lottery, sweepstakes, or casino money consisting of hundreds of thousands or millions of dollars but rather more modest dribs and drabs, such as year-end bonuses, profits from home sales, divorce settlements, sale of assets, inheritances, unexpected rebates, refunds, lawsuit settlements, insurance claims, and other windfalls. Instead of using the majority of this "newfound" money for long-term prosperity building, many use it for consumerism and short-term indulgences and wonder why their investments don't grow faster.

6. **THOSE WHO HAVE AN UNWILLINGNESS TO CHANGE OR IMPROVE.** This is the hardest personal finance situation and one that is all too common. This is realized by the individual who simply is unwilling to change or improve their money management behaviors and habits. It is this group of people that will undoubtedly struggle most with personal prosperity building because they fail to realize that

small adjustments and adaptations in their money management and investing style can often result in large gains down the road.

> ..... Important Self-Analysis .....
>
> It is important now, after studying each of these common financial problems, to do a little self-analysis. Often, we can recognize our shortcomings if we experience them face-to-face.
>
> Are there any of these problems that you feel that you have? If so, what do you feel is the solution? The answer to these questions is usually pretty straightforward and can greatly assist you in your continued prosperity building.

As it has been explained before, it all starts with a
certain level of discipline and commitment.

Understanding the Circle of Competence© Prosperity Concept

Teaching You How to Successfully Become More Prosperous

By the time that many of us enter the working world, we still, unfortunately, lack many of the necessary life, career, and financial skills required to succeed and prosper in our lives. Fast forward ten years or so, home mortgages, vehicle payment, and ever-rising costs of raising a family make it nearly impossible to get ahead, much less even know how to do it.

Jump ahead even further. You enter midlife and start funding luxurious family vacations, buying a larger home, and paying for your kid's college expenses; and we find ourselves dealing with material and "bling" as well as the ever-increasing costs of inflation instead of your retirement nest egg and investment portfolio. In addition to all that, your income does not seem to match your expenses any longer. Guess why.

By the time you have reached your mid- to late fifties, it is clear: you have not done enough of the "cultivating and fertilizing" to be able to begin harvesting your "financial prosperity garden." Instead, it's one that is full of weeds instead of fruit. Enter the **Personal Development Programs®**. This twenty-first-century style of education is proven to be full of the valuable secrets needed to achieve personal prosperity and success. They will significantly and forever change your thinking through a revolutionary concept known as the **Circle of Competence© Prosperity Concept**.

The Circle of Competence Prosperity Concept®

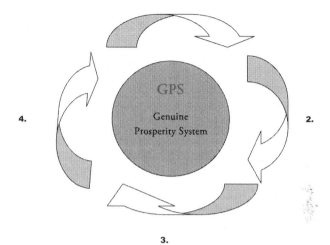

THE FOUR PILLARS OF PROSPERITY ACHIEVEMENT
THAT CREATE *A GENUINE PROSPERITY SYSTEM*

1. **Personal Finance**

2. **Business Entrepreneurism**

3. **Job/Career Success**

4. **Real Estate Investing**

1. **PERSONAL FINANCE** – This is the knowledge and understanding of all the elements of financial literacy, including budgeting, debt, spending, income, and investing and is the essential first step in building a significant prosperity plan. It further includes learning each of the effects of the improper use of money resources. Our money management education can improve your use of financial resources.

2. **BUSINESS ENTREPRENEURISM** – There are only so many ways to build a large income and assets in today's economy, and small business is one of the ways to do this. A business enterprise can become one of the catalysts that can help you create a prosperity rocket ship. Our teaching and training can provide the necessary ingredients to get your business up and running.

3. **JOB AND CAREER SUCCESS** – Even if you have the right technical skills, there is a whole lot more to job and career success than mere talent. You must be able to give your employer value for wages paid. Our training can help you do that so that your career can improve.

4. **REAL ESTATE INVESTING** – Every successful prosperity achiever has a percentage of their investments in income-producing real estate in many categories. There are many opportunities and challenges to overcome in building a large real estate portfolio, and our education can provide the necessary training to accomplish it.

When combined, the total of each of these can take you far in your prosperity-building accomplishments. It is the result of unlocking the secrets to higher levels of personal achievements in your personal prosperity planning and preparation. It is education that we offer and not products or services. What exactly is this? It is a unique, highly focused, and specialized form of education that concentrates on focusing participants on four foundational blocks of personal prosperity that help them accomplish long-term financial goals by teaching and training participants exactly how to do it in a step-by-step process. These are not skills that are taught, like we teach them, anywhere in our existing educational school system—not in high school, not in trade school, not in vocational school, not in college, not in graduate school, and not in business school.

At **The Prosperity Success Institute**™, we teach each of our participants the strategies and techniques necessary to help each of them in achieving a high level of personal prosperity in their lives through each of these areas. It enables them to create a personal prosperity plan that literally will take off like a rocket ship to Mars if followed! Each of the subject areas is separate yet correlate in a highly effective and useful way. They can be used one at a time or combined to create a complete and individual "circle of prosperity competence." In addition, there are three levels of teaching and training available, including basic, intermediate, and advanced, depending on the existing level of knowledge and understanding. Once completed, participants have the tools, the training, the education, and the backup available to take their place on the "prosperity rocket ship."

For more information, you can visit our website at **www.prosperity successinstitute.com**.

Inventing Your Personal Success Style Formula

When closely examining your potential and opportunity for high levels of accomplishment in your prosperity life and career, it is helpful to take a hard look at many of the qualities that compose a successful achiever. The following is designed to help you take a careful look at many of the tried-and-true components that will help you in this process. To which class do you belong?

1. **INITIATIVE TAKER** – Do you need to be *invited* to participate, or do you take the proverbial bull by the horns and jump in as the opportunities occur?

2. **DEFINED PURPOSE** – Are you focused and intense in your pursuit of your goal? Do you have a clear image of what it is that you wish to achieve?

3. **SELF-CONFIDENCE** – Do you believe in yourself first? Do you have a belief in self that makes it easier to convince others?

4. **ORGANIZED EFFORT** – Are you a capable and able planner, preparer, and organizer, or are your efforts mired in chaos and disorganization?

5. **APPLIER** – Can you learn and apply knowledge that you learn as a result of your efforts, research, study, and experience?

6. **LEADERSHIP** – Can you forge a path that others will willingly follow? Are you an Abraham Lincoln or Napoleon Bonaparte style leader?

7. **RESEARCHER** – Do you study and research before making important decisions, or do you shoot from the hip?

8. **ADVISORS** – Do you have an ally advisory team in place that will advise, guide, and direct you in your efforts or when you incur a problem or serious issue?

9. **NETWORKING** – Do you know how to network with others and create a combined effort to accomplish important goals?

10. **MOTIVATOR** – Do you have the proper incentive, and are you properly inspired?

11. **CREATIVITY** – Do you have an imaginative mind that helps you make your dreams come true?

12. **<u>SPIRIT OF CHEERFULNESS</u>** – Do you really enjoy what you are doing, and are you happy doing it?

13. **<u>SERVICE RENDERING</u>** – Are you willing to take on a responsibility for less-than-market compensation for the purpose of learning how to do it better, or are you instead more income-oriented?

14. **<u>SELF-DETERMINATION</u>** – Do you have the necessary resolve and perseverance to accomplish your goals and objectives?

15. **<u>COOPERATIVE EFFORT</u>** – Do you have a spirit and willingness to work together with others who avoid dissention?

It is these as well as other leadership qualities that will help you accomplish your long-term efforts in building your success. When you closely examine all high-level leaders in government, business, and private endeavors, you will see that each of them closely maintained the above factors that helped them achieve their success results. It is not easy to do it and takes a great deal of conscious effort, but creating your own leadership success formula will undoubtedly include each of these—and more.

The Nine Major Fears of Most People

The following are the greatest fears that most people have in their individual lives. They are the result of several exhaustive studies over the years by R. H. Bruskin Associates, a respected research firm. It identifies the biggest fears that most of us have in life. They are listed in order of priority and are the result of several exhaustive studies over the years by R. H. Bruskin Associations, a respected research firm. How many of these fears do you possess? How did you overcome it/them? What strategy did you use? Was it effective? Did it solve the problem completely? Do you still think about it or have nightmares?

In order of priority, they are as follows:

1. The fear of speaking before a group of people
2. The fear of high places
3. The fear of insects and bugs
4. ***THE FEAR OF FINANCIAL PROBLEMS***
5. The fear of deep water
6. The fear of sickness and ill health
7. The fear of death
8. The fear of flying
9. The fear of loneliness

Prosperity Externalities

What's an externality? It is what happens when someone takes an action; but someone else, without agreeing (or possibly even knowing about it), "pays" some or all the costs associated with that action. Some of the common examples of this include secondhand smoke, random motor vehicle accidents that injure people, and even the major negative effects to your spouse and family by failing to create or maintain a long-term prosperity plan. Often, when people aren't compelled to pay the full costs of their actions, there is little incentive to change their habits and behaviors. Not all externalities are necessarily negative, however. Getting a firm grasp on prosperity education creates positive externalities because those who you are closely associated with, such as your spouse, children, relatives, and even extended family members, can all benefit from the results of your prosperity planning and preparation.

After all, the ultimate incentive for every prosperity seeker is not just a $10 Starbucks gift card, is it? Instead, it is a better and more comfortable life and relationships complete with all the positive factors, including improved personal finances, satisfaction, purpose, and most of all, a substantial increase in the joy, happiness, and contentment that make up true prosperity in your life. When it comes to positive externalities, the very best ones, it seems, are those that affect each of you in your "mind" as well as your wallet. This is what makes the science of behavioral change so compelling when it comes to prosperity improvements. Many built-in incentive solutions for prosperity seekers are a large part of long-term efforts in building your unique and successful personal prosperity success program.

Prosperity Building Versus Personal Finances

Prosperity building and personal finances today are very nearly removed from sound economic theory, concept, reasoning, and application. That is why the process to build a high level of prosperity is educating yourself to look beyond what most people do *not see or understand*. It involves looking past merely the numbers into the "hows" and "whys" the numbers were actually created. Too many financial planners, advisors, retirement prognosticators, insurance brokers, and investment pundits focus on the *effects* rather than the *causes* of personal prosperity. They spend a lot of their time, effort, and energies on playing and manipulating the numbers and doing the math and creating complex "what if" calculations and scenarios and very little time teaching their clients the methods needed to maximize their incomes, investments, and prosperity building. (Is this perhaps because of the fact that they are fee-based and commission-based services and that it might adversely affect their long-term compensation?)

A better prosperity strategy is to seek our own road to long-term prosperity success by creating an effective blueprint formula that takes each of our personal, family, career, and retirement situations into account and provides us with a better, more effective paradigm formula that works for you, not those who feed off your investments. The goal should be to establish a plan with the best and highest levels of personal happiness, joy, and fulfillment as opposed to one that only involves mathematics, calculations, and financial projections.

There is also the issue of lost opportunity costs when it comes to the issue of following poor investment strategies. These are the emotional, heartfelt, and strategic expenses for courses of action that were not taken or not taken advantage of because we focused so much of our values on only the numbers and did not include other important factors. They can be explained as the "road not taken" and often result in our making purely monetary decisions and not factoring in happiness values. The very best prosperity plans are those that factor in a happiness element, arguably the very best and truest indicator of real prosperity. It is the ultimate solution to the quality versus quantity question that goes in many individual lives when it comes to financial success. Financial numbers can be deceptive. Who among us have not been disappointed by an overenthusiastic projection by a stockbroker or insurance representative only to learn that the "reality" was considerably more conservative? The better alternative is a balance of monetary prosperity, along with other prosperities, such as happiness, contentment, and satisfaction. Instead of the goal being a "millionaire," how about the objective of being a "happiness-aire" as the best standard of personal prosperity? Many financial predictions are outside of your control anyway. Interest rates, stock market swings, economic factors, the price of oil, inflation, and the value of our currency are all factors outside of your control as well as your professional financial advisors. Happiness is one factor you *can control.*

As a result, taking more personal responsibility of our own prosperity will often result in a higher level of overall effectiveness and results—even in the short term. Learning to question financial assumptions of those who stand to benefit from your investments may be a good technique to achieve higher levels of prosperity. After all, what is the level of *their personal prosperity* success?! And will they share *those results* with you? In truth, will you ever really recover from those 40 to 50 percent downturns in the financial markets anytime soon? What about the effects of inflation and deflation in your investments? Personal prosperity creation isn't all about spreadsheets, charts, graphs, and columns of numbers. It's more about your personal performance on a regular and sustaining basis that creates a thriving, profitable, and sustainable personal, family, career, and homelife. This involves looking beyond merely the numbers. It is ultimately about true, long-lasting happiness and freedom from worry, anxiety, and stress about personal finances. The worst attitude is the belief that having a lot more money will somehow, someway change you. It will only make you *more* of what you *already are*. For better or for worse. Money will not fix your problems. Finding out what makes you happy and using that as your benchmark is the answer to the prosperity question that affects each of us.

Three Options for Improving Your Personal Finances

1. *Increase your overall earnings*
2. *Decrease your personal expenses*
3. *Borrow more money*

> **Question:**
>
> *Which of the above is easier?*
>
> *Which of these is more effective?*
>
> *Which of these makes the most amount of sense?*

Creating Your Forever Prosperity Plan

In your busy day, every minute counts. Time really matters. Nobody can afford to waste their efforts with only concepts, theories, and formulas when it comes to their prosperity development, especially those who cannot or will not work. To understand and create the maximum benefit from your prosperity preparation and planning and to determine the impact that it will have on your life, you need to create a platform or combination of analysis, study, intelligence, education, and commentary that is handpicked and will give you the maximum feedback necessary to establish, maintain, and improve your prosperity growth and awareness. You cannot exceed the everyday norms unless you have the right combination of prosperity intelligence gathering exactly when and where you need it to benefit you in your long-term personal prosperity process journey. To gain a constant, organized, and necessary flow of the right kinds of information, you need to develop a comprehensive intelligence program that consists of the following:

- *Newspapers, magazines, and other periodicals*
- *Highly focused, self-help books and materials*
- *Educational classes, courses, workshops, and seminars*
- *Trusted professional advisors*
- *Technology tools*

- *Documented personal goals and objectives*
- *Formal written prosperity plan*

By committing yourself to this process, you will ensure that you will always have a "forever prosperity plan" in place that will benefit you for many years to come.

Commitment: It's all in your tactical approach to prosperity achievement.

CHAPTER 2

Prosperity Learning and Educational Fundamentals

In this chapter, you will learn about the following:

- *What It Takes to Building a Higher Level of Prosperity*
- *Prosperity Doers and Wannabes*
- *Authentic Prosperity-Building Strategies*
- *Your Financial Attitude "Inheritance"*
- *Do You Have Financial Goals in Place?*
- *Your Educational Prerequisites*
- *Getting to Know Yourself and Your Motivations*
- *Why Is All This Prosperity Education Necessary?*
- *It's a Process, Not an Event!*
- *How Do Really Prosperous People Do It?*
- *Key Elements of Compounding*
- *Personal Emotions That Often Motivate Investors*
- *Maximizing Investment Opportunities*
- *Learning to Avoid Investing Incompetence*

Prosperity Building: This Is What It Takes

*E**ducation** is the first step to discovering and assessing your potential (for prosperity) because it helps you overcome the myths and fallacies that hide your potential from you through fear and misinformation. This is why I constantly stress to people that they must always be reading good books, attending seminars, seeking out and engaging with mentors, working at certain jobs to learn specific skills and doing anything else that they can possibly do to increase their knowledge and awareness.*

—Garret B. Gunderson, Author (with Stephen Palmer)
Killing Sacred Cows, p. 132 (2008, by Greenleaf Book Group)

Prosperity "Doers" and "Wannabes"

< Separating the Venerable Sheep from the Goats >

Ultimately, we must make the distinction and separation of the prosperity sheep from the goats. We must put the sheep, the good and obedient followers, on the right and the goats, the stubborn and self-serving critters, on the left. Each category must be left alone to handle its own goals, aspirations, thoughts, and planning and learn to overcome their personal challenges by aligning them carefully with the peace and harmony that is described as prosperity. Creating a connection between our long-term goals and objectives and directing our daily lives toward the accomplishment of those desires is the fundamentals core of a carefully constructed prosperity plan. As you develop this mind-set within yourself, you will find that each of your actions will gradually become a part of your overall plan and success. Nothing will be too large for neither it to accomplish or anything too small for it.

Likewise, it will be accomplished with careful planning and resolve; and you will begin to witness that if it is done properly, it will lead you to health, happiness, joy, improved personal finances, and prosperity. Letting go of old ideas, habits, and behaviors that have hindered your ability to create higher levels of personal prosperity must be replaced with newer and better ones through change. Each of you has the power to be able to do this. Letting go of the old and taking hold of new ideas and concepts that form the core of prosperity thinking is the ultimate formula in achieving this.

The Role of the Trainer as "Border Collie"

< Herding the Sheep >

How will you accomplish this? Where will you get the money? What changes will you have to make to achieve it? There are opportunities all around you when you open your prosperity thoughts. Learning to let go of previous views and attitudes and making room for better and improved prosperity thinking means learning how to let go, to give up, and to replace those old thoughts and ideas that promise to improve your condition with others that will actually change it. Eventually, you will find the right combination of ideas that will bring to you that which you desire. It is an age-old process of growth, progress, and development. Just as youngsters outgrow their clothes, you outgrow your ambitions and broaden your thinking. It is a natural evolution that involves elimination of the old, which can hinder your growth and perhaps even stop it completely. This purging of old ideas is at the very heart of prosperity thinking. It is never wise to do this until you are sure that the new ones are better than those that take their place, yet the truth is that prosperity laws are eternal. They are not for only a select few or are they achieved through a secret process. They are for everyone to be able to use once they are disciplined and committed in doing it. Throughout the process, a competent teacher/trainer/mentor can be of tremendous service in guiding you. Just as the Border collie herds the sheep with laser-like focus and ability, a properly trained instructor can educate and assist you in the successful building of your personal plan by guiding and directing you through the process.

Authentic Prosperity Building

We live in challenging financial times today. Our fast-paced, high-tech, information-based global economy is contrasted sharply by a cross section of scammers, schemers, and fast-buck artists who prey upon your personal identity and financial assets at an alarming rate. Many of these crimes were not even conceived or thought about as recently as twenty years ago. It seems that we now live in the "best of times and the worst of times" as described in the immortal words of Charles Dickens over 150 years ago in the book *A Tale of Two Cities*. Today such a book might be more appropriately called *A Tale of Two Value Systems*.

It seems that our entire capitalistic system has been challenged today like never before, and the very element of one's ability to create even a modest level of personal prosperity in their lifetime in this country appears to be an increasingly fleeting concept now. Indeed, in one of the most symbolic pillars of visual prosperity today in America, homeownership has fallen on hard times as evidenced by record levels of foreclosures, repossessions, short sales, and auctions that have become more and more frequent at alarming rates not witnessed since the Great Depression.

This entire financial situation is made even worse when we realize that most Americans are now saving less money than any other capitalistic country on earth where they have also created a level of personal indebtedness consisting of credit cards, equity loans, and other consumer debt at a rate never witnessed before in our entire history. We, as a nation, are literally in hock up to our very ears based on overspending, overindulgence, and even overeating. We are too trendy, too wasteful, and too overweight. So what is the solution to this enigmatic problem? Is it for us to merely go on a "debt diet" (as well as a food diet)? Is it a need to simply outwait the national financial storm that has befallen us? Or is it something far deeper than all that? The solution to the vexing problems facing many people today is perhaps the greatest single challenge facing this entire generation and will not cnd very soon. It appears that many people have lost their financial momentum, similar to a pump when it loses its prime and can no longer pump any liquids.

Prosperity building is not a type of modern-day sorcery. It is neither a form of magic, voodoo, or hocus-pocus nor an unsolved mystery. It is instead a subject that has been taught in the past for thousands of years from generation to generation and has existed throughout the ages in both good times and bad. It is something that many people aspire to create in their lives, but far fewer ever realize its results or even their own potential to accomplish it. They are, it seems, often their own worst enemy in achieving it. It was a technique that at one time was passed down from father to son and family to family yet today seems to be lost in this age of indulgence. It is also something that arguably appears to have a more of a willing audience during bad times than good times.

Just as computers and the Internet have changed the way information is accessed and available today and how cell phones and text messages have changed the way we communicate, perhaps it is time to look at prosperity building in a whole new light. Instead of simply desiring it, maybe we ought to take a closer look at how it is created and what the necessary ingredients are to build it so that we can determine if we really want it or are willing to do what it takes to achieve it. Perhaps it is time to look closely at our personal goals and ambitions to see what it is realistically going to take to achieve prosperity and what the cost will be both in terms of monetary expenses as well as personal and emotional efforts. Maybe it is time to take a step backward to take a few steps forward. Maybe, just maybe, in the words of Austin Powers in the eighties movie *The Spy Who Shagged Me*, we just might need to find our "mojo" again.

As we go forward in your reading, we will go right to the source of many of the problems facing individuals today and explore each of the core prosperity principles that can serve to jump-start prosperity in our individual lives. We will delve into many of the causes and effects as well as the reasons that people today are mired in excessive personal financial problems and then offer a unique set of solutions as well as an assortment of techniques, strategies, formulas, and models that can be used to get aboard the prosperity speed track.

Our concepts are not necessarily new; but our style and manner of explaining each of them in a practical, commonsense, and useful manner certainly are unique and are the reasons that we have been successful in building our own prosperity. Because the author has, as Jimmie Johnson, legendary head pro football coach of the Super Bowl Champion Miami Dolphins, "walked the walk," he highly qualified to be able to "talk the talk" and will do it in a manner that virtually anyone can duplicate in their personal life. It is from this carefully created ancient set of financial codex beliefs and principles that are presented in a modern format that can benefit anyone willing to become disciplined and committed to learn them.

It is, indeed, TRUE AND AUTHENTIC PROSPERITY BUILDING!

Your Financial Attitude "Inheritance"

Many of our attitudes, beliefs, and personal financial habits are the result of our inherited family values and attitudes about money. Much of our present-day views concerning personal finances are often woefully inadequate compared to the complexities of today's twenty-first-century economic arenas. Indeed, many people face their personal finances with an angry, hostile, defensive, helpless, overwhelmed, or frustrated attitude that is due, in part, to a lack of understanding or ignorance of the principles of personal finance. This is one of our key roles of this book, to teach you the knowledge and know-how so that you will be able to make better future financial decisions in spending and saving instead of an out-of-control feeling.

Think back to your growing-up years. Did you ever have someone sit down with you and explain how to handle your money? Were your parents planners or savers? Did they complain about not having enough money frequently? Unfortunately, there are more people with negative feelings about their personal finances than positive ones, so the solution to overcoming your attitude about personal finances is to recognize that changes have to be made if your situation is to improve.

Do You Have Documented Financial Goals?

<< The Best Laid Plans All Start with Goal Setting >>

One of the first steps in the process of attaining financial independence is to create a list of personal financial goals. This process provides a realistic, written plan that will allow you to develop a strategy to accomplish your aspirations. Like many other areas in life, it is necessary to spend an appropriate amount of time, effort, and energy in documenting personal, family, career, and professional goals.

Like any other journey, unless you have clearly defined goals, objectives, and aspirations, you will never be able to arrive at your ultimate destination on time and intact. This is a thought-provoking exercise that cannot be accomplished in just one setting. Instead, the successful completion of a goals list is achieved after much deliberation and contemplation, and only when you have prioritized each of them are you in a position to begin assessing an action plan to accomplish each of them. The *work gloves process* is where many prosperity goals fall short of their goals, and it should be remembered in the planning stages that opportunities come along for each of us. Just because you do not feel that your existing level of income will generate any high level of prosperity does not mean that there won't be something that occurs in the future to change that.

The advice is simply this: create the financial goals anyway! You can concern yourself with funding each of them later. *The workbook that accompanies this book illustrates exactly how to develop each of your short- and long-term goals and objectives.* Refer to it as you begin to document each of your aspirations.

The Many Benefits of Goal Setting

A unique aspect of personal prosperity building is the process of goal setting, which is another word for setting priorities. This is the opportunity to document your dreams and ambitions so that you can build a personal template formula on how you will be able to achieve each one of your objectives in the future.

It is an important time to use your imagination and creativity to harness each one of your aspirations so that they can become your realities in the future. Make sure to give each one of these elements of your planning plenty of time, or you might somehow forget the purpose of the plan itself. For some, it might become an ironic challenge since you may have to get ready to increase your acceptance of those things in life you really want. Sometimes it is difficult to do this since it requires stepping out of your comfort zone to do it, and you may even feel unworthy to desire many of these items on your list.

One of the biggest challenges in creating personal goals is recognizing that you are both deserving and capable of achieving the results. When you start moving in the direction of your dreams, you begin to shed the self-created perception of your limitations. A good strategy if this occurs is to ask yourself this: what would your life be like if you could have anything you wanted? The "how" is what we will focus on later. Perhaps it's even time to go back to your childhood and start thinking bigger again. Children are the epitome of dreamers and make-believe, and maybe your dreams all began to shrink a little as your "life" and all its frustrations began to take over. It's now time to revisit those hopes and dreams. It's time to remember how to think larger again.

What exactly is it that you *really want* in life? To achieve each of your new goals in life, you must even be a little selfish for a while now. Each of your goals needs to be clear and specific in your mind. Most of all, they need to be written down and documented. Dare to create the affirmation of *exactly* what it is that you want in life. Remember too that this is a private experience (for now anyway), so you don't have to worry about how others will think or feel. It's nobody's business what your dream list looks like or even includes.

Part of the process of reading your newly established goals involves the ability to give up those things that you really determine you don't want or need. Knowing what you don't want or need is somehow, magically, just as important as determining what it is that you *do want*. This process involves taking a realistic look at many of the things in your life that you may feel are important but in the final analysis aren't really that earth-shattering. Does your lifestyle get in the way of your prosperity goal somehow? Are you sure that the McMansion you are considering is worth the monthly mortgage payments? Do you have a handle on your personal debts to be able to achieve your monetary goals? If not, it's a sign that perhaps that should be one of your goals as well.

In her book The Four Spiritual Laws of Prosperity, author Edwene Gains describes her ten-step formula that has become wonderfully successful for her and others. Those ten steps are briefly described as the following:

Step 1: Write down each of your desires in a spiral notebook. Carry this notebook with you in your pocket, briefcase, or purse; and as you think of new ideas and dreams, write each of them down and document them in your notebook. This is an effective way to begin creating your life priority items.

Step 2: From the above list, choose your most significant and important goals and desires and prioritize them. Be specific here. If you can't be specific, it may be an indicator that your dream might have to go to the bottom of the list or go on the back burner for a while. Make sure that these are *your personal goals* and not the goals of someone else (spouse, significant other, parent, friend) that has been imposed on you.

Step 3: What are the action steps that you will need to take to achieve each of your goals and dreams? This exercise will become the difficult part, ascertaining what exactly must be done to get to where you want to be, but do it anyway because the results will surprise you.

Step 4: Create your own personal timetable for each one of your newly created goals. This will be the date you wish to accomplish each one of them. If you get near that date and have not yet achieved it, it's time to develop a more realistic expectation of it.

Step 5: Refer to your list of goals and objectives frequently—several times a day. Focusing on these will help you affirm that they are important to you and your future life and will benefit you by drawing power to it.

Step 6: Use your creative imagination and see yourself in your mind's eye, subconsciously accomplishing each one of them. The more you do this, the easier it will be for you to attain each one of them. The power of the subconscious mind is significant, and many books have been written by successful people who have learned to do exactly that to be able to achieve their personal and career goals.

Step 7: Take the attitude that you believe that it is possible to achieve each of them. Accept that the successful completion of each of them will be the result of a lot of hard work, but it will occur. Taking this proactive position approach will become a major part of your accomplishment of each of your objectives.

Step 8: Keep this private. There will be lots of time to disclose your dreams and ambitions to others, but for now, keep the list between you and your Creator. This will avoid the inevitable criticism and doubt by others. Only your most trusted friend and loyal supporter can know about your plan (if you, indeed, are lucky enough to have one).

Step 9: Cross off each of your goals as they are accomplished and achieved and become part of your reality and continue to add new ones regularly to replace the ones you cross off. This should ideally become an ongoing process and not a single event.

Step 10: Develop an appreciation for everything that you have and how you were able to finally achieve it. It is simple for many to develop *convenient amnesia* the moment that they have successfully accomplished a difficult goal and forget the work, sacrifice, and effort that went into achieving it. Maintaining a healthy appreciation for the time, effort, and energy that you (and others) have put forth will send a strong message of sincere appreciation as you continue to do it in the future.

By following each of these steps, you will be on track in being able to develop, document, seek, and create an effective plan to get you from here to there. It is not easy, however, and having an *accountability partner* can help you in the process. This can be a trusted friend, spouse, or family member whom you confide in and "report to" on a regular basis that can encourage and motivate you to achieve your dreams.

You are well on your way now with a sound and effective strategy map showing you how to do it.

Take a Bow, Catch Your Breath, Set Your Notebook, and Pen Down for A Moment. You Can Start Feeling Prosperous!

Seven Steps for Setting and Reaching Goals

1. **STAY FOCUSED** – It is easy to get bogged down in the demands and details of the day and lose sight of your larger goals. Appreciating and focusing on your larger objectives turn ordinary activities into achievements and every effort into an adventure and learning experience. By embracing the fundamental principles of successful living, you will learn to eliminate hindrances to be able to achieve your most important life goals.

2. **SET REALISTIC EXPECTATIONS** – The key to staying motivated is creating realistic expectations. Evaluate your previous experience and current situation. What is a realistic, reachable goal for you in the area you are considering? Achieving a small goal is more valuable than brooding over impossible expectations. Dreams can become realities or nightmares, depending on the size of the steps. *Remember, it's a cinch by the inch, but it's hard by the yard and a trial by the miler.* Little steps often can lead to big victories.

3. **EXPECT CHALLENGES** – We can turn our mistakes and failures into victories if we learn from them, become more vigilant, adopt new strategies for successful achievement, and grow in wisdom. Successful people are not mistake-free; they just don't give up or give in when things go wrong. Mistakes can be the greatest stepping-stones to realizing your goals if you refuse to be defeated by them.

4. **MAINTAIN A POSITIVE ATTITUDE** – Leave those negative thoughts at the door. To a large extent, we have the ability to choose how we think and feel about any situation regardless of the type. Make the choice to focus on solutions rather than problems. Look at difficulties as opportunities for gaining strength to meet new challenges. Find a valuable lesson in every hurdle. Most importantly, cultivate thankfulness, optimism, and trust in a Higher Power in the situations that you cannot change. If you are naturally negative, give yourself time to grow in this area but keep a record of your progress such as in a journal.

5. **SEEK SUPPORT AND ACCEPT REPONSIBILITY** – Spending time and forming relationships with those who have positive life skills is

one of the ways to learn new habits and new ways of thinking. We become what we surround ourselves with. Social ties create mutual accountability and give you the opportunity to demonstrate and build responsibility and consistency into your life. The principles of support, accountability, and responsibility enable you to create deep and meaningful relationships with others, and the results will amaze you.

6. **PRACTICE NEW CHOICES** – Extreme makeovers may work on television and in home remodeling programs, but remodeling your financial life is a process that takes place over a period. Fast is fragile, but slow is steady and stable and comes to maturity over time. It is the steady process of repeatedly making positive choices that build mind, body, and spirit. Never underestimate the power of carefully chosen, small, and daily positive choices in overcoming bad habits. Repetition and patience are the keys to crafting a positive future.

7. **CONNECT WITH OTHERS** – Circumstances alone cannot change the heart. The best of intentions can plunge your plan with the preserving power of self-belief and eternal faith. The recovery of broken habits and the restoration of hope and happiness come through focused attention and perseverance. A network of trusted friends and advisors can be a critical line in the attainment of your long-term achievement of your goals and objectives.

Your Educational Prerequisites

"Desire Is Important but Not Nearly Enough."

The first step in this or any other meaningful course of study and learning is old-fashioned **desire** and "want to" that is also properly flavored with personal motivation. Desire, however, is not nearly enough to achieve prosperity. You must also have the willingness and the thirst to learn everything you can about it; and that all starts with reading, studying, and even attending highly specialized, focused education at locations that teach the key fundamental and core principles of prosperity building.

The second step in obtaining the required knowledge is **commitment**. Without a pledge of engagement, the necessary learning will not occur on a timely basis. This is one of the most important steps in the evolutionary process since it is an emotional attachment of wanting to "do better" in life and helps to define the level of endurance, just as in many of our other personal relationships. This has been explained by many motivational speakers and others who say that "nothing significant in life really ever happens until you are committed to doing it regularly and consistently." This is called commitment and is the literal definition of success in personal prosperity building.

The next step or third on the list is **perseverance**. Even with the requisite desire and commitment, many fall short when the learning becomes challenging or difficult because of a lack of resolution, grit, or pluck, especially when the educational training becomes detailed, complicated, or difficult. As we all know, it is the degree of dedication that we submit that often produces the results we seek. Without it or when subjected to only a half-hearted effort, a sustained and accomplished prosperity plan is not more than merely a dream or idea instead of a reality or actuality, which will have little resemblance to a successful result.

The fourth prerequisite step in the series is choosing the right **format** to use in the learning process. There are significant benefits to each of the previously mentioned category formats, and they each have inherent advantages but do not create a one-size-fits-all advantage for every person.

The following highlights some of the advantages and disadvantages of each format:

1. **SELF-HELP BOOKS AND MATERIALS** – There are many of these available today, and some of them include DVDs, video, and audio tapes that serve to explain many of the key learning point details.

2. **INVESTMENT SEMINARS** – These are a popular form of financial education today and are held frequently at minimal cost or even no charge for qualifying persons. You will learn something at each seminar; however you should be advised that there is always a seller motivation on the part of the host (stockbroker, investment firm, or insurance agent/company), and it is essentially designed to sell participants a product or service in the guise of personal financial education. You can gain *some knowledge* but should be warned that these are more of a marketing gimmick than true prosperity or financial education.

3. **USE OF FINANCIAL PLANNER OR ADVISOR** – This is an excellent method to achieve a successful prosperity plan model and will usually result in a highly effective set of techniques and strategies that can be used. The downside, however, is that these professionals are *very expensive* and will often charge clients in one of two ways: 1) by the hour (typically from $200 to $300 per billable hour with a minimum charge) or 2) by compensation via commissions on the products or services that they recommend (usually between .5% percent and 1.5 percent) and/or a percentage of the annual portfolio that you have invested with them (with a minimum fee amount).

4. **COMMUNITY COLLEGE OR ADULT EDUCATION COURSE** –
    This method is also very useful to consider, and you can benefit from
    educational training because of the style of classroom learning, but
    they are not offered frequently and are often taught by institutional
    instructors or professors who may not have succeeded in accomplishing
    any significant amount of personal prosperity themselves and, as a
    result, teach only dated concepts and theories. Usually, these courses
    are devoted to only concepts and financial/investment theories that
    result in little real-life experience, guidance, or planning.

5. **LENDER SYMPOSIUMS** – Often, banks, credit unions, and similar
    lending institutions offer seminar and symposiums at different times
    of the year to "teach and train" their clients, customers, and prospects
    about investing and planning. However, just like investment seminars,
    the question arises: are these educational in nature, or do they merely
    offer a heavy dose of marketing of products and services in the mask
    of education? The phrase "You get what you pay for" comes to mind
    quickly here, and if you are not paying very much for the seminar or if
    it is offered free of charge, then the chances are that you will not gain
    much knowledge from attending, and you just might walk away with a
    commitment to buy some sort of financial investment from them that
    you hadn't planned on.

6. **NEWSPAPERS, MAGAZINES, NEWSLETTERS** – Each of these is a
    useful method to gain further knowledge or stay up-to-date regarding
    financial prosperity building. However, it must be remembered that
    each of these offers highly focused and many useful insights, up-to-
    date information, and knowledge to *enhance* individual strategies and
    techniques yet often are so focused and specific that unless the reader
    already has a previously prepared plan in place, they are of little use
    and often confuse more than educate the reader.

7. **PROSPERITY TRAINERS AND MENTORS** – This, obviously, is
    the optimum choice; yet, as previously discussed, they are difficult to
    find and have little inclination to want to do it, especially for a longer
    period and without charge. Some exceptions to this may include family
    members, relatives, or friends who are willing to share their individual
    prosperity secrets with you.

So where does that leave you? Again, there *are* highly specialized and
focused institutions and learning centers around the country that offer classes,
courses, workshops, and seminars that are highly informative and educational
in style, format, and content that can teach people how to build their individual
prosperity plan through the use of an outline and design that will help build
and engineer your own prosperity plan while working with each member every

step of the way. The style of that educational training and how it differs from any other type is that it deals personally and directly with real-life opportunities and events that are used in real-time circumstances while coupled with numerous quizzes, test, carefully created personal experiences, and examinations that guide, direct, and coach participants into being able to successfully prosper themselves based on their needs and desires. This training is often a shared learning experience by all members that emphasizes a hands-on approach to achievement.

Getting to Know Yourself and Your Motivations

"Know thyself" is a commonly used term when seeking many of the fundamental truths in life. The same is true with prosperity building. A few of the key factors that might help define the individual prosperity building for many individuals include the following:

1. **AGE** – Your age is an obvious factor in the planning process because the strategy used for twentysomethings is vastly different from midlifers or those in their more senior years. Age plays a *huge factor* in the overall planning process.

2. **INCOME/OCCUPATION** – Another helpful determinant in the creation of a realistic personal prosperity plan involves income production based on job/career and even the type, frequency, quantity, and quality of that income production. Is it stable, consistent, increasing, or a result of being an employee or self-employed; and is it subject to fluctuations, such as bonuses, incentives, and commissions?

3. **BACKGROUND** – Does the participant's background in any way prevent them from achieving their prosperity building? Is their marital situation strong and bonded, or has divorce wreaked havoc on their personal finances? Do they have a large family or a smaller one? What are the ages of their children? Are there parental caregiving issues involved? Do they live in an expensive city or a less-costly rural or suburban setting? These are all factors in the category, format, and type of prosperity education needed.

4. **EXPERIENCE** – Does the participant have an existing knowledge of where they are and how they may choose to arrive at their prosperity destination? Or, on the other hand, are they just getting started or changing their job or career field or perhaps seeking to "test their wings"? Here too, the relative amount of prosperity experience is a big factor in the education necessary.

5. **GOALS AND OBJECTIVES** – One of the most critical factors in determining the necessary type of education is in exploring the goals

and ambitions of the participant. Are they modest, moderate, or extreme? The answer to each of these questions largely determines the category and intensity of the prosperity education that is necessary to improve it.

6. **INDIVIDUAL AND RELEVANT DETAILS** – Any and all other personal and individual information and details that make the personal prosperity planning experience unique to your situation, such as number of children, whether you are an employee or self-employed, if you have other income opportunities, and even if you have an existing strategy plan in place, are all relevant to creating your individual prosperity planning.

Why Is All This Prosperity Education Really Necessary?

The answer to this question might be answered by asking another key question: why is *any important* personal education necessary? It is the process of gaining key insight, perceptions, and lifelong experiences of a skilled instructor that makes prosperity education so necessary and compelling. It is more than learning how to become more financially comfortable. It is understanding each of the underlying principles and components that create an awareness of how they all correlate and fit together in formulating your particular prosperity plan and the one that is unique to Y-O-U.

It is the process of becoming financially literate and knowing while understanding each of the techniques and strategies that are used in creating your one-of-a-kind formula. It is a method to discover *how to* ratchet your existing earnings and income into a powerful prescription that produces exponential financial growth year after year for the rest of your life, which makes this education so useful and important. Prosperity education teaches participants how to achieve a more balanced view of the asset-building process and should ideally do it in a practical, commonsense, and sensible way without any undue emphasis on money, wealth, or materialism but instead on well-being, happiness, and peace of mind.

We all know that there are many more "lookers" and "seekers" than "accomplishers" and "achievers" in life. The former can be termed "prosperity explorers," who search for the right combination of opportunity and resources to capitalize on them yet concentrate on speculation more than knowledge. The latter are those who recognize that they lack the necessary skills and training and choose to become educated by those who have "been there and done that" to achieve a high degree of prosperity by taking fewer or more calculated risks while experiencing much greater rewards in the end.

Which category do you fit in? Are you a looker or seeker or an accomplished and achiever?

The answers to these questions lie within each reader's personal attitude regarding knowledge and education. If you are prosperity educated, you will know and understand the right moves to make and when to make them and will be able to accomplish predictable results. If not, you might take a too-cautious approach, resulting in the inability to achieve your goals and objectives. On the other hand, a too-aggressive approach could cause you to put your entire plan at risk like the fable Goldilocks, who carefully tested each of the bowls of porridge that were "too hot" and "too cold" and finally found that one that was "just right." You too want your prosperity plan to be "just right."

This comes about as a result of **P-r-o-s-p-e-r-i-t-y E-d-u-c-a-t-i-o-n !**

The Golden Principle:

Sound economic lessons need to be learned and developed early in life.
Prosperity cannot remain static;
It either grows or diminishes,
Depending on your efforts to preserve it.

—L. S.

Prosperity Education and Learning:

"It's a Process, not an Event!"

Prosperity is a term that is used a lot in our teaching and training at The Prosperity Success Institute™. The reason is simple: learning how to do it is a lifelong process and not merely an event in life. Often, really desirable situations in our lives are understandably sought after with zeal and anticipation, yet it should be remembered that those same situations also need to be tempered with the necessary amount of patience. To effectively arrive at the destination, it takes a requisite amount of time, energy, and effort to understand how to do it. By the time that many of us leave high school, college, or trade or vocational school or even graduate school, we are tired and weary of "hitting the books" and are only too ready to embark on a lifetime of working, earning money, starting a family, or having leisure and fun activities. One of the problems is that in most cases, the anticipated prosperity in life has no real formal plan or preparation. It often becomes a haphazard and trial-and-error experience replete with many missed financial opportunities that defines the lives of most people.

Interestingly, most of us spend many years working, earning a living, providing for our families, and preparing for other important events in our lives, yet somehow we seem to neglect one of the most important aspects of life. Over the years, we plan for a great many events. We save for those things that are, indeed, important to us and then at some point in midlife begin to worry. Will we have enough money for retirement? Will our children be able to go to college? Will our jobs remain secure? Sometimes the very future seems so insecure. How can we ever manage to plan enough? There is seemingly a daunting list of "what if" questions that needs to be answered.

The solutions to these questions are not as difficult as they may seem. Planning and preparation are some of the obvious answers, but what kind? Where does one get the real, no-nonsense, practical, commonsense approach that provides the strategies, techniques, and know-how and that produces the needed results? The financial meltdown of Wall Street in the fall of 2008 is a highly visible example of those who tout and sell prosperity building, but we are left to wonder whose prosperity is being created. Theirs or yours!?

In the end, the necessary planning and preparation involves many particular aspects of prosperity building that you can and should understand to gain the required comprehension. This does not mean that you should become a stockbroker or sell portfolio investments, but you should understand how to live within your current income and avoid flagrant use of credit cards and consumer loans. It doesn't mean that you should invest your lifetime savings into a risky business, stock, or speculative property investment; but it does mean that you should understand how compounding works for and against you and that a well-directed investment portfolio can reap enormous long-term returns if it is properly invested.

How Do Well-To-Do, Really Prosperous People Do It?

There are countless methods that can be used and implemented to improve personal prosperity in each of our lives. We see and experience them in a number of ways, yet usually, it comes about as a result of buying something that is offered by an extremely talented and experienced salesperson. The unfortunate result is that often, this approach becomes an emotional event rather than a rational or logical one. When we think of the vast number of investors who experienced huge losses in their portfolios in 2008–2009, we are reminded that sound portfolio investments are the result of diligent planning and preparation that is accomplished by studying and evaluating the options available and *not* merely by choosing the latest stock or investment tips. Personal prosperity producers don't all wear suits and ties or dresses and skirts. Many of them are "working class" people, such as nurses, insurance agents, mechanics, teachers, truck drivers, firemen, law enforcement persons, and other whose motivation includes a desire for a comfortable living, along with a compelling desire to help and give to others.

Many of them are active in church and community organizations as well as with their families. They put those ahead of the materialism and consumerism that represents many Americans today. Their levels of debt and borrowing are substantially lower than their contemporaries in their age group, and they have a resourceful and conservative attitude toward their money management and personal finances. They are more apt to have investment accounts that they regularly contribute to and often save toward specific goals and objectives through a logical approach rather than an emotional one.

Prosperity builders invest their money into appreciating assets like small business enterprises, real estate property, and financial portfolios rather than spending top dollar for new vehicles, large homes, jewelry, and other outward displays of wealth. Saying "no" comes easily to them concerning spending their money on materialism and bling as easy as saying "yes" to areas of prudent financial investments that they know and understand, which will produce respectable and predictable gains year after year. To say that they are good with their money is an understatement. The U.S. government would do well to have these personal prosperity producers running the nation's budgeting and spending because they excel at it and know how and when to make the right choices. Yet money management is not really what these people are totally all about.

You will find them engaged in volunteer groups, church activities, passionate pursuits, and many aspects of giving in their lives, jobs, and careers. They have learned how to strike a balance between giving and receiving that earmarks them as prosperous. They have become engaged in the passionate pursuit of *true prosperity*. Their lives and those around them are much richer as a result of it.

Prosperity Wisdom

Put your trust in education, preparation, and skill
when developing your prosperity template formula
and not in emotions, anticipations, or instincts.

—L. S.

Investing Your Money

"Creating a Personal Financial Portfolio"

Successful investing techniques and abilities are a huge factor in achieving long-term personal financial goals. But how do you create the necessary know-how to go about it? What are the necessary steps to do it?

Similar to many of the other facets of knowledge that you are gaining in this course in personal finance, successful investing is an acquired learning skill. It is *not* something that anyone is born with. It is *not* an innate talent or skill. It *is* something that you can learn.

This session deals with helping your efforts as a potential investor understand many of the options available to you when it comes to creating and managing those types of assets. It also will help you navigate through this detailed and complicated arena. It should be remembered that high-risk investing can be compared to speculative gambling, while the logical, unemotional approach to investing more of a long-term growth strategy. If done properly, your investment portfolio should serve you well over the long run.

> *"If you want to lose weight, talk to a skinny person; if you want to learn how to invest, talk to a successful investor."*

- *Risk-taking* is one of the first considerations of investors. You have to know and understand your tolerance for risk since there are a great many of them to consider in investing.
- Exactly what is *risk*? It is the possibility of losing some, part, or all your chosen investment regardless of the type. Most risks are proportionate to the potential gain. In other words, the more potential gain, the more risk. Less risk equals less potential gain.
- Every investment carries with it a certain amount of risk-taking. Even *the* most secure savings account produces the risk that inflation or cost of living will outweigh the potential overall gain. At the other end of the scale, others like technology stocks carry high risks when you consider that the company may be a shining star one quarter and then merely fizzle out and die in a few years based on its market share, ownership, and management.
- To succeed as an investor, you must determine where you are in terms of your investment risk tolerance and objectives. This is what a risk model looks like:

GROWTH   **CAPITAL**

Growth   Income   Income   Preservation

High Risk   **Low Risk**

The secret is to understand what risk is and to know your tolerance for risk-taking so that you are comfortable managing your investment portfolio regardless of the market conditions, up or down. Taking a logical rather than an emotional approach to investing can create better overall investing results.

Two Personal Emotions That Often Motivate Many Investors

< Fear and Greed >

The underlying effects of each of the emotions of *fear* and *greed* are highly significant and compelling factors in overall investing and prosperity building. They are largely governed by personal feelings, including the following:

FEAR – A willingness to accept low risks and rewards.
GREED – A desire to accept and focus on high risks and potential rewards.

Everything else is in the very middle of these extreme emotions. One of the secrets to long-term prosperity building is to create a highly useful and proportionate balance between each of these opposite and polar extremes. In fact, it is commonly known that a well-balanced personal asset portfolio is usually a combination of each of these financial emotional extremes as well as many others in between.

Understanding each of these two emotions (and everything between them) is a critical first step in evaluating your unique and individual money personality and style, a strategy that involves the extreme end of either one of them, as opposed to the proverbial "middle ground," which is never a sound approach and seldom works successfully for very long.

Maximizing Investment Opportunities

To increase and maximize your investment returns and yields, you need to increase your chances of winning at the investment game and decrease the opportunities of losing. As a direct result, the better you manage your risks, the higher the returns can build. It does not necessarily mean that you have to accept high risks for high returns and instead focus on taking personal responsibility for your choices. Investing is something that you *can control*, and there are numerous ways to successfully achieve it:

- **ONE OF THE BEST WAYS IS TO ESTABLISH ACCOUNTABILITY.**
  Any investment that involves high risk, large uncertainties, and the factor of luck is gambling and not investing. Instead, the true, valid investment is one that is a result of honest value creation.

- **THE BETTER YOU MANAGE YOUR RISKS, THE HIGHER YOUR RETURNS WILL BE.**
  Prosperous and successful investors learn how to reduce risks while increasing returns. They do this by understanding that *they* are their most important asset and educate themselves constantly to better able do it.

- **THEY REALIZE THAT PASSIONATE LIFE PURSUITS ARE ALWAYS GOOD INVESTMENTS.**
  Those things that you really enjoy, understand, and committed to are always good investment choices in your time, energy, and capital resources. Investing in yourself is a critical part of this process. You are always your own best investment.

- **REDUCING RISK INVOLVES DOING EVERYTHING POSSIBLE TO INCREASE YOUR CHANCES OF WINNING.**
  Using this approach, the most profitable investments are a direct result of how you decrease the risks associated with them. It involves analysis, study, and research to know the type of investment you should consider.

- **SUCCESSFUL INVESTORS UNDERSTAND GAMBLING VERSUS INVESTING.**
  Putting your money into the stock market does not automatically make you an investor if you have no idea of what your money is invested in or what type of returns to expect. Fear and greed are the marks of gamblers and not investors.

- **HIGH-YIELD INVESTMENTS ARE A RESULT OF KNOWLEDGE COUPLED WITH EDUCATION.**
  The difference between those who do well in investing and those who don't is that successful investors have learned how to secure them through a higher level of financial IQ than others. They have studied, learned, and adapted certain unique formulas to achieve better results.

- **FINDING A GOOD MENTOR OR COACH TO HELP AND ASSIST YOU IS AN EXCELLENT STRATEGY TO USE.**
  Someone who has successfully maneuvered the investing experience over time and "been there and done that" can be an invaluable tool in achieving higher levels of investing returns.

In the end, each of the above techniques has the effect of transferring risk rather than retaining the risk. This is what typically separates all successful investors from everybody else and has the effect of producing long-term predictable results.

What's Your Stock Market Investing Style?

On Wall Street, the word that investment pros most often use to determine the types of stocks and investments that an individual chooses to purchase is called **style**. Your choice of investments helps define your perspective. Some of the commonly used styles are as follows:

- **Growth Investors** – These investors purchase stocks with earnings that are rapidly growing.
- **Value Investors** – These investors purchase stocks that often appear to be undervalued compared to their current price or assets.
- **GARP Investors (Growth-At-Reasonable Price)** – These investors purchase stocks that are a mixture of both qualities: growth and value.
- **Momentum Investors** – These investors purchase stocks that display lots of growth momentum with anticipation that profits will grow even faster than expectations.
- **Technician Investors** – These investors are those who purchase stocks by studying trends and patterns over a period.

What is your particular and unique style?

Consistency Beats Luck Every Time

Experiencing a "hot hand" is exciting. Every win is exhilarating and makes your heart beat faster and even makes your blood rush. It's a thrill to take chances and do it over and over. But what happens when Lady Fortuna looks the other way, and everything comes crashing down? Sadly, the law of averages promises that it *will happen* to you one day.

This is the reason that consistency is more important than luck in building your personal prosperity plan (think: tortoise and the hare). Don't make the mistake of being too conservative or too aggressive. Create a balanced investment portfolio. Set realistic standards and meet them with your investments year after year. Be realistic. Be relentless in your pursuit of it. Be unwavering. Be the person whom everyone tries to emulate. Build a solid track record of prosperity planning achievements. The best strategy is to choose those investments that perform year after year and do it through good economies as well as recessions. They may even appear to be slightly boring or ho-hum but continue to grind out predictably good result year in and year out.

Consistency trumps luck or a hot hand every single time. There's literally nothing better for your long-term prosperity-building plan.

Sage Investment Advice

It's a whole lot easier to lose money *in investing than it is to* make money *doing it.*

—L. S.

Key Prosperity Learning Lesson:

To reduce the odds of loss, you should *educate yourself* in the process of how to do it!

This generally does not happen from the ones who are selling the investments to you.

Ancient Asset Allocation

Please note that the concept of asset allocation presented is not a new idea. The first asset allocation formula was written in the Talmud over two thousand years ago. It exhorts investors "to invest a third in land, a third in business, and a third in reserves." It seems that this formula is one that has worked successfully for many years.

Creating an Investment Policy Statement (IPS)

When building personal investment securities portfolio, it is important to create an investment policy statement (IPS) for many reasons, including many of the specific reasons why certain investments were selected as opposed to others. It also provides documentation of those reasons so that during more challenging periods, you can reflect back as to why they were originally chosen.

An investment policy statement is a carefully detailed, long-term investment plan that helps you outline your financial objectives and strategies for you to stay on target and avoid financial blunders in your overall prosperity-building investing. Ideally, it is a document that is created during calmer financial times and lists many items that comprise your investment philosophies. It serves to remind you of your decisions and includes such things as risk tolerance, risk capacity, asset allocation, performance predictions, and personal goals and objectives.

In addition, its use is a custom-designed, long-range blueprint of your investing philosophy that helps determine all the relevant issues that will help you avoid surprises and bring clarity to future decisions and adjustments. It can be altered, changed, edited, and updated from time to time as personal and career circumstances change; and it needs to be created over a period. Like all worthwhile projects, it helps to work with someone who has created an IPS before and can guide and direct you to its successful completion.

Efficient Versus Inefficient Prosperity Investment Markets

One of the fundamental advantages of real estate property investing is the ability to get good deals based on a number of variables, including the buyer's or seller's personal motivations or even through other events, such as death, divorce, inheritance, loss of income, health factors, and other personal reasons as well as factors, including zoning issues and changes, real estate assessments and taxes, geographic location, condition of the property, and many others. In the final analysis, it is a highly *inefficient market* and one that is driven by numerous variables that can be mutually advantageous to either party.

There are also many inexperienced buyers and sellers who are able to capitalize on these situations. Add to this "opportunity mixture" the role of real estate agents who are more driven by commissions instead of creating value or better pricing, and you have a nearly perfect real estate prosperity investment scenario for those who understand how, when, and why to invest. In addition, you can find real estate that is priced below the market if you are willing to take the time and effort to find and locate the properties. You can also invest if you can recognize good value and if you have the necessary cash or access to the cash to make the purchase. You can also succeed if you have a good personal real estate property investment formula that you have created and developed over the years.

Now let's compare this to the traditional stock-picking financial investment market: In the stock market, securities of every company are offered to potential stockholders for *exactly the same price*. There are not "deals" available for the average consumer or investor. For that reason alone, it is a *highly efficient market*. Investor *A* is simply not going to find a better deal on a given stock than investor *B* or anyone else at the same time because of this efficiency. This is also the reason that it is nearly impossible to create large, significant profits on a regular basis from stock-picking investments. This is especially true with large cap stocks (those huge corporations that have more than one billion dollars' worth of total capitalization). Even if it does occur, it does not do so on a regular and frequent basis. This is the basic underlying reason why real estate is often and usually a significant portion of every prosperity investor's investment portfolio and why we endorse the investment in it as part of your long-term prosperity-building plan. Real estate ownership investment has been a major factor in nearly every prosperity investor's portfolio since ancient times.

So now you know.

Stockbrokers Versus Handicappers

A detailed investigation of the real value performance of many stockbrokers can be compared to an activity that has similar characteristics: **betting on horses**. In both arenas, it is necessary to study the facts, view the research, weigh the "wins and losses," estimate the odds, and then decide where to invest your money. **Investing, it seems, is not really so different from horse race betting using handicaps.** What makes the results so compelling (other than the fact that it is really your own hard-earned money that is at stake in **both situations** but much higher in investing) is that the timely accuracy of forecasting the odds is a highly complex process. Many factors have to be considered, and how they relate to one another is significant. In truth, handicappers use models that are arguably more complex than those used by the most savvy and experienced stockbrokers, so-called manipulative models, in which the values of some factors, such as the conditions of the track, altered the importance of others, such as the last race speed.

In the end, it is the results that count, so it is important to know and understand **how** the process works from an investor's perspective. The way to do that is to gain a fundamental knowledge of how stock market investing really works by taking a class, course, workshop, or seminar and by choosing a stockbroker only after careful research and analysis. The next step is to ask questions, lots of them, to understand the broker's personal strategies and techniques used. Ask them to see their "track record" (if they refuse, that is a bad sign). Ask to see their investment philosophy when it comes to **your** investments. What is their rebalancing timetable?

In the real world of stock market investing, knowledge is important, and most successful brokers often appear to be highly intelligent. Yet the link between intelligence and high achievement is not nearly as powerful as we commonly suppose. The results are the prerequisite to extraordinary achievement in the business of stock picking. Measurement of this ability is relatively easy. What are the stockbroker's overall yields for their clients? **Ask to see the evidence!**

Defining an Effective Personal Asset Allocation Portfolio

A finely tuned personal asset allocation portfolio recognizes that there are three main asset categories:

1. **INTEREST-EARNING CATEGORY** (Protection against deflation)
This category consists of two broad asset classes: cash and bonds. It provides capital preservation as well as cash flow while keeping this portion of your total investment safe.

2. **REAL ESTATE CATEGORY** (Protection against inflation)
This category of allocation consists of three basic asset classes: personal residence (a place to live), productive property (rental property, commercial property, and REITs), and nonproductive property (vacant land, second homes, and limited partnerships). The ability to create financial leverage via mortgages as well as many significant tax benefits make this one of the most inflation-defeating assets to own and invest in. This is a long-term investment and is frequently illiquid.

3. **EQUITY SECURITIES CATEGORY** (Profits during periods of prosperity)
This is the "locomotive growth engine" of the total personal portfolio but is subject to the most volatility. This category involves stocks, mutual funds, international monetary funds, precious metals, and employer stocks.

The Magic of Compounding

What exactly is compounding? All the money you invest and put to work in an investment creates interest or yield, and all that interest then creates more interest, and all that interest that the interest earns creates even more interest. This goes on every day, every month, and every year that you own it. That's pretty powerful when you consider that all you have to do is to choose the right kind of investment. Compounding does all the rest!

It has been said that those who fail to understand how compounding *can work for them* are destined to pay compounded interest *to others*.

LEARNING LESSON: If you want the mental illustration of the huge effects of compounding that *you pay others*, look at the amortization of your thirty-year home mortgage. For example, the $100,000 that you originally paid for your house will create over $200,000 in compounded interest accumulation to the bank or mortgage company. *How would you like to be on the receiving end of that loan?*

The Reality of the Power of Compounding Over Time

The ultimate power of compounding can be illustrated by the following example:

Let us say that Russell begins as a teenager to save money for investing. Each year for the next five years, he saves $3,000 per year from his part-time earnings, holiday gifts, birthday gifts, allowance, and other incomes. He places the funds into an investment that produces a 10 percent annual rate of return. At the age of twenty, after a total of five years, he never saves another dollar and instead allows his $15,000 investment to grow for the next forty years, untouched, at the 10 percent rate (this is not difficult to do in the stock market through a diversified mutual fund).

His best friend, Bates, however, waits until after college, at age twenty-five, to begin his investment plan. He also diligently saves $3,000 of his earnings and does it every single year of his entire working life until he reaches retirement age of sixty-five (a total of forty years). This is the same investment as his best friend, Russell, and is earning a 10 percent annual return on investment.

At age sixty-five, Russell, who saved for only five years and only $15,000, will have accumulated $1,468,512 in his account, while his best friend, Bates, who saved $120,00 over forty years, has realized slightly less, $1,463,555.

How could this possibly be achieved? It is through the magic of the *power of compounding*!

*   *   *   *

This is an example of the powerful effects of compounded investing when it begins at an early age since it allows your investment money to grow over many years. Think of how far you would be if you started an investment program in your teens. If not done early, you will undoubtedly spend the rest of your life catching up.

Despite the recent period, over the past seventy years, the stock market has increased at an average rate of 11 percent per year.

More on the Magic of Compounding

If you can save $100 per month and you can do this faithfully for forty years or more (for example, from age twenty-five to age sixty-five), you will have well over $700,000 in your retirement nest egg as a result of the magical power of compounding. This is created by an S&P 500 stock market index rate of just 10.2 percent. Curiously enough, the eighty-year track record of the New York Stock Exchange is even better than this.

Talk about magic!

<< *Pearl of Wisdom*>>

The problem that most people have is not that they cannot save $100 per month. It is that when they see this investment build up to $5,000 or even $25,000, they want to pull it out and spend it on materialistic "stuff" like a new vehicle, boat, RV, motorcycle, etc. This results in the exponential effects of compounding ceasing, and then the process has to start all over again with far less long-term results because we have "picked the fruit too early." Then as we get older, we run out of time to be able to keep duplicating this process over and over, which leads to depreciated assets and nothing in our portfolio account to live on at a critical time in our lives.

Key Prosperity Learning Lesson:

Many people feel that compound interest is the eighth wonder of the modern world and one of the key reasons that the capitalized world has witnessed such explosive and consistent growth since the end of World War II. Compounding means exponential growth, and money works exceptionally hard because the interest earned also earns interest, which, in turn, earns more interest. The result is the most pleasant increase in growth, earnings, and yield in an account.

Prosperity Nugget

Now comes the financial "rule of 72"

The rule of 72 is a simple method to calculate the way to see how long it will take for money to double in value. To calculate it, divide the number 72 by any interest rate, and that is approximately how many years you will need to be able to double your money.

A 6 percent rate, for example, you will need 12 years to double your money (72 divided by 6 equals 12).

A 15 percent return means your account will double in nearly 5 years (72 divided by 15 equals 4.8 years).

This is an easy method for many investors to use in figuring growth in investment accounts.

The Rule of 72 Explained

The most powerful force in the universe is compound interest.
—Albert Einstein
(And it is rumored that he knew something about numbers!)

Net Worth Compared to Cash Flow in Investing

Definitions:

1. **<u>NET WORTH</u>** – This is your assets less liabilities or what you own less what you owe (think: stored financial potential).
2. **<u>CASH FLOW</u>** – This is a combination of net, sustainable, and productive income created by your assets (think: continuous income cycle).

What good are assets if you don't or cannot use them? Putting your net worth to work not only is a good idea, but it is a sound, effective prosperity strategy too. It is a highly useful method to achieve many of your personal goals and objectives, increase the level of your personal happiness, and add value to others. Simply, asset utilization is all about learning the difference between fixed assets and cash flow assets.

For example, a piece of real estate property owned by you is an asset and adds value to your net worth. It becomes a cash flow asset when you have it rented or leased out and if it produces income for you. Once you pay down or pay off the mortgage, it then creates *significant* cash flow. In this example, the real estate property is a nonperforming asset until it is leased to someone. The same is true of other personal assets.

After all, is not one of the key concepts of building greater prosperity about what we use our capital resources for as opposed to merely having them? By investigating and examining our assets versus cash flow, we may be able to figure out a better way to produce investment cash flow. This is a highly useful technique that can help supplement your personal income.

It also includes something known in the financial industry as the **velocity of money**, a term used to describe exactly how much benefit is produced by a given investment. In other works, *output* versus *input*.

An example of this is if you had $100,000 invested in a mutual fund or stock account, and it was producing 8 percent or $8,000 per year annual yield, and you made the decision to invest that money into a small business, where you could potentially get a 35 to 40 percent annual return. You have essentially increased the velocity of your money by 300 to 400 percent. Learning the process of developing your assets into better, velocity-driven cash flow will enable you to build your financial prosperity at an even higher level. This is one of the reasons that real estate property investments and business enterprises are good uses of your money asset.

Learning to Avoid Investment Paralysis and Incompetence

Be very careful who you listen to when it comes to your personal finances and prosperity building. There are many so-called experts or professionals in the financial world who are anxious, clever, and very willing to give you their advice but are perhaps more concerned about making their sales goals and commissions than they are about helping you achieve *your* goals and objectives. The truth is that much of what these individuals *say* passes for good theory in many cases yet isn't.

This is also true in other phases of financial products and services, including insurance providers, mutual funds, brokers of all types, informational organizations, and even others, including financial advisors and planners, who can be motivated by portfolio fees and commissions. Many of these don't always have your personal objectives in mind as much as their own. It is important to always ask a lot of questions and even seek second opinions when it comes to building your long-term prosperity program and to recognize that there is a lot of marketing that exists.

On the other hand, you might just have more control than you think in many areas of your prosperity plan, including taxes, investment diversification, resourcefulness of money management, earnings, percentage of income devoted to savings and investing, and other areas. The secret is to be *proactive* rather than *reactive* in the process of each one of these. Select the right investments that will boost your overall prosperity building over time and not attempt to do it quickly or overnight by accepting only the advice of so-called experts and financial marketers.

Your Personal Prosperity Success-Building Paradigm (PPSBP) is not realistic, functional, or complete unless it addresses each of these critical factors:

1. **A Diversified Asset-Class Base** - A mixture of several different investment categories is always recommended.

2. **An Element of Real Estate** - Property investing is still one of the best long-term investments for virtually any portfolio and any investor.

3. **The Impact of Taxes** - Taxes are one of your biggest expenses in life and play a significant role in prosperity building. If there is not an effective strategy in place to keep them proportionate, you could be paying more than your share of taxes.

4. **The Dimension of Liquidity of Some Assets** - You need a certain amount of access to cash and cannot have everything tied up in long-term investments.

5. **The Necessary Flexibility of the Inevitables in Life** - Birth, death, marriage, divorce, accidents, sickness, financial needs, life challenges, and opportunities are all part of life.

6. **An Emphasis on Financial Literacy Education** - If you are going to succeed, you need to know how to play the game. It all begins and ends with a good understanding of the "rules."

The learning lesson here is that personal prosperity planning is a *highly personal* experience and needs to be addressed in that manner. All the sophisticated computer printouts, charts, graphs, and statistics in the world *do not* represent your unique, individual, and personal life situation. It is the same difference between finely crafted heirloom furniture and the off-the-shelf varieties sold in countless home improvement stores by the thousands.

Ask yourself which is more valuable: custom-created personal planning or boilerplate ones? The evidence shows that boilerplate financial advice is simply not very effective for most prosperity seekers. It is absolutely amazing how much advertising gets passed off for insightful financial advice in magazines and investment programs in the media today. The conflicts of interest, abusive marketing practices, and self-dealing in financial markets are alarming to witness.

In addition, it is a myth to think that there is any single person, group of people, or even any financial institution that can accurately predict what's going to happen next in the financial markets (arguably, they have enough of a challenge in even deciphering what happened in yesterday's results, so how could they accurately predict tomorrow's?) If there were, indeed, a really hidden investment opportunity out there, what makes investors think that they would be even inclined to share it with others?

In truth, the odds of predicting the next hot investment opportunity are not necessarily a result of keen analysis, insight, or psychic capability and more commonly known by many economists as the theory of large numbers (i.e., at best, there is only a fifty-fifty guesstimate probability). Even if correctly selected, luck promises to run out eventually. In the end, investment advice frequently comes down to sophisticated marketing more than a solid investment possibility or opportunity. The solution to this financial investment conundrum is that your ultimate financial prosperity building lies where it should be—squarely on your shoulders and within your prosperity map plan that has been carefully prepared through the input of others but recognized as being your own.

It is *your plan* after all, and you are the one who will benefit from it or not. Know what it takes to create it and follow the steps that will take you where you want to go.

Useful Investing and Financial Educational Questions

The better our investing and financial educational questions, the better our chances to improve ourselves. In his book entitled *Killing Sacred Cows* (2008), author Garrett B. Gunderson has created a basic list of compelling questions when considering an investment choice, proposition, or educational teaching. Among them are the following:

1. *Why is this being taught? What is the background that led to the development of the teaching, concept, or theory? Is it based on sound economic principles that are relatively easy to understand?*

2. *Who benefits more if this lesson or investment is trusted and believed in? Who has a vested interest in seeing that it is believed, followed, or bought into? How will it benefit me?*

3. *After identifying where the interest lies, ask yourself this: what is the motivation of this person, financial institution, or advisor?*

4. *Is this teaching or opportunity in alignment with my own best interests, passions, and values? If so, how is it? If not, why isn't it?*

5. *Does the approach used utilize my passionate pursuit in life? What else is involved in it other than my money?*

6. *Is this proposition an immediate return or, instead, merely a hope for the future? Is it an existing value or a potential "stored" value for my future use/benefit?*

7. *What is my level of active management with it? What relationship is necessary with other people, institutions, or markets?*

8. *What are the opportunity cost tradeoffs of it (i.e., what else could I be doing with my time and money?)*

9. *Am I educated enough to be able to follow it and to make the decision? What information am I lacking, and how do I go about securing it?*
10. *Do I have a financial coach or mentor whom I can seek advice from or get additional information?*

By asking yourself each of the above questions, you are more likely to define the key elements of the investment, proposition, or teaching that is being offered and better and more able to make a better decision. This is by no means a complete list, and you should feel free to add your own personal questions to it. Never be afraid to question opportunities. It is the best method to prevent making a financial mistake or error.

STYLE

Style refers to the various types of investment choices that various investors use to choose to purchase their investments. Your choices determine your "style":

A. **GROWTH INVESTORS** - These are investors who choose investments that grow rapidly.
B. **VALUE INVESTORS** - These are investors who choose investments that appear to be undervalued compared to their current costs.
C. **GARP** (Growth and Return Prospects) - These investors choose an equal balance of growth and value returns.
D. **TECHNICAL INVESTORS** - These are investors who choose investments as a result of studying charts, graphs, and patterns of various investments.

CHOICES

The two fundamental types of paper investments are *stocks/mutual funds* where you own a piece of the company and purchase it, hoping that its value will increase over a period. It is also based on many external factors, including the industry, marketplace, and timing of the purchase.

•   The other type of paper investment is *bonds and notes*, which are essentially IOUs that pay a stated interest rate over a defined period on the investment purchase. At the end of the contract, you can review the investment and choose to take the initial investment and do something else with it or renew it again. Some, including municipal bonds, are state and federally tax-free.

Virtually all the Wall Street paper investments fall into one of these two choices, and there are thousands of derivatives of each of them, some simple and some very complex.

RULE OF THUMB: The shorter the period of your investment horizon or timeline, the more conservative you should be in your investing. Conversely, the longer the period of your investment horizon or timeline, the more risk tolerant you can afford to be. The rationale with each of these should be obvious.

An Effective Four-Pronged Investing Approach

Listed below is a very practical investment priority approach for the average investor to consider:

1) **RAINY DAY FUND** - This is an emergency fund that should be created initially.
2) **RETIREMENT NEST EGG FUND** - This is your long-term investment for your golden years of retirement.
3) **HOME PURCHASE FUND** - This is the money to set aside for your initial home purchase.
4) **BROKERAGE ACCOUNT FUND** - This is the money that will help supplement your senior years.

Detailed Discussion of Each of Them

Applying the four-pronged approach to your long-term prosperity plan creates a solid set of building blocks for your future.

How much should you put in each of them? Because of the power of compounding (we will go into this in a few minutes), if you can just put $50 per month into each of these accounts (more if you can afford it during certain months), you will have nearly $1,000 plus compounded interest (depending on where/how you invest the money) in just eighteen months.

Starting out the program is always the hardest part. But as you move along and apply the discipline and commitment to continuously do it, the money will start to grow and build in just a few years, and you probably will not even miss the money!

1. RAINY DAY FUND

One of the most important foundational blocks of personal finances is the creation of a rainy day fund or emergency fund equivalent to three or four months of monthly earnings. Ideally, this should be created even before you consider making any other portfolio investments. Where do you place this rainy day fund? The best choice is in a savings account or money market account, where you have total liquidity or complete access to it in case you need it. "Emergency" is a broadly defined term. Here are some specific examples of bona fide emergencies that you could use this fund:

- A vehicle accident where you need cash to pay for your insurance deductible
- Health-care injury where you need cash to pay for the hospital deductible
- Damages to your home or property that are under the deductible amount or not covered by insurance
- Sudden loss of income from your job because of layoff or downsizing

Here are some examples of nonemergencies that your rainy day or emergency fund should never be used for:

- Weekend trips or vacation excursions
- Shopping sprees
- Clothing purchases—even if the articles are on sale!
- Restaurant and hotel expenses
- Holiday shopping or gift buying

(Incidentally, when you use the rainy day fund, you must *always replace the money*).

By taking this step, you are insuring yourself against an unexpected incident that may cause you to have to borrow the money or to use your credit card. For this reason alone, it is a good idea to fund this account first.

2. RETIREMENT NEST EGG

People entering retirement today could conceivably spend as much time in this period as they did in their working careers. This is because, in part, of longer lifetimes as a result of better health care and longevity. It is for this reason alone that each of us must start planning for this important period in our lives at an early age. This is again where the power of compounding can create significant gains in your investments if they are left to multiply over your lifetime.

A retirement nest egg is the sum of all your investing and savings that have been made over your lifetime. It may consist of an IRA, CDs, a 401 (k), various mutual fund and stock market investments, a ROTH, and other financial security investments, such as bonds and bond funds. It also might include real estate investments, small business enterprise investments, and even some higher risk investments. Using a laddering approach allows you to invest on a regular basis and average your investments on a consistent level so that the result increases in value over the years.

The mistake that many people make is that they borrow money from their investments, which has the dramatic effect of curtailing the compounding effects. Few people realize that virtually 80 percent of their stock market and other investments increased value occurs in the last ten years of their investments. Borrowing from your retirement funds has a significantly negative effect on the opportunity to build through compounding.

3. HOME PURCHASE FUND

Despite the current real estate downturn, it is a fact that an investment in your home is of significant value over one's lifetime, and the positive effects of homeownership and long-term equity cannot be overlooked. As a result, it is important to set up a fund to start saving for an initial down payment for a house immediately as opposed to renting. For buyers, this is indeed the time of your life to consider purchasing a home since prices are at an all-time low. Real estate values will slowly rise again, and a purchase of a home real estate property will always be a good value when you can purchase it at a discount. **TIP:** Don't make the mistake of borrowing on your home equity via various loans created and offered by banks, mortgage companies, and other lenders to entice you to borrow against the equity of your home. This is where many people got into trouble during the housing crash in the Great Recession.

4. BROKERAGE FIRMS

There are many options in choosing a broker to invest your money for your retirement nest egg fund and a brokerage account fund, including the following:

A. **FULL-SERVICE BROKERS** provide stock recommendations, advice, strategies, and research at a significant annual cost. These firms are the right choices for investors who need assistance in creating a portfolio and managing it. These are typically either commission based or fee per account based.

B. **DISCOUNT BROKERS** are firms that are designed for those investors who choose to make their own investments and who choose to make their own decisions (think: do-it-yourself), and their fees are based on this provision. Their charges are "per transaction," and they offer a no-frills approach providing basic services. They do offer a full range of investment products above stocks and bonds, including bonds, mutual funds, CDs, annuities, life insurance, and even checking accounts and credit cards services.

Discount firms are good choices for those who do not trade frequently and those who choose to make their own investment decisions.

There are literally thousands of books, media programs, and DVD's that can help and assist you with learning about investing. The biggest question to ask is *whose money is it anyway*? And this should serve as your guiding light in how actively you are in maintaining and cultivating your investment portfolio.

There are also more investment options than merely paper investments. For example, investment real estate has always been a viable option for many prosperity builders. Another is a small business enterprise, either as a start-up entrepreneur or as an investor in an existing enterprise. Still, others include art and collectibles and gold and precious metals. The ideal portfolio should include a mixture of various types of investments to balance your personal investment portfolio.

CHAPTER 3

Ten Rules of Personal Prosperity Building

Building a higher level of prosperity requires adhering to a certain set of rules that allow you to be able to achieve it. It prevents you from wandering or developing a haphazard way of building it that could jeopardize the final results. Each of these rules has been carefully thought out and conceived so that it can act as a guide in assisting you in customizing your personal prosperity plan. These rules can help you achieve your overall results. In this chapter, ten of the most important ones are described in detail and will serve to have the largest effect in the necessary overall planning and preparation in your formula. Together, they offer a significant step in creating your unique, personal paradigm.

In this chapter, you will learn about the following:

- *Prosperity Laws Defined*
- *The Personal Prosperity-Building Rules*
- *Learning the Language of Prosperity*
- *The Ten Rules of Personal Prosperity Building*
- *Details and Descriptions of Each of the Rules Involved*
- *Creating an Effective Financial Regimen in Your Financial Life*

Prosperity Laws Defined

The word "law" is frequently associated with the legal process that government uses to punish. It seems that many people are unable to perceive that these are principles created by others to protect them from transgressions. They forget that the primary aims of laws are a defensive measure to ensure the security of everyone and that the secondary purpose is that of punishment when they are violated. The same is true with the laws of prosperity building. They are formed to protect and guard you from the pain, hardship, and suffering that will be the result from the failure to follow them. They are universally applied and not partial. Properly followed, they act as a guide to the highest levels of wealth and prosperity achievement.

The protection factor serves as the "guiding light" of its compliance, while the punishment aspect results in the likelihood that you will not be able to achieve your goals and objectives if they are not each followed one by one. These same laws that protect and preserve our ambitions will also punish us if they are not each complied with. As we progress through a process of learning and knowledge, that same process involves a certain amount of personal pain when the laws of prosperity are not followed.

In addition, it is the desire for some people to be able to achieve a high level of prosperity success without having to undergo compliance of these laws. They feel that the laws, principles, and beliefs should yield to their will and desire as they want to experience the gain without having to undergo compliance of these laws. However, the most successful prosperity seekers are those who know and understand that they must submit to each of these laws and bend their will while subjecting their desires to create the desired results.

Those who understand this are able to proceed in the planning via a proven process of established fundamentals that can keep them within the boundaries of prosperity building through these carefully chosen set of laws that are designed to eliminate as much of the potential pain as possible. After all, isn't any good, effective formula the result of carefully chosen "ingredients" and a process of blending them together in the right method that creates the desired results? Prosperity laws serve that very same purpose. They serve as the defining rules of the game.

Creating a Unique Personal Finance Success Formula

Many financially successful people share similar habits and views when it comes to money and have many things in common. Among them are the following, which help create a personal financial success formula:

- *They are passionate about the work/career they choose.*

- *They realize that there is no such thing as a GRQ (get-rich-quick) scheme and instead choose to get prosperous s-l-o-w-l-y.*
- *They recognize the importance of living within their means.*
- *They have learned how to handle and save money, many at an early age in life.*
- *They have developed good spending habits even before they started making large amounts of income.*
- *They fully understand the difference between needs versus wants as well as what is meant by materialism and consumerism.*
- *They pay off their credit card balances every month.*
- *They exercise self-discipline when it comes to the use of their money and always use a monthly budget or spending plan.*
- *They understand the use of insurance and the value of protecting their assets.*
- *They know how to create passive portfolio income in addition to earned income.*
- *They maintain a giving attitude and seek to be involved in philanthropy and volunteerism in a chosen area of their lives.*

When you carefully analyze financially successful people, they each follow the above pattern and principles.

Five Things You Should Know About Building Your Personal Prosperity

1. *It's Possible for Anyone to Do It* – Like any other successful undertaking in your life, prosperity building is something that can be achieved with the right blend of desire, willingness, focus, perseverance, and knowledge.
2. *It Doesn't Happen Overnight* – The mistake that too many individuals make in their building plan is that they think that it can be accomplished in a few days, weeks, or months. Instead, it may take a year or possibly more from the time that you start until you begin seeing the results of your planning and preparations.
3. *It Requires Both Knowledge, Strategy, and Implementation* – Personal prosperity building demands education to know and understand the entire process and how it can be used to create your unique individual strategy formula. Then it takes implementation to make it happen.
4. *It's a Team Effort* – There are frequently many people involved in the undertaking. Specialized professionals, including accountants, lawyers, financial advisors, coaches, tax advisers, spouse, family,

children, and others, must all work together to achieve the objective results.

5. ***It's Not Just About the Money*** – Prosperity building doesn't only involve finances and money management. It is a much higher level of personal achievement in life and the virtual *tipping point* where receiving and giving come together that create true happiness and job in life.

Three Common Misconceptions About Personal Finance and Money Problems

> I.   *It is something that I will somehow grow out of.*
> II. *It is something that I will earn my way out of.*
> III. *It is something that I will inherit my way out of.*

Reality:

Where you are right now will make a huge difference in where you will be five, ten, fifteen, twenty, or even twenty-five years from now!

Common Misunderstandings About Money and Finances

Many of us have developed misunderstandings about money and the use of it in our lifetimes. Here are some common misconceptions:

> ➢ *Using debt to identify some of the various ways to justify the use of credit*
> ➢ *Using good credit to create bad debts*
> ➢ *Inheritance perspectives that are passed down from parents to children*
> ➢ *Using emotional attitudes that alter poor spending habits*
> ➢ *Failing to look far enough into the future when we are young and thinking only in the moment*
> ➢ *Not understanding or comprehending the concept of compounding and how it works both for you and against you*
> ➢ *Routinely buying "bigger" than what your budget allows*
> ➢ *Not aligning your career, your spending, and your personal financial plans*

Changing Your Perspective About Personal Resources

Here are some useful tips when considering your future retirement needs and applications:

✓ *Keep your eye on your long-term financial objectives. It will help you avoid the bad short-term investment decisions that can ultimately cost you hundreds of thousands of dollars at retirement time.*

✓ *The prosperity process is a long-term program. No doubt you have eroded your potential future wealth by doing a number of nickel-and-dime mistakes, and it didn't happen all at once. Become a plumber and stop the leaks!*

✓ *Some of the big leaks: big balances on charge cards, large and expensive car loans, exorbitant credit card debt, and frequent dining out.*

✓ *Eliminate vices like smoking, illegal drugs, alcohol, gambling, and lottery ticket purchases. This alone can save you a lot of money over the course of a year's time.*

✓ *Create better shopping habits, such as not going to the movies so regularly, minimizing restaurant eating out, and using cash instead of credit cards. These alone can save you hundreds of dollars per month that can be invested in your retirement nest egg.*

By doing some of the above, you can stop the financial roller coaster that you may have been riding on for years. Remember the occasional stories of the janitor or manual laborer who died and to everyone's surprise left a fortunate to his church, school, or favorite charity? This is how they were able to do it.

It indeed takes maturity, responsibility, self-discipline, mental change of heart, decision to change your lifestyle, long-term as opposed to short-term thinking, the need for less *stuff in your life,* and a change of heart about consumerism. The result will be an independence from personal debt and no need to rely solely on Social Security to take care of you at retirement.

One of the enduring challenges is that the sacrifices are immediate, yet the payoff is long term.

Essential Money Skills That You Need to Learn

The following is a list of seven money skills that are a priority foundation to begin the process of developing solid money techniques, along with a brief explanation of each of them:

i. **Know How to Value It** – Make a point to plan your spending, especially the big-ticket items. Look for discounts. Create long-term (ninety days or more) planning strategies.

ii. **Know How to Control It** – Be sure to account for every dollar of your money. You can do this with computer software programs like Microsoft Money or Quicken. Use credit cards only for emergencies instead of day-to-day expenses and only when you can pay them off at each month.

iii. **Know How to Save It** – Prosperous people save first and then live on what's left over. *The key to good personal financial planning is to manage your cash flow and save/invest your surplus or disposable income.* It's so much easier to save a dollar than earning an extra one, just like it's easier to control spending than to increase income.

iv. **Know How to Invest It** – There are basically three risk levels: conservative, moderate risk, and high risk. All these are based on your age, retirement timetable, and level of risk. Knowledge and research are the keys to investing.

v. **Know How to Make It** – Simply put, when you earn it, you value it. The key is to create more than one stream of income, such as passive income, from investments and real estate and the kind that is reoccurring, such as an entrepreneurial business.

vi. **Know How to Protect It** – Understand and familiarize yourself with the various types of insurance and deductibles that are available to protect your assets.

vii. **Know How to Share It** – Develop a charitable attitude through a system of planned giving that is good for the giver as well as the receiver(s).

In Real Life, You Really Will Be Eaten by the Big, Bad World If

- ✓ *You don't learn to develop a competitive spirit*
- ✓ *You don't understand basic personal finance and economics*
- ✓ *You have an entitlement attitude*
- ✓ *You cannot balance taking with giving*
- ✓ *You think you do your employer a favor by showing up to work every day*
- ✓ *You don't learn from your mistakes, failures, and experiences*
- ✓ *You don't use your creativity and imagination whenever and wherever possible*
- ✓ *You don't develop good financial habits early in life*

✓ *You don't stay in touch with what's going in the global world when it comes to finances*

✓ *You think that your education ended when you received your diploma*

✓ *You don't maintain a reading and studying habit*

✓ *You are afraid to speak up when you see something going wrong with your finances or investments*

✓ *You don't listen to those who are wiser and more experienced in certain areas than yourself*

✓ *You develop a spending habit and don't balance it with a savings and investing one*

✓ *You don't create personal goals, dreams, and ambitions for the future*

The Essential Personal Prosperity-Building Rules

Rules are designed to guide many of our actions. Let's face it, without rules, where would we be in life? If there were no rules, there would be chaos; and we would seldom, if ever, receive the necessary guidance to achieve our goals and objectives. Literally, they are created to help keep us on track, emphasize key elements of learning, and otherwise they serve as a method to obtain higher levels of success in our undertakings. This is also true with the prosperity-building rules that follow. By their very nature, rules offer little flexibility since they are essentially a series of guiding light statements that lead us to logical and rational conclusions. They don't focus on the "how-to" but instead are based on significant and important statements or a formula that helps achieve the desired results for each of us.

As children, we wanted to believe that all rules were meant to be broken; yet as adults, we know and understand that rules are created and meant to be followed to accomplish our objectives regardless of the type or category of them. In nearly every situation in life, we use rules to direct our actions for accomplishing results in our endeavors. In the following pages, we have listed ten of the fundamental rules for prosperity building. Each of them serves a specific purpose in creating long-term prosperity in life. When followed, these rules work together to form a strong foundational formula for individual prosperity. By following each of them regularly, you join thousands of others who have learned the secrets of building significant prosperity in their lives and careers.

After reviewing them, you will find a full description of the purpose and use of each of them, and then you can begin to understand why they are so very important to your personal prosperity planning and preparation and how they will affect the achievement of your personal financial goals and objectives in life. Study them carefully and completely. They were created based on the author's study of hundreds of prosperity seekers over the years and are the reasons that you will achieve major success in your efforts if they are closely followed.

Learning the Vocabulary and Language of Prosperity

Successful prosperity achievement is similar to learning a new language. It is mentally stimulating and even exhausting at times. The results yield slow but discernible progress over time. You eventually learn to figure out what you have to work with and what you don't. The process of learning to integrate each of these takes time, not days or weeks but often months or years, yet it is achievable for each of you. Furthermore, it is a project that offers many challenges and often speaks in terms and phrases that are not always very easy to understand the first time around. In the end, after repetition and practice, it does yield many personal benefits and is well worth the effort.

Also, just like learning any foreign language, you need to take it slowly and build on every success and not get discouraged in the process of doing it. It pays to also remember that like any other difficult undertaking, there are rules, and there are disciplines that must be followed. It is not always easy to interpret the language of prosperity either, but it does need to be understood and comprehended over time to arrive at the right destination. Those of you who have tackled learning a new language can understand this process. They understand that often, there is no exact duplication of a concept or idea from one language to another. Foreign language also involves learning and working with customs just like the unique process that we often must use in prosperity building.

To be fluent in prosperity takes effort, but the result is *always* worth it!

The Ten Rules of Personal Prosperity Building

RULE #1 – *You Must Develop a Savings Attitude Instead of a Spending One*

RULE #2 – *You Should Understand That Money Is Often an Emotional Experience Rather Than a Rational or Logical One*

RULE #3 – *You Need to Understand That How You Use Money Says a Lot About Who You Are and What You Are*

RULE #4 – *You Must Learn That Planning and Preparation Is Essential to Accomplishing Your Personal Financial Goals and Objectives*

RULE #5 – *You Must Learn to Live Within Your Income and Means*

RULE #6 – *You Must Learn That Bigger Does Not Necessarily Mean Better Just as Quantity Does Not Equal Quality*

RULE #7 – *You Must Develop a Carefully Detailed Personal Prosperity Formula*

RULE #8 – *You Must Learn the Contrasting Difference Between "Think" and "Do"*

RULE #9 – *You Must Be Disciplined and Follow a Carefully Created Monthly Budget*

RULE #10 – *You Must Understand the Critical Difference Between "Want" and "Need" and Be Able to Distinguish Between Each of Them*

The Ten Rules of Personal Prosperity Building Explained

RULE #1 – DEVELOP A SAVINGS ATTITUDE

This rule was placed at the very top of the list for a very important reason: no prosperity-building plan will succeed until you have achieved the discipline of developing a savings attitude instead of a spending one.

Without such a view, your plan will always fall short of its potential.

What is a savings attitude? It is one that recognizes that you cannot and should not spend every dollar of your regular earnings regardless of the amount. It is a view that you must set aside a percentage (5 to 10 percent is recommended) of your net or take-home pay and invest it for the future. It is an understanding that life has its proportionate share of ups and downs and that setting aside a percentage of your earnings is not merely a good idea, but it is also a **cardinal rule** of effective prosperity building.

One of the best techniques and strategies to use in accomplishing this is the familiar phrase "Pay yourself first" concept, where you factor a certain percentage of your net income into an investment of some type or category and regularly write a check for it each and every payday or have it deducted from each paycheck. Either way, it becomes a sustaining prosperity booster.

A savings attitude also applies to many other areas of your life, including the judicious use of your earning in many other ways. For example, learning to use warehouse stores, such as Sam's Club or Costco or others, for many consumable purchases as well as Dollar Stores or similar discount stores for many other basic items. It includes always looking for good deals, discounts, and the use of coupons and effectively being able to barter or negotiate large purchases.

It also includes understanding the differences between "depreciating" assets like vehicles, furniture, clothes, and similar items and "appreciating" assets, such as real estate property investments, small business enterprises, and portfolio investments. It involves building an overall personal investment strategy for down-the-road use instead of spending every dollar that you earn (and then using credit cards or consumer loans to supplement your spending habits). It also means using a proactive approach to your use of a carefully developed household budget or spending plan rather than a reactive one that leaves you short at the end of every month. Creating and developing a savings attitude is a single, most important step in your prosperity-building strategy plan, and it cannot be sidestepped or compromised for any reason. It is also an effective way to teach your children and help them improve their financial behavior at an early age.

Finally, it is a philosophy that you will make every dollar count in your life. To paraphrase our twenty-first-century version of a familiar Benjamin Franklin expression, "A dollar saved is (literally) an investment dollar earned."

RULE #2 – MONEY IS OFTEN AN EMOTIONAL EXPERIENCE

We like to think of the use of money as a faceless, detached, unemotional, and pragmatic transaction that is more about the use of the "mind" as well as the wallet or purse than the "heart." Studies have shown, however, that this is often not the case. Money emotions play a major and contributing factor in the handling and effective use of it. There are many personal emotions that are often linked to our use of money both good and not so good, and the ways that we use it and abuse it have a lot to do with our emotions toward our finances and use of it.

Learning what motivates your money emotions is the first step in the better use of it and positively improves our financial behaviors. Personal prosperity building involves using your earnings to create more and better long-term results; and emotions play a substantial role in it and, in addition, how and to what degree your prosperity is ultimately achieved. There is a place for rational and logical money handling (think: investments and securities portfolios). Those who have learned to handle money in a more detached manner often achieve better overall results. Each of us needs to understand that money emotions play a big part in the use of our finances in our lives. Discovering each of our emotional "triggers" can also go a long way in developing better perspectives about better money handling. It is also important to how we can more effectively use it and its potential.

Emotional money management can, however, create less-than-desirable results if the results are purely and entirely heartfelt and not coupled with a sense of meaning or purpose. Many fortunes have been squandered because of the illogical and irrational use of it as opposed to a more deliberate and carefully planned strategy. Think of the countless stories we read or watched on the television news media of those who suddenly and unexpectedly won huge lottery or sweepstakes winnings and, within just a few short years, have lost every bit of it and perhaps even filed bankruptcy, all because they let emotion override logic. Soon, it was gone as quickly as it arrived.

Often, we discount the effects that emotions have in the proper use of money in our lives, yet there is an element in it in every financial decision we make, good or bad.

RULE #3 – HOW YOU USE MONEY SAYS A LOT ABOUT YOU

How you use money in your life says a lot about you and who you are. The ways that it is used by us helps define our very character and perception of others. What then is your unique *money personality*? A list of unique yet common descriptions of various money personalities is attached that can perhaps help you determine your own personal money style. It can assist you in defining your individual money personality. A cautionary note, however. You might not like everything that you will see as it is slowly revealed to you.

Your money personality is a highly intense and helpful method of examining your personal use of money and in developing a financial composite of your individual money personality. You may even be surprised to learn about yours. It offers a rare glimpse into many of the contributing factors, including how you use money in your dealings with others. Your money personality may also be a mixture of several different types. This is often the case since few of us have a single all-of-one-kind type. It is often a mixture of two or more of them with one specific and dominant one that eventually emerges.

Your money personality offers a rare look at who and what you are and further reveals many aspects of your character, attitudes, motivations, and other personal qualities that affect your use of money and how you earn and spend.

Save and invest your money resources. They help define who you are and what you are all about when it comes to your relationship with money.

Do you use it as a status symbol, as a reward, for controlling others, as a sense of manipulation, or in a generous, giving, thoughtful, and philanthropic expression of your personality? These money personality extremes serve to define your use and application of your money resources and are a significant part of your very life.

RULE #4 – PLANNING AND PREPARATION ARE ESSENTIAL

What's the first thing we all do when planning a vacation or extended trip? What are the steps that we take to arrive on time, intact, and with enough money to enjoy the experience? At the beginning of the process referred to as the thinking stage, don't we pull out the map or atlas to locate our destination, gather as much useful information and data, find points of interest, mark out our stops along the way, and then create an overall timetable? Don't we also locate a notepad and pencil and begin making lots of detailed notes, including budgeting our expenses so that we will have enough resources to make the trip worthwhile? Doesn't it then make a lot of sense that we should follow the same process or even *more extensively* for creating a long-term personal prosperity plan? Aren't the results of *that* journey truly worth it?

Many people go through life without making very many plans for the future. They then wake up one day in midlife (or conceivably later) and suddenly and profoundly realize that they haven't done enough in the P&P department (planning and preparation). They then become stressed out, fearful, and apprehensive that perhaps it is too late to recover from their *lack* of preparation. Understand that it *is never too late* to start building your prosperity plan. It will quite obviously take more discipline and commitment (as well as more money set that will need to be set aside each month) to achieve any significant level of personal prosperity if you wait until midlife to get started, but it is still possible.

A modest $100 set aside and invested every month in your twenties will grow into a great nest egg. At midlife, it would require $500–$600 per month or even more to achieve the same results in your investments. Why? Because you have lost many of the magical benefits of compounding! That's why. And there is no way to get that investment time back, so you have to simply ante up more money later in life.

The upside to midlife is that you should have a clearer vision of your future since you are further down the road. You should also be a lot more realistic and focused about your life goals and objectives. You need to know where you are now and where you want to be later more than when you are young. That can work to your distinct advantage in prosperity planning (think of the Aesop's Fable of the Tortoise and the Hare). In any regard, even if you aren't yet disciplined or cannot afford to set aside money early in life, at least you should consider some of the preparatory steps, the thinking, and the planning as you go along in life. Having a good "game plan" is all about the P&P. Watch a Broadway play, go to a symphony orchestra presentation, and attend a college or professional sporting event and think of all the planning, preparation, and practice that went into it before the final presentation and outcome.

Then ask yourself, "Isn't my like prosperity planning equally important?"

RULE #5 – LEARN TO LIVE WITHIN YOUR MEANS

We all like nice things and want to enjoy a comfortable lifestyle. That is the common denominator within each of us. Yet those who use credit cards, consumer loans, and equity lines of credit to purchase too many "toys" are creating mountains of debt that start piling up as opposed to their investments and prosperity building. They don't seem to realize that personal debt is the biggest budget buster in achieving any significant long-term level of prosperity building.

It is certainly okay and all right to buy and own "stuff" within reason or course, but when you have to borrow money to finance it and your other comforts and craving, then it is arguably time to take an inventory and ask yourself if you are living within your means or are sacrificing your future prosperity through the use of borrowing money in the present. On tip of this, you are *paying* compound interest to someone else instead of *receiving it* from your investments.

In interviewing hundreds and thousands of people over the years, the issue of living within your means ranks near the very top of the successful implementation of one's personal prosperity plan and can provide a major negative factor in being able to get ahead of your personal financial life as well. Debt caused by overspending doesn't allow you to create needed discretionary income (money that is left over as a result of net or take-home earnings less expenses). For that reason, it is difficult, even impossible, to ever have any money to invest in the future. If you are spending 100 percent (or more than this if you are using credit cards or consumer loans to buy your "stuff"), chances are that you should closely examine your lifestyle and begin the necessary discipline of living within your means in the future.

What's more important than your financial future?

RULE #6 – BIGGER DOESN'T ALWAYS MEAN BETTER: QUANTITY VS QUALITY

Let's face it. We live in the land of *big*. As Tom Hank's character showed in the 1980's movie *Big*, he learned the effects of bigness when his world suddenly turned upside down, and everything became *big* for him. Today we see bigness in virtually everything we see and do—bigger burgers and fries, bigger clothing sizes (when was the last time you saw a "small"? It seems that the smallest size now is large or supersized), bigger coffee servings, bigger types of furniture and beds, and even bigger homes that are termed McMansions. It seems that we experience bigness in nearly everything that we see and do today. It is such a descriptive term that many have even forgotten (or worse, never learned) other descriptive terms, such as "good, better, or best" and instead use *big* as the catch-all phrase substitute.

One of our fifty states even has a well-known and well-used expression to describe its status and perspective in the United States—"Everything is bigger in Texas!" Let's ask ourselves if bigger doesn't usually come with a (ahem) "bigger" price. If bigger is all we ever seek, then it would seem that other terms should be removed from the vocabulary and dictionary. What purpose would "good, better, and best" serve? The same is true with quantity versus quality. Even here, the perception seems to underline the perceived reality that largeness always trumps quality.

So isn't prosperity building all about creating larger and B-I-G-G-E-R assets and net worth? Isn't bigness a good thing when it comes to incomes, assets, and financial statements? The answer to these questions is both "yes" and "no." "Yes" if it means that you have chosen the right prosperity-building formula so that you can achieve higher levels of results but "no" if it means that in the process of doing it, you are stressed out as a result of the risk-taking, active asset management, inability to take needed time off, and using a formula that does not adapt well to the ups and downs of the periodic cycles of the economy and the marketplace.

A good, effective prosperity plan doesn't have to be (pardon the pun) *big*. A better one is one that produces consistent gains and value and does it month in, month out and, year after year, is much preferred over one that produces "big" peaks but equivalent "big" valleys. It seems that "big" is only a useful term when it comes to net incomes after taxes at the end of the year and not in everyone else's perception of *big*, or perhaps the best and most useful definition of *big* is the one that is used to describe the type of giver and philanthropist you are?!

RULE #7 – DEVELOP A DETAILED PERSONAL PROSPERITY FORMULA

Isn't developing a personal prosperity formula what this book is all about? The answer to this is obvious but not the individual formula that you use to do it. Everyone's personal prosperity plan is unique based on their individual goals and objectives, incomes, risk tolerance, education, background, financial strength, and willingness to commit to achieve higher results based on effort and persistence. Creating the personal formula that works best for you is not something that can be done in an evening, a weekend, or even in a month. It is a detailed process that will often and usually take many months, possibly even a few years, to accomplish it via a step-by-step and move-by-move strategy that is based on many key factors. The most important of these factors are your knowledge and education in how to do it wisely and effectively as well as your discipline and commitment to implement it.

This is what this book is all about: how to do it well and for the optimum results. It must be remembered that it is not an event but an entire process in your life that if carefully prepared and planned will achieve substantial levels of personal prosperity for years to come and continue to work for you even after you are gone. The key, of course, is to develop a unique, individual formula that serves as the basis for your entire prosperity-building program.

It requires and involves reading, studying, and learning many of the options that are available to you. However, even when the formulas and techniques are learned and understood, the process is not over. Learning without implementation is like a vehicle without any fuel to power it. It is useless until it is added. Therefore, you must be able to implement the strategies that you have learned into a useful method that puts the sizzle in your long-term, carefully thought-out prosperity plan. Why go through all this effort? After all, ask yourself the following revealing and compelling question: who is ultimately going to benefit from it?

RULE #8 – THE DIFFERENCE BETWEEN "THINK" AND "DO"

When growing up in the 1950s, there was a popular and widely used series of elementary schoolbooks used across the country known as *Think-and-Do* books that were designed specifically for adolescents and published by the Houghton Mifflin Harcourt company. These books taught the fundamental life skills and concepts needed for growing and maturing while covering everything from reading, writing, language, and other important and fundamental principles. These principles were taught in a continually advanced level, depending on the grade in school. They were highly successful because they taught a foundational principle, and then they followed it up with a useful personal application. The concept behind this series of educational workbooks was to closely examine a particular issue or situation and then choose the correct response from a list of questions, answers, and other options that best fit the problem.

This is the same application that you can use in your personal prosperity plan. After learning the various options, strategies, and techniques, you can then implement the "think and do" phase of your personal prosperity building. We are all familiar with the expression, "When all is said and done, there's always more said than done." This, unfortunately, is true of many prosperity-building plans.

The same concept of "think and do" holds true with the concept of adult thinking and doing. The only way that the learning will ever develop into a full-fledged action plan is if it turns from one to the other. That means carefully considering the options, developing the strategies, taking the risks, making the commitments, and following a prosperity-building plan by staying on track with it and refining it from time to time. In the end, the difference between "thinking and doing" is very similar to dreaming versus doing. Putting your ideas to work to create a beneficial result is the goal. This is the literal defining point where action replaces concept and theory and the portion of the process that puts teeth into your prosperity-building plan.

The thinking portion of the personal prosperity plan is very important. Without it, there will be little chance to create the correct formula that fits your particular needs. As a result, you should spend a considerable amount of time, energy, and resources planning, preparing, and creating it for your long-term use. However, equally important is the "doing" aspect of your plan since concepts and ideas are worthless unless they are coupled with action. It is these same "actions" that will produce the necessary results.

PEARL OF WISDOM: *Why not create your own version of a* Think-and-Do *workbook for your personal prosperity plan?!*

RULE #9 – YOU MUST BE DISCIPLINED AND FOLLOW A BUDGET

As a former U.S. marine who served in Vietnam in 1968–1969 as an infantryman, I can personally attest to the positive effects of discipline when involved in a challenging personal life-threatening situation (or albeit a financially threatening one when it comes to your overall prosperity planning).

Self-discipline can be a very useful and needed tool in life, especially when coupled with a well-designed, positive, life-changing personal prosperity plan. It can provide a powerful method to achieve many of your personal goals and objectives. It can also provide the necessary self-motivation and gut-level personal desire that never says "good-bye" when things become difficult or adverse. Is this an exaggeration for use with a personal prosperity plan? Think about this question for a moment: have you ever thought about creating a personal prosperity plan before? If so, did you do it? The effects of discipline can move mountains if used objectively and correctly.

Often, we face many distractions and demotivators in life. Our daily family and work routines, job and career challenges, weekends, holidays, and other responsibilities all have a profound effect on each of us; and the result is that we don't always do the things that need to be done and opt to do things that are frequently more fun and enjoyable. What is the common denominator with many of the reasons why things fail to get done? Frequently, it is a money factor (and *usually*, it is from having too *little* of it as opposed to too *much* of it). More often, however, one of the reasons that we do not have enough of it is the lack of intestinal fortitude, a polite word used to describe willpower or discipline. One of the most significant areas that it can be used in our lives is via the active use of a carefully prepared household budget or spending plan document.

The very term "budget" can create a negative attitude within many people. "It means that I will have to go without things I really like!" say many. "It will result in my not being able to do things and go places that I really enjoy!" say others. Or "It will result in my not being able to have as much fun!" say some. The answer to each of these responses is that you can continue to maintain the lifestyle that you are accustomed to but maybe just not quite as often or quite as much. Cutting back in just one or two critical areas, such as those in the "big four" expenses discussed elsewhere in this book, can result in the needed funding that you can use to immediately start building discretionary income through your household budget.

Virtually all financially successful people share this personal character quality. Admittedly, they may have personal "indulgences" that they favor; but ultimately, they also realize that there are *limits* on everything in life (even very good thins) and can easily justify some of them because they have the discipline to cut back in other needed areas of their lifestyle to be able to afford their fun. This is why many of them can afford to spend money on expensive "toys." They know how to budget for them and have the discipline and willingness to sacrifice in getting them. Discipline can always be a positive motivator. One other way to describe it is to ask yourself how badly you really want something. The "fuel" that you can use to eventually secure it is called *discipline*.

RULE #10 – UNDERSTAND THE DIFFERENCE BETWEEN "NEEDS AND WANTS"

Some of the best salespeople in the world are children. Their innocent and apple-cheeked, cherublike expressions are simply irresistible when it comes to their badly "wanting" something. We often excuse this behavior because most of the time, they don't realize the distinction between a "want" and "need"; and if they have a "want," they predictably also think of it as a deep-seated "need" because they have not yet learned the contrasting differences between these two desires.

Adults, however, should realize the vastly and proportionate differences between these two extremes. On one hand, "needs" are characteristically viewed as shelter, transportation, food, clothing, medical care, and associated expenses that are basic necessities in life. These are the core essentials that are "needed" to sustain each of us in our lives. "Wants," on the other hand, cover virtually everything else in our lives, including such things as dining out, concerts tickets, cruises and exotic vacations, designer clothing and accessories, boats, country club memberships, and virtually everything else above and beyond basic necessities. It is virtually a long list of material possibilities. The problem often occurs when people confuse the two of them and feel that just because they have a desire for something or anything, it is a "need" when actually, it is a "want" that is being expressed. It is also very easy for each of us to justify turning our "wants" into "needs." As adults, many of us have the financial freedom to buy nearly anything we want and don't always look carefully enough at whether our purchase is affordable in our budget or spending plan regardless of the price. Many feel that if there is enough left on our credit card balance or equity line of credit to buy a new boat or RV or other "want," then we can, indeed, afford it. Sadly, this is the wrong barometer to use. A better strategy would be to understand how much value that putting aside an equivalent amount of money into an investment account would create for them over a period of a few years. This coupled with the appreciating efforts of the account (10 to 15 percent per year) plus the magical effects of compounding the investment totals is a far better comparison and use of our discretionary incomes.

Which of these money management approaches do you feel *appreciates* in value over a time? Which of these *depreciates* in value and earnings in a few short years? Which of them do you feel you will be more pleased with over a longer period? Identifying the differences between "need" and "wants" is an important core principle rule in developing and creating your personal prosperity plan and will significantly impact your prosperity-building results.

CREATING AN EFFECTIVE SHORT- AND LONG-TERM PERSONAL FINANCIAL REGIMEN

For the purpose of this illustration, let's say that you have made a successful prosperity move whether it was securing a promotion that results in better earnings, starting a small business and watching it begin to grow, purchasing a real estate property investment, or buying a block of stock that suddenly increases in value. What do you do now? Do you simply pat yourself on the back? Do you develop a sense of triumph? Do you experience malicious delight? Or do you identify and isolate another prosperity opportunity to capitalize on and go forward?

Long-term prosperity success stories are usually a direct result of careful consideration, planning, preparation, and strategic moves similar to a competitive chess match that occur move by move and step by step, which build your personal prosperity through an effective financial regimen. These moves focus on making the *right moves* at the most opportune time instead of series of haphazard moves that come about once in a while when you feel motivated for whatever reason to do it. Given a choice, a carefully conceived, disciplined, regimented approach will always produce the desired long-term results. Prosperity building, after all, is a systematic course of events consisting of "game winning" strategies that are carefully thought out in advance and implemented just like a patient, experienced angler who knows exactly where to cast his line into the water and at what time of day or night and along with the proper bait. Knowing the "how" and the "when" to be able to successfully do it creates the desirable results.

Prosperity builders are made and not born, and it all starts with education and an effective personal financial regimen. Without it, your efforts are, at best, a crapshoot and, at worse, merely a guessing game that can produce major blunders in your long-term personal prosperity success "scorecard." When properly put into action in your personal prosperity plan, the use of a properly designed regimen similar to your daily exercise routine can significantly help your planning and preparation and results. It is through this discipline that major effects can be witnessed in your ultimate outcome. When properly applied, it will have a virtual layering effect that can produce the very best results.

Besides, have you ever met a fisherman who was content to catch just one fish and who didn't want to catch the next biggest one?

CHAPTER 4

Prosperity Thinking Versus Poverty Thinking

In this chapter, you will learn about the following points:

- *A Streetwise Sense of Prosperity*
- *What Is the Silver Bullet in Prosperity Building?*
- *Financial Education*
- *A Prosperity Testament*
- *The Divine Mind*
- *In Defense of Prosperity*
- *Some of the Primary Causes of Poverty*
- *Survival of the Financially Fittest*
- *Overcoming Many Money Disorders*
- *Poverty Versus Prosperity Views*
- *Primary Causes of Poverty*
- *Prosperity Optimists Versus Poverty Pessimists*
- *Your Financial Personality*
- *Ten Common Money Personalities*
- *Extreme Money Personalities*
- *Flat-View Thinking*
- *The Psychology of Prosperity Thinking*
- *Personal Economic Reform*
- *Arriving at the Epiphany Moment*

Prosperity Versus Poverty Views

The wealthy and the poor think very differently about money and its use,
Without a significant shift in thinking, it is difficult to move from one group to another.
—Brad Klontz, Psychologist, and Ted Klontz, PhD
Authors of *Mind over Money* (2009)

Prosperity Thinking Versus Poverty Thinking

Our attitudes play a critical role and an important factor in significant personal prosperity building just as they do in other aspects of our life. They are often the critical difference between long-term successes and failures and evidenced by examining every high-level prosperity builder and their accomplishments. Developing and maintaining a positive prosperity-building attitude will play a big role in your eventual long-term results and even the size of those results. Some of the specific factors that involve prosperity thinking as well as poverty thinking are discussed in great detail in this chapter. They can function as your positive prosperity attitude and will affect the entire process.

A Streetwise Sense of Prosperity

There is a pervasive view that if you are rich, then you are smart. It seems to say that the wealthier you are, the more intelligent you must be. Following that view, the wealthiest people must also be the smartest ones. *Wrong!* Unfortunately, that correlation simply does not exist. To be wealthy is to be wealthy, just as to be smart is to be smart. Occasionally, they are one in the same but only by coincidence. Some highly wealthy people got that way from a streetwise sense of opportunity and ability to be able to make money. However, they might not even be a good role model or be able to give good personal advice. The same is true for prosperity success. Wealth does not always require a high IQ or commerce or investing MBA degree. It does require desire, discipline, and commitment, along with a willingness to create a step-by-step plan to be able to follow and achieve.

Academic underachievers, on the other hand, have the same opportunity, or even better, to create long-term prosperity as highly educated intelligent ones. That said, remember that well-to-do people do not have to be intellectually smart just as those with high IQs often struggle with high levels of prosperity just like anyone else.

In the end, they are often two separate and entirely distinct issues.

What Is the "Silver Bullet" in Prosperity Building?

Just exactly what is the magic solution to prosperity building? Is there one? We have included many possibilities, techniques, strategies, formulas, and templates in this text writing that are proven prosperity success achievers. Each of them can individually help accomplish our goals, and collectively, they can go a long way toward prosperity building. But is there another more direct or better method of accomplishing it? Is there a process that has been overlooked? Have we missed something? Is there anything that will be more effective in bringing the desired results?

As it turns out, the silver bullet in personal prosperity building can be summed up with two simple words:

F-i-n-a-n-c-i-a-l E-d-u-c-a-t-i-o-n

It is through financial education that individuals gain the insights and knowledge to learn what it takes to create the unique and individual template formula that will power the engine of your prosperity rocket ship like nothing else. It is through prosperity education that all the various techniques bring about the knowledge and understanding that will put you on the right track and keep you there. It is through this form of education that the blueprint map is ultimately achieved. It can be enhanced through the advice of those on your professional prosperity team consisting of advisors, planners, brokers, agents, realtors, mentors, teachers, and trainers; but it is, in the end, a uniquely personal effort that begins and ends with you knowing enough about all the prosperity-building options. This knowledge is what can help you make the right decisions and selections that serve to steer your prosperity rocket ship in the right direction at the right speed and following the right course so you end up on Mars and not Pluto.

By using your financial education, you will be in the driver's seat. *Get ready, get set, blast off!*

The Divine Mind

In the book *Prosperity* written by Charles Fillmore in 1936, he discusses "Man, the Inlet and Outlet of Divine Mind" in lesson 4. It is yet another example of prosperity thinking versus poverty thinking mind-set. In it, he says,

"Do not hesitate to think that prosperity is for you. Do not feel unworthy [of achieving it]. Banish all thoughts of being a martyr to poverty. No one enjoys poverty, but some people seem to enjoy the sympathy and compassion they can excite because of it. Overcome any leaning in that direction and every belief that you were meant to be poor. No one is ever hopeless until he has resigned to his imagined fate. Deny every appearance of failure."

He also documents a poem that he adapted entitled

A Prosperity Testament

(A revised Twenty-Third Psalm of Prosperity)

The Lord is my banker, my credit is good.
He maketh me to lie down in the consciousness of omnipresent abundance;
He giveth me the key to His strongbox,
He restoreth my faith in His riches;

He guideth me in the paths of prosperity for His name's sake,
Yea, though I walk in the very shadow of debt,
I shall fear no evil for Thou art with me;
Thy silver and Thy gold, they secure me.

Thou preparest a way for me in the presence of the tax collector;
Thou fillest my wallet with plenty; my measure runneth over.
Surely goodness and plenty will follow me all the days of my life,
And I shall do business in the name of the Lord forever.

In Defense of Prosperity

With money in your pocket, you are wise, you are handsome, and you sing well in the shower.

—Old Yiddish Proverb

What does it take to become prosperous? Hard work? Energy? Good opportunity? Income? Or all this? It is becoming increasingly harder in this era of high taxes and governmental regulation to achieve prosperity, but millions still have managed to be able to gain prosperity in their lives in spite of the challenges. Only in capitalistic societies where people are allowed to take personal chances and risk security in exchange for gain to improve their lives in many ways can it be accomplished. It is through the process of their own choosing that individuals are able and free to prosper and grow. It is a process that needs defending because it is no sin to be prosperous. It is a right for every American based on the free enterprise capital system.

It is a personal prosperity book that can be written by laymen, practical people, and individuals rather than economists or the "masses." To have the audacity to become prosperous and have a little "extra" should not create an opportunity for others to be less motivated or for them to pass instant judgment on those who seek to pursue it. To enjoy prosperity is to even expose ourselves to criticism by symbols of it; and there are those who feel compelled to make judgments on those who have learned to do better in life, which is an age-old problem, including issues such as what should they be allowed to earn and how they should spend their money.

Much of this questioning is done in the name of equality, which differs greatly from equality of individual opportunity. Much of modern-day prosperity can be credited to the capitalistic free market system that was fathered by Adam Smithy, a Scottish philosophy professor who wrote the classic book of economics entitled *Wealth of Nations* over 250 years ago. Its basic point was that people work best in their own self-interest, and therefore, they should be allowed to do exactly that in their personal lives, careers, and futures.

Those who were born in twentieth-century America take the freedom to develop their personal prosperity for granted. To them, it seems a natural state of mankind as opposed to the unique prosperity-building opportunity that others in the rest of the world cannot engage or participate in. The epitome of prosperity lies within the legendary families, including the Vanderbilts, the Peabodys, the Carnegies, the Goulds, the Gettys, the Rockefellers, and the Fords. It is they who have been the target of persistent and hysterical abuse and often resentment because of their formidable wealth and prosperity. It didn't matter, it seems, what they did with the vast money resources; it is enough, apparently, that they just had it. Yet these families have each done much to improve and add value to our civilized society in such areas as art, music, libraries, medical research, and education. It is a too-soon-forgotten fact that many prosperity achievers accomplish monumental charitable and philanthropic giving and forever change millions of American lives.

It seems that we really do need prosperity seekers after all.

Some of the Primary Causes of Poverty

Poverty is often caused by a problem or combination of problems that are seemingly unsolvable to those affected and are not, as many people feel, a result of only financial issues and situations.

Some of the compelling reasons for poverty among people today are the following:

- ✓ **Compulsive disorder behaviors like alcohol, gambling, or drug abuse**
- ✓ **Low skill levels, lack of technical training, or substandard education resulting in a low-paying job**
- ✓ **Health-care issues resulting in frequent medical treatments without adequate insurance coverage in place**
- ✓ **Improper money management resulting in excessive debt, foreclosure, or even bankruptcy**
- ✓ **The inability to borrow money because of an inferior or below-average credit or payment history**
- ✓ **Previous criminal record resulting in not being able to secure any licenses or good-paying job or career**
- ✓ **Creating a large family with the result of no practical method of supporting them**
- ✓ **Getting married early in life to someone who you are incompatible with resulting in a costly divorce**

These and other problems, factors, and issues are the reasons that many people cannot seem to break out of the poverty cycle to become prosperous.

On top of this, many social and economic problems are perceived as those that only the government can solve. Make no mistake. The method to steer yourself out of the poverty cycle has nothing to do with dependence on the government. *Their solution lies squarely with you.*

Only you can do it for yourself.

Survival of the Financially Fittest

As we know only too well, life can have its share of prosperous periods as well as survivalist ones. Often, when things seem to be performing at their best, we are subjected to an event or series of events or circumstances that force us to look at the bigger life picture and realize that somehow, someway, it can and will all average out (hopefully, that is).

Some people take a similar view of their prosperity building. Instead of a conscious and disciplined effort to set aside the necessary funds for emergencies or rainy days, they feel that life will somehow "balance out" the various ups and downs and that there is little need for them to interrupt their lifestyle until it is absolutely necessary to do so.

The well-known fable of the ant and the grasshopper comes to mind in considering this. As you may recall, the ant, noted for its hard work, discipline, and perseverance, busied himself every day throughout the summer months with his efforts of putting away food and other supplies and provisions, while his counterpart, the grasshopper, whiled away his time during the same period, fiddling away in the sunshine. Alas, when winter eventually arrived, the grasshopper had nothing to carry him through the cold, dreary months, while the ant remained warm and secure as a result of his work.

The same situation exists in real life too. Many of the "grasshoppers" in life are content to merely have fun, enjoy themselves, and refuse to even think about what might happen to them if a personal financial crisis should occur. When it inevitably does, they panic and become anxious, not knowing what to do, much less have any finding to be able to accomplish it. These grasshoppers have literally "fiddled away" their prosperity-earning years by engaging in too much consumerism and materialism and did not create enough "financial provisions" to carry them through a potential "down" period that occurs frequently. For them, surviving during a low point or calamity is something that they didn't want to even think about, much less were willing to prepare for. They frequently have few or limited resources because they lived paycheck to paycheck and worse, may even have subsidized their lifestyle by using and abusing credit cards, consumer debt, and home equity loans. As a result, they are ill-prepared to handle an emergency or other disaster when it arrives at their doorstep in any form whatsoever.

Meanwhile, the "ants" of the world know only too well that life hurls many objects at them from time to time. Many of these are minor inconveniences and can be quickly addressed. Others are more serious and require a longer-term financial solution. Some of them are bona fide economic calamities that can forever shape their future life and existence. Ants know and understand the differences between a spending and a savings attitude. They wisely use insurance as asset protection in their prosperity building. They also create rainy day or emergency funds and make no pretense of trying to merely *look* prosperous. Instead, their motivation is to *become* prosperous in their life. Secure in their "burrow," they are ready to endure life's financial storms because they have judiciously, prudently, and carefully set aside a percentage of their earnings, bonuses, incomes, and even windfalls into a series of sound and adequate financial investments that function to get them through tough, difficult, and challenging economic periods in their lives.

Many people experienced such a "financial survival mode" in the fall of 2008 when the entire financial world was turned upside down as a result of too much consumerism and personal indebtedness that resulted in a "swarm of locusts" that darkened the economic skies and sent many to ruin as they eventually started to examine their lifestyle and spending patterns. On one hand, those grasshoppers who did not bother to set aside any of their earnings quickly became victims of this financial crisis and devastation. On the other hand, the corresponding ants of the world were able to rely on their stored financial provisions and, together with their savvy and expertise in learning how to do it over the years, were able to survive and even thrive during this cataclysmic period that many say even rivaled the Great Depression of the 1920s and 1930s. They were able to do it because of their preparation and planning plus a learned ability to be able to take advantage of their past efforts to get through this dark period of American personal finance history.

Ironically for the ants, this period also resulted in many significant financial opportunities for them that occurred as a result of many discounted prices, reductions, numerous sales, frequent auctions, foreclosures, downsizing, and other events that were the result of too many grasshoppers and too few ants. Many would argue that it has been this way since the down of mankind, the contrast between the "haves" and the "have-nots," but the secret (if there really is one) lies in the *discipline* and the *commitment* of those resourceful individuals who know and understand the fundamental differences between life's ups and downs and who know the value of setting aside adequate financial "supplies and provisions" to carry them through similar dark periods.

Sadly, many of those under age fifty who went through this recent major economic downturn had never experienced a similar down period in their entire lives, leaving them totally unprepared in dealing with the losses, much less even knowing *how to* deal with the losses. Their unwillingness to prepare and plan literally changed their lives forever. *Meanwhile, the ants continue to prosper and take advantage of the numerous opportunities that came up as a result of the grasshoppers' numerous misfortunes.*

Overcoming Many Money Disorders

Many people have an existing complex, complicated, and perhaps even dysfunctional view and relationship with money and finances that causes frequent personal hardships. Our troubled attitudes and views often are the result of a lack of knowledge, which has created many incorrect beliefs, behaviors, and habits that can even go back to our childhood and upbringing. In addition, they may also be shaped by some of the financial errors, mistakes, and blunders that we have made in our lives, which resulted in painful personal finance experiences. However, even information is not enough to overcome all the challenges that you may be faced regarding money issues. These beliefs and behaviors are often so deeply imprinted into our subconscious mind that they can shape the way we interact with our money and our relationships with others throughout our entire lives.

By taking a close look at our relationship with money and personal finances, we can learn to examine, analyze, and recognize these negative behaviors that are self-defeating and can have the effect of threatening marriage, career, prosperity building, and our ultimate joy, contentment, and happiness.

A few of the more common compulsive money disorders are the following:

- *Compulsive Overspending*
- *Using Money to Influence Others*
- *Creating Financial Enabling*
- *Obsessive Money Hoarding*
- *Avoiding Personal Money Problems*
- *Using Money to Buy Friendships and Love*

The answer to many of these issues is the ability to learn to recognize many of the symptoms and disorders while learning how to better deal with each of them to overcome them. Developing a healthy view and better perspective of your relationship with money and personal finances will help you to be able to enjoy a better and more prosperous life.

DEBT: A Four-Letter Word Meaning "Too Much Spending"

Of all the prosperity-building hurdles and pitfalls, none of them will wreak more havoc on your personal economic success than this particular issue. No matter what your income or asset level is, knowing how to effectively deal with debt can be a convincing prosperity lesson for each of us. However, did you know that debt can work in your favor and that good things can actually happen when you incur debt? It is because essentially, there is such a thing as good debt and bad debt, and prosperity builders need to know and understand the effective use of each of them to achieve their goals and ambitions. Ignorance of these fundamentals differences can often result in a major negative financial impact over a lifetime. *In this writing, I am going to briefly explain both bad debt and good debt and give the reader some compelling reasons how to distinguish between each of them so that you know and understand how each of them is created.* I will also demonstrate to you what the effects are to your prosperity plan long-term wise. A thorough knowledge of the differences between these types of debt can alone alter and improve your prosperity-building efforts over your life.

First, let's start with bad debt since that seems to be the cause for so many personal finance failures and economic calamities. Bad debt can be broadly defined as a term referring to consumer debt. This is the personal debt that is created through the use of credit cards, department store cards, and other types of buying and spending methods. It often includes wasteful or even frivolous shopping and spending for items and merchandise that depreciate quickly in value or have no long-lasting effect (other than perhaps memories). Some examples of this type of debt are expensive clothes, furniture, vacations, trips, high-cost autos, vehicles, expensive gifts, boats, costly jewelry, regular attendance at major sporting events, and other similar types of expenses. Often, the use of credit cards for these types of expenses is a signal that the purchaser cannot really afford to be buying this type of merchandise; and therefore, it must be paid via *borrowing money* aka credit cards.

It should also be mentioned that paying too many taxes is also a sign of bad debt since it is an indicator that you have not taken the precautions of building a viable tax-minimization strategy to offset the tax liability you are responsible for. Granted, taxes do pay for many municipal and governmental services at the local community, state, and national level; but you are legally responsible for only paying your *fair share* of them, and overpaying taxes is not a cause of good debt. Bad debt has a tendency to snowball, creating the need for HELOC (home equity lines of credit) loans, remortgages, personal loans, and other types of borrowing. When studied, those who make a habit of regular borrowing of these categories of expenses are the ones most affected when there is an economic slowdown. The result is what we have witnessed as a result of the economic downturn over the past few years in America. Those with significant consumer debt are the ones most affected by this situation.

The critical difference between the issues of affordability of each of these items is whether you can pay cash for each of them or pay them off when you receive the bill in the mail at the end of the month on your credit card statement. However, affordability in and of itself is not necessarily a key indicator that they are good investments in your income. This is especially true when you consider that, by comparison, you could be investing this *disposable income* in some sort of investments that will pay regular dividends and will appreciate over a longer period. *What is the best description of good debt, and how does it impact each of us?* Good debt can be best explained as debt that is assumed by an individual who will produce income and/or will produce an asset that *appreciates over time*. This is the type of debt that does not go down in value but instead goes up in value. Obviously, there are fewer of these types of items available as compared to bad debt; but to build long-term prosperity in your life, you must know and recognize what they are.

Specifically, they include your home and other real estate investments, such as rental homes, condos, duplexes, foreclosed property, and tax lien certificates to mention only a few; an assortment of several types of small business investments; tools and equipment if they are used to produce an income stream for you; and other paper investments, such as those that are found in the stock or bond markets. *Virtually anything that can be considered as a good source of income-producing can be considered good debt.* Even insurance coverage, since it has the effect of protecting your personal and business assets, can even be categorized as good debt. Education for you, your spouse, or your children is also acceptable good debt as the result positively affects the effort in building a greater amount of wages and income for you over your lifetime.

Poverty Versus Prosperity Contrasts in Thoughts, Feelings, Attitudes, Emotions, and Actions

POVERTY VIEWS:

• Emptiness • Problems • False Beliefs • Failures • Inadequacies • Fear • Ignorance • Worry • Lack • Pain • Sorrow • Limitations • Dissatisfaction • Difficulties • Losses • Resentment • Anger • Guilt • Misery • Darkness • Trouble • Envy • Covetousness • Jealousy • Suffering • Frustrations • Disappointments • Despair • Doubts • Sadness • Torment • Hopelessness • Bondage • Anxiety • Grief • Despondency

PROSPERITY VIEWS:

• Joy • Freedom • Peace of mind • Harmony • Abundance • Faith • Satisfaction • Happiness • Comfort • Fulfillment • Supply • Integrity • Bliss • Contentment • Purpose • Desire • Ambition • Growth • Trust • Honesty • Success • Achievement • Light • Confidence • Accomplishments • Multiplicity • Constructiveness • Magnifying • Multiplication • Solutions • Poise • Calmness • Serenity • Relaxation • Vibrancy • Buoyancy • Inspiration • Objectivity • Wisdom

Which One of the Above Best Describes You?

Prosperity Thinking Versus Poverty Thinking

As many of us have already learned, attitudes are often an essential and important part of our jobs, careers, and lives. They help us shape many of our emotions, thoughts, and feelings about our sense of worth and even self-esteem. In the end, it is far more than assets versus liabilities; it is all about the proper attitudes, commitments, and disciplines. In between "savers" and "spenders." On one hand, prosperity thinkers typically have more positive attitudes about their future and what they can and will accomplish. Poverty thinkers, on the other hand, spend most of their time in the mere acceptance of their fate and don't often choose to take a more active role in altering, refining, or otherwise changing their attitudes. Let's look at a few of the contrasting views of prosperity thinking versus poverty thinking:

PROSPERITY THINKING – *"I may not have my perfect career job yet, but it is in my sights!"*
POVERTY THINKING – *"I'm destined to work at this dead-end job forever."*

* * * * * * * *

PROSPERITY THINKING – *"I have learned to become resourceful and to make better use of my money because of my present economic situation."*

POVERTY THINKING – *"It is never going to get any better, so I might as well complain about it."*

* * * * * * * *

PROSPERITY THINKING – *"Despite my finances, I am still putting away money every month!"*

POVERTY THINKING – *"I need every penny I can get my hands on to support my lifestyle."*

* * * * * * * *

PROSPERITY THINKING – *"Keeping up with the Joneses is not important to me!"*

POVERTY THINKING – *"I do not want people to think that I cannot afford it."*

* * * * * * * *

PROSPERITY THINKING – *"If I do not have the cash, I simply don't buy it!"*

POVERTY THINKING – *"If I do not have the cash, I simply use my credit card."*

* * * * * * * *

PROSPERITY THINKING – *"Cash, equity, assets, and net worth are my ongoing financial priorities!"*

POVERTY THINKING – *"I spend every dollar I make just to keep up my image."*

* * * * * * * *

PROSPERITY THINKING – *"I willingly pay my fair share of taxes for community services that I also use."*

POVERTY THINKING – *"I cut a lot of questionable corners in figuring out how much tax I owe because it will not matter much anyway."*

* * * * * * * *

PROSPERITY THINKING – *"My work is more than a job. It helps define who I am."*

POVERTY THINKING – *"I work because I have to, and I need the money."*

* * * * * * * *

PROSPERITY THINKING – *"My friendships with others often resemble my own attitudes and views about work, life, and values."*
POVERTY THINKING – *"I live to party and party to live."*

* * * * * * * *

PROSPERITY THINKING – *"Sacrifice and occasionally going without are worth it in the end. It makes me appreciate things more."*
POVERTY THINKING – *"I live for today. Tomorrow can take care of itself."*

* * * * * * * *

As you can see, prosperity thinkers don't just live for the moment. They are planners and organizers who have created personal goals and objectives in their lives. They recognize that if their lives are going to change and improve, it will only do so if they have summoned the discipline, courage, and commitment to achieve the changes that need to be made.

Poverty thinkers do not often think about the future, or maybe they are simply fearful of it. They are the ones who do not invest their money in an investment portfolio; they spend it on lottery tickets and the casino. Instead of being focused on goals and priorities, they are content to live just for today. They tend to focus on the past instead of the future.

Some of the Primary Causes of Poverty

Poverty is often caused by a problem or combinations of problems that are seemingly unsolvable to those affected and are not, as many people feel, a result of only financial issues and situations.

Some of the compelling reasons for poverty among people today are the following:

   ✓ *Compulsive disorder behaviors like alcohol, gambling, or drug abuse*
   ✓ *Low skill levels, lack of technical training, or substandard education resulting in a low-paying job*
   ✓ *Health-care issues resulting in frequent medical treatments without adequate insurance coverage in place*
   ✓ *Improper money management resulting in excessive debt, foreclosure, or even bankruptcy*
   ✓ *The inability to borrow money because of an inferior or below-average credit or payment history*

✓ *Previous criminal record resulting in not being able to secure any licenses or good-paying job or career*

✓ *Creating a large family with the result of no practical method of supporting them*

✓ *Getting married early in life to someone who you are incompatible with resulting in a costly divorce*

These and other problems, factors, and issues are the reasons that many people cannot seem to break out of the poverty cycle to become prosperous.

On top of this, many social and economic problems are perceived as those that only the government can solve. Make no mistake. The method to steer yourself out of the poverty cycle has nothing to do with dependence on the government. *The solution lies squarely with you!*

Only you can do it for yourself.

Prosperity Optimists Versus Pessimists

"Positive and Negative Prosperity Thinking"

A prosperity pessimist realizes that they have made a lot of personal financial mistakes and errors in their life. They berate themselves for being thoughtless enough to make so many of them with their personal finances and feel trapped. They direct their anger at others—family, friends, relatives, neighbors, and coworkers—and become irritated at tall of the people around them. Mostly, however, they are mad at themselves for the circumstances that they find themselves in. They realize that they could have done better and are now completely frustrated, unhappy, and disorganized. Worse, they don't even seem to have a plan to help them get out of their misery. Pessimists tend to feel that many of life's events are caused by either their behaviors or by outside forces beyond their control. They tend to give up more easily and to give in, which produces further negative behaviors. Does any of this sound familiar? Let's compare this behavior to the optimist.

The essential elements of a prosperity optimist's attitude underline planning, goal orientation, and continuous personal development. Optimists tend to have a "gratitude attitude." They see situations as events that are carved outside of themselves and are temporary and occur for specific reasons. They realize that there are, indeed, some "do-overs" that they would like to try again but realize that things are the way they are, so they will simply make the most of it. They will make the best of their circumstances and even take advantage of the learning lessons experienced to avoid similar events in the future. They take the time to make better decisions, think through them thoroughly, and plan and prepare for the future. They also maintain their discipline and commitment until another good opportunity presents itself so that they can possibly take advantage of it.

The difference between these two approaches is an example of how different styles impact personal prosperity building and how we tend to react to and resolve financial challenges in general and how they can be changed, depending on how we look at a given set of circumstances. This is regardless of whether it is a traumatic financial event of just an everyday irritation. Optimistic people seem to take more risks, and that makes sense because they feel confident in their decisions and results. They believe they will succeed in their goals and objectives. They remain open to life's opportunities, challenges, and possibilities, which are important to their life prosperity achievement and long-term success.

*   *   *

A positive, optimistic attitude is not something that merely happens to you. It is created by a personal decision that occurs in advance that involves a choice of the most resourceful response to a given set of circumstances and an attitude that you will deal with adversity in a manner that is consistent with the goals and objectives you are seeking and the person you want to become. There have been a number of books written over the years concerning positive attitudes, most notably the well-known book *The Power of Positive Thinking* by Dr. Norman Vincent Peale. This is the literal textbook of modern-day positive thinking even though it was written in the 1950s, which discusses the many advantages of using positive thoughts to improve our attitudes and our lives.

The power of an optimistic, positive attitude cannot be overstated in the development of your personal prosperity-building plan. Used effectively, it results in identifying a sense of thankfulness regardless of life's circumstances and a method of turning financial challenges into financial opportunities for personal growth. It can often lead you to develop an even more optimistic outlook, a more positive mood, better problem-solving techniques, improved social skills, and even better health. Optimistic and positive people take more risks because they feel confident in their decision-making process. They believe that they will succeed in their efforts and undertakings. By maintaining better and more optimistic attitudes, they realize how much better off they are than many others that, in turn, creates a sense of gratefulness in their attitude. It can also help them find hope and courage when faced with despair and adversity.

Remember, you alone have the power to be both positive and optimistic.

PROSPERITY OPTIMISM VERSUS PESSIMISM

<< Are You Scared of the Future? >>

The decade between 2010 and 2020 may well find many people in the uncomfortable position of running scared when it comes to their personal finances and prosperity building. In a Gallup poll conducted by *USA Today* in late December 2009 and published on the front page of *USA Today* on January 6, 2010, over 75 percent of Americans don't like the way things are going in the country. Given the level of economic uncertainty, political diversion, terrorism threats, war, unemployment, and looming national deficits, many suspect that they are facing the worst of times; and they must then attempt to make the most of their personal situations. There is even a persistent view that as a nation, our best days are, indeed, behind us.

Yet our assumptions that we are at the brink of collapse might well be one of the motivational factors that can save you from going over it. It might be the key to establishing or redefining your personal prosperity plan formula. As the future develops over the next ten years, there will be more and more changes and modifications necessary for you to be able to keep up the pace in your personal prosperity planning and development to achieve more meaningful results.

So exactly what can you expect in the next decade according to this report? Among many of the leading issues are the following:

- *Over 16 percent will become age sixty-five or older, the largest level of seniors living that has ever been witnessed in America.*
- *Energy costs will continue to skyrocket at an ever-increasing rate that could conceivably make this one of the leading personal costs for everybody in the next decade.*
- *Smaller households and smaller homes will become more of the common denominator eclipsing the previous decade of "larger and bigger."*
- *Job growth will continue to be weak as they will continue to move overseas or be replaced by automation and technology. By 2008, the government estimates another two million jobs will be eliminated in the United States.*
- *Consumer spending is anticipated to grow at 2.5 percent in the decade, down from 3 percent according to the Bureau of Labor Statistics (BLS).*
- *The United States will continue a period of weak economic growth overall and major industries, such as auto and steel will continue declining.*
- *Technology will be the guiding trend in education, and there will be more monitoring of outcome results as well as more and better testing of students. The key, it is felt, will become accountability in education.*
- *Healthy lifestyles will offset many previous life-shortening diseases with Alzheimer's replacing cancer as the number 1 public health enemy.*

What does this all mean? Each of the above factors points to a real need to increase your prosperity building to improve your personal results and to further uncover new methods to be able to significantly improve it. The key in doing this is through education and learning the techniques and strategies that are available to do it. It is through the building and refining of a prosperity plan that will serve your needs now and over the next decade. Educational sources like The Prosperity Success Institute™ Learning Center located in Gold Canyon, Arizona, are the type of specialized and focused educational programs that serve that unique need. They emphasize prosperity building through better knowledge and training in personal finance, business entrepreneurism, success training, and real estate investing and are completely education-oriented.

You can contact them at **prosperitysuccessinstitute.com** or for additional information and a schedule of their available classes, courses, workshops, and seminars in all levels of education.

Your Financial "Personality"

What does your financial personality say about you? Who are you financially speaking? What is your money style? Are you a credit card user, a check writer, or a cash user? Are you a "charger" or a "saver"? Do you spend more money on fun and leisure or in your career? Are food, eating out, clothing, and lifestyle interests the descriptions that define you? Are you tight-lipped about money? Do your spending habits resemble your parents, siblings, or close friends? How you perceive yourself and your financial personality has a lot to say about your self-image. By developing a positive self-image of your money personality, you will be more able to enjoy your life and to feel more secure about your future. To a large extent, money is an emotional state of mind.

Take the time to begin to develop a sense of who you are in relation to your finances. Figure out what you want and when you hope to be able to afford it. How will you go about purchasing the really big things in life that you either want or need? How do you spend your money? Plan, create, imagine. Read financial publications that extol the virtues of "smart money habits." Familiarize yourself with the world of finance. Knowledge is, indeed, power in this critical and important area of your life; and understanding the complex world of personal finance is the key in benefitting from everything that it provides.

The Ten Money Personality Category Descriptions

1. **SPENDERS** – These are people who compulsively and often purchase things whether they even need them or not. Their goal in life is to buy "stuff" to feed their spending habit regardless of the type of purchase made. They have not been able to distinguish between "wants" and

"needs" and usually are maxed out on their credit cards and maintain a disproportionate amount of consumer debt compared to their income generation.

2. **SAVERS** – These individuals are people who carefully and judiciously save a certain percentage of their discretionary income that they use to make portfolio investments or other types of investing for the future. They demonstrate resourcefulness in all their money management habits and consciously control their levels of indebtedness. Savers rarely have money problems.

3. **WORRIERS** – These are people who regularly and consistently undergo anxiety over money management issues. They never seem to be able to get a grip on the best use of their personal finances and fret over everything that relates to income, spending, and investing. Often, their irrationalities do not permit them to take advantage of very many financial opportunities as they ponder too long while these same opportunities slip through their fingers.

4. **CONTROLLERS** – These are people who make every effort to control others with money. They frequently accomplish this in subtle ways and are particularly clever in doing it. Controllers are those people who accomplish their objectives by handing money to others and at issues and hoping to solve them in that manner. Even though prosperous and wealthy people have been accused of being the ones who do this, it is a behavior that is emulated consistently in virtually all levels of income.

5. **SOOTHERS** – These are people who attempt to use money to eradicate and eliminate all sorts of problems in their lives or the lives of others who are close to them, such as family members, friends, and others. They dole out money that way a pharmacist writes prescriptions, just at higher personal costs. They fail to recognize that money can be used as a lethal drug when improperly used, which can create an "enabling" situation that can stifle the receiver's motivation.

6. **MANIPULATORS** – These are the folks who attempt to get others to do what they want by waving money in their face. They know precisely how to "up the ante" until their needs are met based on the degree or the intensity of the issues involved. They are both cunning and clever in the ways that they can do this, and it is one of the frequent misuses of money.

7. **COMPETITORS** – These individuals look at everything as a game where money is the ultimate "scoreboard." They use their personal finances to "win" the contest by the number and cost of the things they buy—bigger vehicles, larger homes, more exotic vacations, designer clothes, better schooling for their kids, and so on.

8. **REWARDERS** – These are people who offer or give monetary gifts to others in the same manner that the infamous Pavlov trained his famous dogs. They provide money to others as a frequent means of satisfying an emotional or perceived needs, and the results produce more dependency on the giver by the receiver, which is even greater than the value of the gift itself.

9. **INFLUENCERS** – These are individuals who have a need to provide frequent gratification by money contributions that they feel will have an impact on others. It is similar to offering a tip to a waiter for good service or to a hotel doorman for hailing a cab and opening the door for you. This personality tends to puff their chest out a little just as Robert De Niro's character in the movie *Goodfellas* when he would meet someone and then tuck a $100 bill in their shirt pocket.

10. **BLINGERS** – These are people who feel compelled to display ostentatious levels of wealth and prosperity via necklaces, chains, watches, rings, clothing, vehicles, McMansions, or even other things like schooling, jobs, and careers that say, "Look at me!" and "See how successful I am!" For them, if you can't view it, wear it, drive it, or live in it. It really doesn't matter.

Four Major Extreme Money Personalities
(Adapted from the book *Why Smart People Do Stupid Things*
written by Bert Whitehead, MBA, JD, 2007 by Sterling
Publications)

Listed below are four of the **major** and **extreme** money personalities that comprise many people. These are the types of personalities that serve to define who they are and how they use their money resources. Look and study each of them and see if *you* fit in any of these extreme personalities:

1. **THE SCROOGE** – This is someone who is motivated by a compelling desire to accumulate extreme levels of wealth for themselves. They are savers and typically are business people who have created large amounts of cash wealth. They frequently have a very controlling personality and fail to understand that even though they may be very successful in their personal enterprises, they are not necessarily good financial investors, nor do they always spend their money well or wisely.

2. **THE GAMBLER** – This is someone who has a strong desire to *appear* that they have great wealth and, as a result, take many high risks. They also have more of a spending personality bordering on an addiction. They are also characterized by heavy personal debt and even other patterns of substance abuse and who are eternal optimists when it comes

to investing and money management. They are frequently depressive personalities because of the investing mistakes they have made in the past because of their involvement with many GRQ (get-rich-quick) schemes. They are guilty of lying to themselves and bragging about their winnings while at the same time denying their losses.

3. **THE MISER** – This is someone who is both strongly motivated by fear but also bay a basic desire to save. These are good savers yet have little to show for it. They are the consummate "bury it in a can in the backyard or putting it in the mattress" types and have a tendency to keep their money in ultraconservative bank savings accounts and other similar investments. They avoid all long-term commitments, and they are often motivated by fear rather than guilt. They are not very financially savvy. Essentially, they have developed a wrong perception about the whole business of investing and money management.

4. **THE SHOPAHOLIC** – This money personality is usually motivated by fear plus a desire to spend. They like to give gifts to others and or pick up the tab for a meal but put the expense on their credit card. They come from deprived backgrounds and confuse their wants and their needs. They literally become euphoric during a shopping experience and frequently hide their purchases and seldom even use any of them. They also use money to "get even" with others.

Next, we reveal another group of money personalities. These are more common and can be seen among many of those whom we know—even ourselves.

Four Common Money Personality Types

As opposed to the extreme money personalities previously discussed, these common money personality types can be seen in many places:

1. **THE ENTREPRENEUR** – These are the personality types that are willing to embrace risks, and many even seem to thrive on it. For them, money is their way of "keeping score." They have the ability to perform with long-term financial horizons but are frequently undercapitalized. They usually invest all their money into the business enterprises and don't always understand how to investment their personal money into other more diverse long-term investments.

2. **THE NESTER** – These personality types are able to save, and their favorite all-time investment is their home. They are totally committed to fixing and improving it. Nearly every dollar they earn goes into it rather than other investments. They are family-oriented and are concerned about college and higher education for their kids. They

also have a very practical nature. Time shares and vacation homes are both areas that nesters invest in and eventually lose money on. They feel that they should only invest in their residence because everything seems too complex and difficult.

3. **THE TRAVELER** – These personality types prefer to spend their money on experiences rather than "things." They are antimaterialistic and love anything that has an educational factor to it. Another term for them might be that of a "professional student." They enjoy travel and trips and enjoy a modest, simple life. One of the greatest treasures is their photo albums of their trips and journeys.

4. **THE WORKAHOLIC** – These personality types are those who are driven in their work and careers and make good incomes. They love gadgets and are techno freaks. These people are concerned about appearances, status, and materialism; and this is how they reward themselves. Name brands are important to them. Their long-term investment strategy is "a little of this, a little of that" because they are susceptible to sales and marketing people as well as temptations. Many of them confuse hobbies with investments.

Advantages and Disadvantages of Each

Each of these personalities and personality types has proportionate advantages and disadvantages. Chances are that most people can identify with one or more of them. This is especially true when relationships are added to the scenario. It is not uncommon for one person to choose an exact opposite of their personality for a relationship to even offset their own failings. For example, misers often choose gamblers, workaholics often choose entrepreneurs, nesters often choose travelers, and scrooges often select shopaholics. As people go through life, it is not uncommon to move from one personality type to another as they mature or learn to adjust with other factors that make up their prosperity lifestyle. The most well balanced are those who have experienced one or more of these money personality types and now have found a suitable balance.

Prosperity "Flat views"

Many prosperity seekers are guilty of viewing their world only in "flat view." Flat view, according to an obscure 1884 British high school math teacher, Edward A. Abbott, in his book called *Flatland,* is a world where people exist only in different geometric shapes. He posted this theory and concept in the book, which became a classic, even today, not because of its uniqueness but because of the startling perception that many people use in their cognitive thinking patterns. This view has a dramatic effect on their decision-making and success in life. In *Flatland*, the concept of width and depth does not exist. Its inhabitants are mere geometric shapes, and society is organized along strict class lines. The more sides to each person's shape, the higher their individual status. For example, in the book, "squares" are teachers, "triangles" are workers, simple "straight lines" are women, and priests, who have the highest rank of all, are "circles." One of the characters in the story has a dream one night and finds himself caught up in a one-dimensional world called *Lineland*, where all the creatures are nothing more than points moving up and down a single geometric line. Sadly, they do not realize that there are other dimensions in life. When the hero attempts to demonstrate this to the Linelanders, they are incapable of understanding or conceiving it. To them, the concept of "sideways" is foreign to them, and they cannot comprehend it.

Another creature introduced is called a "sphere," which provides a fourth dimension called depth, and the hero cannot understand what upward or downward means. Finally, in the end, the hero is able to grasp the priceless truth. He understands that the world is not as he always viewed it. It could be different than he imagined and in many and varied ways. He has freed himself from the confinement of a flat world. Flat views are any rigid perspectives that constrict our imagination to only one dimension. It is binary thinking, extreme one way or the other, without regard to the shades of gray that compose many problems. As a result, they lead to only the most simplistic solutions. In prosperity thinking, it is important to recognize that there are literally many ways to achieve your long-term prosperity goals and objectives and not merely a single method. For that very reason, it is important to create a personal prosperity formula that takes into consideration a multitude of factors and events—from your talents and skills to your family situation, to your ambitions, and to your life timetable to be able to achieve all of it.

It further involves seeing the world in color and not in black and white. For instance, did you ever take a careful look at a black-and-white photograph? Did you notice that there is literally *more gray* in the image then *either* black or white? Flat views result from not using creativity and imagination in your thinking and prevent you from speculating on many of the "what if" scenarios and how your life could potentially change and improve.

The Psychology of Prosperity Building

More on Flat-View Thinking

Often, people look for simple answers to complex or complicated problems. While this could be classified as simply human nature by some, human behavior defies simple explanation whether we are talking about the causes or the effects of such things as prosperity building. As discussed previously, most of the time, the damage to potential prosperity lies far below the surface. A flat view or simplistic answer to a complex personal prosperity problem can constrict your thinking concerning the *real cause* of the problem. Looking at an issue in a one-dimensional frame of mind will often not solve a multi-complex, multifaceted problem. It can also lead us to approach the issue of prosperity-building problems in a narrow "either-or" mentality mind-set when actually, it can be a result of several, even many, specific factors. Rigid views, such as "I don't have enough money to even pay my bills, much less set any of it aside," can conflict with broader thinking, such as the possibility that you are not living within your present income. Those firm views can even imprison better judgment over a period, further complicating the prosperity enigma.

The key to solving personal prosperity challenges is not to look at them in simplistic one-dimensional terms, which can even cause the problem to be misread. An unimaginative flat view can lead to many prosperity traps and the rejection of sound principles and beliefs. The same is true when you use a "herd" mentality, such as "Doesn't everybody know that making more money is the solution to prosperity?" (Answer: it isn't, and it involves far more than this.) Remember that flat-view thinking is any rigid thought process that restricts your ability to focus your approach to more than just one dimension. It's extreme thinking—all of nothing, all good or all bad, the maximum or the minimum. It limits our imagination and therefore leads us to simplistic solutions to problems that often cause personal mistakes in prosperity success. It is further often caused by a lack of creativity, imagination, and speculation. When you open your mind and look at all the possibilities that can contribute to your long-term prosperity achievements, you will realize that there are many solutions, indeed, to the process.

Personal Economic Reform

A higher degree of prosperity in our life cannot be achieved until you carefully understand the need for personal economic reform. Many people mistake "wants and desires" for needs. Taking a close look at your spending habits and behaviors can often result in our being able to curb excessive and needless spending and to be able to use that income in a better, resourceful, and more productive manner. One of the keys in accomplishing this, as previously mentioned in this book, is to create an effective yet flexible budget or spending plan. This allows you to capably and predictably figure your future expenses in advance so that overspending is minimized or eliminated. Sadly, only the government has the power to overspend on a regular and consistent basis since all *they* have to do is print more "monopoly-style" money. Literally, there is no remedy to solve the ills of prosperity seeking until you understand this law of prosperity.

The ability to become more efficient in your use of personal financial resources will have a major impact in your prosperity-building plan in the future. Those who can manage to learn to do this effectively are often rewarded with a greater *amount* of resources to manage.

Learning to do this is one of the **Seven Laws of Prosperity Building:**

1. *Learning How to Make More Money*
2. *Learning How to Budget Your Money*
3. *Learning How to Better Borrow Money*
4. *Learning How to Productively Use Personal Debt*
5. *Learning How to Protect Your Money and Assets*
6. *Learning How to Invest Your Money*
7. *Learning How to Better Utilize Your Money and Assets*

Arriving at the Epiphany Moment

<< The Ultimate Prosperity "Aha" Moment >>

At some point during your study, training, and education, you will arrive at the ubiquitous epiphany moment. For some, it will be shortly after the training and instruction begins. For others, it will be partly through it, perhaps even midway. For still others, it will be at the conclusion when each of the strategies and techniques has been explained and summarized. It is not necessarily at what particular point you have the "aha" moment or event. It is far more important to make sure that you *do experience it* in your educational study and training.

Exactly what is the moment of epiphany? It is the period when you suddenly begin to comprehend and understand how each of the various pieces of the financial and personal prosperity jigsaw puzzle comes together. You begin to witness how they apply to one another and to your personal situation. Instead of it being an abstract concept or theory, it starts to become very personal to your specific situation in life. It is no longer merely a vague or elusive idea; it has become a useful and defining formula that you can relate to and apply in your career, family, relationships, and personal life.

It is a lightning bolt moment when you now understand how it really works. *You have reached the "aha" moment.*

CHAPTER 5

Some of the Largest Income-Producing Opportunities

In this chapter, you will learn about the following points:

- *Income and Earnings Opportunities*
- *The Key Difference Between a Job and a Career*
- *Some of the Large Income-Producing Opportunities*
- *Which Options Are More Likely for You?*
- *Choosing the Right Job/Career*
- *Job Versus Career*
- *What Do You Sing About, Cry About, and Dream About?*
- *Playing It Safe in Your Career Can Cost You!*
- *Ten Reasons for Starting an Entrepreneurial Business*
- *The One to Two Punch of Major Prosperity Achievers*
- *Exactly What Is Financial Security?*
- *Consider the Hardworking Ant*
- *How to Financially Succeed in Your Life and Career*
- *Important Success Qualities*
- *Bettering Our Self Assessments*
- *Fifteen Master Strategies for Personal Achievement*
- *Twenty Laws of Extraordinary Success*
- *The Success Formula That Will Not Fail*
- *Inventing Your Personal Success Style Formula*
- *ORGANIZATION: The Core of All Successful Achievement*
- *Intelligently Failing*
- *Setting Yourself Free from Your Fear*
- *Conquering Our Demons*
- *The Key to Overcoming Fear: CONFRONTING IT!*
- *Your Personal Mission Statement*

Income and Earnings Opportunities

Prosperity building all starts with income and earnings. The ability to create a solid income-producing strategy is essential in achieving a high level of personal prosperity in your life. Equally important is the wise and efficient use of that income and earnings. Without the necessary income, which is funded partly by discretionary earnings (the difference between your net or take-home pay and your expenses), your plan will certainly stall and not grow.

Some of the other details in creating additional income and earnings include the following:

- *What Are Your Personal Options?*
- *Your Personal Options Practical Exercise*
- *Choosing the Right Occupation in Your Life*
- *Choosing the Right Occupation Practical Exercise*
- *The Personal Prosperity Success Codex®*

OPPORTUNITIES

Our lives are determined by opportunities, even those we do not take advantage of.

—Larry Snow

The Key Differences Between a Job and a Career

There is a distinct difference between what is known as a job and a career. A rare glimpse of the difference between them is seen in a stand-up presentation by Chris Rock,* who offered a few of those differences in the following narrative description:

- *One of them has too much time, and the other has not enough time.*
- *One of them involves passion and creativity, and one involves drudgery and a feeling of being stuck in a rut.*
- *One of them you look forward to all the time and the other you dread every day.*
- *One of them you check to see how much time you have left and the other you check to see how much time passed.*
- *One of them makes you happy to get up in the morning, and the other makes you want to keep hitting the snooze button and not want to get out of bed.*

- *One of them makes you want to talk about it all the time, and the other makes you want to forget about it.*

Now Guess Which One Is a Career and Which One Is a Job?

*Adapted from a Comedy Central's presentation by stand-up comedian Chris Rock at a Chicago, Illinois, performance.

Passionate Work Versus Constrained Work

There is a vast difference between the types of work that is performed in the process of personal income production in your life. Essentially, it can be divided into two separate and distinct types: *passionate* and *constrained,* and there is a huge difference between the two of them. On one hand, passionate work is the type of labor that you look forward to every day. It is vocation of the heart where little effort is necessary to become impassionate with the daily tasks involved. It is the type of work that you dream about, think about, and shout about every day. Passionate work can be difficult, time-consuming, detailed, or complicated; but it makes little difference to the worker because they have the *fire-in-the-belly* type of devotion to performing it. Often, it has little to do even with compensation (*thinking: starving artists*) and is undertaken more from the heart than from the head or pocketbook.

Passionate work can be the result of an early childhood even that forever made an impression, a love of a certain ideal, a result of hero worship, or even a tragedy that occurs in life. Regardless of the motivation or reason, passionate work is what builds bridges, sculpts magnificent statues, motivates people to climb tall mountains, and causes young men and women to go off to war. It is the sort of stuff that motivates people from every age, background, gender, and ethnicity to undertake the really big things in life.

Constrained work, on the other hand, is often described as drudge work. It is the sort of work that is done through obligation, force, and pressure. It is effort that is needed to pay personal finance obligations and performed as drudgery. Constrained work is generally work that involves physical labor, but this is not always true. It is often menial labor that is done as a result of a need to produce regular income to pay one's living expenses. Seldom does constrained work result in a sense of internal personal achievement, and frequently, it is not the type of effort that is looked forward to on a daily basis. It is a sense of have-to-go-to-work type of toil, and frequently, the only real benefit is the money that is earned as a result of the undertaking and possibly some of the social benefits of coworkers who are also performing it.

People perform constrained work every day out of a sense of obligation to put food on the table and to put a roof over their heads, yet it somehow also shapes their attitude toward life and their sense of prosperity building. The opposite is true of passionate workers who seem to gain a sense of purpose and creativity when engaged in their passionate pursuit of their occupation, career, vocation, or profession.

Some of the Large Income-Producing Opportunities

"What Are YOUR PERSONAL *Options?"*

Making the choice of what long-term, income-producing strategies to use in your life is an important decision. Finding the best and most suitable one depends on a number of key factors, including personal ability, skill, education, experience, desire, and opportunity. It is critical to choose the best one since it forms the basis to fund your lifelong income and lifestyle. Theoretically, the larger the income, the more options you will have in life and the more independence and personal freedom to do it.

Which of These Options Are More Likely for You?

1. **BECOMING A DEGREED PROFESSIONAL** – This can be done by attending college or graduate school or by obtaining an advanced or specialized degree to become a lawyer, physician, scientist, professor, dentist, veterinarian, or other high-skilled professional. However, it frequently takes many years and possibly even hundreds of thousands of dollars in education to accomplish this option.

2. **BECOMING A PROFESSIONAL SPORTS ATHLETE OR CELEBRITY** – If you have outstanding athletic or artistic prowess and are at the very top in your field, you have the opportunity to secure a lucrative performance contract complete with numerous endorsement possibilities. However, there are only so many star athletes, and "starving artists" is more than merely a term.

3. **INHERITING A FAMILY FORTUNE** – If you are fortunate to come from an existing well-to-do family or are "heir apparent" to an existing fortune, you can easily jump on the high-income bank wagon if you are from the right gene pool.

4. **ENJOYING A LUCKY DAY AT THE CASINO, LOTTERY, OR SWEEPSTAKES** – This approach involves being a high-risk speculator or gambler that could result in an enormous amount of money by sheer lady luck. Yet the odds to do this are not in your favor, and many, many thousands of dollars will be lost in the process.

5. **OTHER PERSONAL CHOICE POSSIBILITY** – *(complete here)*____
   _____

6. **<u>BEST OPTION</u>** - *Developing a Detailed and Well-Thought-Out Personal Prosperity Plan* – If none of the above sound like viable options for you, perhaps you should consider creating a carefully thought-out, detailed, and effective prosperity plan that includes outlining your personal success opportunity formula.

Some of the items to include in this strategy are (a) possibly starting a small business; (b) buying real estate investment property; and (c) investing in a personal investment portfolio of various stocks, bonds, mutual funds, CDs, and others as a supplement to a good-paying job/career income. In the final analysis, when you consider what the available options are, which of them make the most sense to you? How will you go about achieving it? What is the likelihood of achieving it? What is the really *best choice* of you? In any case, your passion in pursuing your career will serve as a guiding light in whether you have chosen the right field.

Choosing the Right Job/Career

"It All Starts with Income"

Did you choose your job or career, or did it somehow sort of choose you? Often, locating a suitable job or career is a matter of timing or opportunity rather than a concerted effort to find the right type and category of work that best suits your personality, style, and temperament. Unfortunately, it often is decided by the issue of compensation or earnings rather than a consideration of whether it's well suited to the worker. When you consider that you will spend many thousands of hours working at your job and career in your lifetime, it's important to recognize that finding employment within a field you really enjoy and are passionate about is just as important as the re-numeration factor. Yet isn't this another example of being "easier said than done"? Isn't it more difficult to find work that is *both* enjoyable and pays well?

Work occupies such a large part of our life that it demands careful consideration. That is why it is termed "occupation." It frequently involves over 50 percent of your daily waking hours. For that reason, it is important to carefully choose it rather than let it choose you. Since it is also one of the biggest factors in personal income and prosperity building, it should also be a choice that is carefully considered and thoughtfully planned. For these reasons, it is important to wisely choose your job and career field. Because you will spend over seventy thousand hours of your lifetime pursuing your chosen work, it makes sense to spend a great deal of time evaluating exactly what you choose to do for income. In the end, you might ask yourself, did you choose your job, or did your job choose you? In other words, did your job/career come about as a result of a need for making some money, and did you accept the first offer that was made to you, or did you take more of a pragmatic approach and search out your chosen field of employment?

A Job Versus a Career

What is the real difference between a job and a career? By many standards, the chief difference is that a job is merely a source of income, and it may or may not be necessarily a passionate pursuit. A career is quite literally a "job on steroids" and one that largely defines your life and your personality. Often, the mistakes that many make in their life's work is that they find a job or career field because they need income and have bills to pay rather than finding one that passionately motivates them. Understandably, most people need to earn an income to pay their expenses and lifestyle, but many remain in their jobs/ careers even if they are unhappy with performing it regularly. They may lack the courage, engage in procrastination too long, or not have the necessary skills to change their field of work.

What qualities really define a job/career? Is it skills, environment, industry, coworkers, effort, compensation, or some other factor? Examining the factors that constitute a "good job" will help determine if you have the proper personality, traits, and other human factors to successfully accomplish it. A good job/career is a method to actively pursue a personal passion while also earning the necessary income to fund your living expenses. The key to matching you to your work is to be able to adequately matching you to the type of work that you desire. It simply has a lot to do with your type of personality than any other reason.

The four basic personality types are as follows:

1. **CHOLERIC** – This is the individual who is totally in control. They have high energy and control situations rather than letting them control them. Examples of these personality types include business owners, motivational speakers, and other take-charge people.
2. **MELANCHOLY** – These personalities are detail-oriented, list takers, and very exacting in all that they do. Examples of these are accountants, government employees, and computer programmers.
3. **PHLEGMATIC** – These personalities include those who experience very few highs and lows in their lives and are very even-tempered. Nothing ever seems to bother them. Examples of these individuals are musicians, artists, health-care workers, and employees engaged in manufacturing services.

4. **SANGUINE** – These personalities are enthusiastic, bubbly, love working with people, and enjoy being "cheerleaders." Examples of these are salespeople, hairstylists, and coaches.

What Do You Sing About, Cry About, and Dream About?

Passion is one of the most compelling emotions in life. In his book *Talent Is Never Enough*, author John C. Maxwell emphasizes what constructive passion can do for you in your career.

1.) <u>**PASSION IS THE FIRST STEP IN MAJOR ACHIEVEMENTS**</u>
     The only way to accomplish anything of significant value is to really want it badly enough. Passion provides that ability.

2.) <u>**PASSION INCREASES WILLPOWER**</u>
     Our accomplishments in life are based more on how much we want them rather than what we want.

3.) <u>**PASSION PRODUCES ENERGY**</u>
     When you have passion in what you do, achievements become easier to accomplish.

4.) <u>**PASSION IS THE FOUNDATION FOR EXCELLENCE**</u>
     Passion is the difference between average and excellence. It fires your desire to achieve and energizes your talents.

5.) <u>**PASSION IS THE KEY TO SUCCESSFUL ACHIEVEMENT**</u>
     Enthusiastic passion is the number 1 quality for success in anything you set out to do. It takes more than mere talent to do it.

6.) <u>**PASSION IS CONTAGIOUS**</u>
     Passion is an inspiration to others, and it is easy to catch from observing others.

If your career seems to be stalled and you don't seem to have the right amount of enthusiasm to accomplish your work, you might want to check to see if it is the kind of work that promotes your passion in performing it. Passion is one of the most compelling categories of emotion and is a requirement for successful achievement regardless of the type of work involved.

Playing It Safe in Your Career Can Cost You!

<< *Going from Ordinary to Extraordinary* >>

There is, it seems, a price to be paid for long-term career comfort; and those who enter the job market working for someone else often pay it. A steady, secure paycheck masks the many other growth opportunities that are available in private business ownership aka entrepreneurism. Perhaps they risk-taking aversion or a fear of failure, but many people just haven't given themselves much of a chance to advance in areas such as a small business venture.

Ironically, during many economic downturns, such as the one that we are currently experiencing since 2008, private business start-ups always significantly increase. Often, this is fueled by the fact that many people have lost their jobs and have the time and motivation to focus on other sources of earnings. Coupled with that is the on-the-job (OJT) training that they have already received from their employer(s), which helps qualify their ability to be able to succeed at small business. Note, however, that small business is not to be confused with self-employment even though it frequently is a result of it. Self-employment is defined as a person who works for himself/herself. Small business entrepreneurism involves other employees, many customers, an off-site office and work environment, and many investments in technology, equipment, and systems.

Many people have trouble distinguishing between guaranteed income as in a job and the often much higher earnings opportunities of a private business enterprise. In a survey that was taken in 2010 by the Kauffman Foundation, the majority of people opt to choose the secure income rather than to take the risk of higher and longer-term option of entrepreneurism. Perhaps this too is a matter of the instant gratification factor (IGF) that many younger workers seek and find in a conventional "job" that is a clearly defined figure, along with benefits, as opposed to a much higher, albeit riskier, private venture and feel that they must position themselves securely to prepare for marriage, children, and a mortgage in the suburbs.

The lengthier your time horizon, the more you want to avoid relatively low-yielding, conservative career investing in favor of perhaps a riskier career choice that offers significantly higher opportunities and possibilities over time. The current economic climate doesn't seem to offer a lot of compelling reasons for job enthusiasm, except in one area: entrepreneurial start-up businesses. Like most downturns, there are a record number of new businesses being formed every day; and by the time this period is over, there will be thousands more of them. These new entrepreneurs have learned that there are opportunities literally around every corner, and through their start-up businesses, they are seeking them every day. There will be arguably more millionaires made during this down period than any time in our nation's history, just like during the Great Depression.

Many of these individuals have "sensed" these opportunities and possibilities. Small business ownership certainly isn't for everyone; but for those who are willing to seek a higher risk, higher reward career opportunity, it can become an exciting personal career adventure that offers unimaginable returns in the future. When you think of it as an "investment" (which it is by the way), would you make the choice to invest any of your capital resources now in simple savings or a CD at an early stage in your life, knowing in advance of the meager return? Or would you instead choose to be more aggressive in your approach, such as a mixture of stocks and mutual funds that would, over time, create a more substantial return for your portfolio? Apply this same strategy to your career choice and add in the element of compounding, and what is the result?

The main lesson to be learned here is that risk can and does affect each of us, either positively or negatively, depending on your tolerance; and you should differentiate the difference between risk-taking, speculation, and downright gambling. Job income is designed to provide secure income comfort and is the method that many seek, but even jobs have been subject to elimination through downsizing during this current downturn, and we have seen many layoffs and job cut-backs.

As it turns out, the biggest risk for many career seekers may just be not taking one.

Top 10 Reasons to Consider in Starting an Entrepreneurial Business

1. To create a work environment where you have the ultimate responsibility for the results.
2. To pursue your career at the highest possible level of competence.
3. To make the key decisions that will positively affect others and yourself.
4. To improve yourself and others through the application of developing continuing skills.
5. To help others achieve their short- and long-term personal and financial goals.
6. To be able to totally immerse yourself in the pursuit of your dreams.
7. To explore all the details of your chosen career passion.
8. To develop a continuing sense of purpose in your work and career.
9. To keep your mind sharp by continually improving yourself and your organization for a lifetime.
10. To maintain an unlimited cap on your happiness and income potential.

The One to Two Punch of Major Prosperity Achievers

These Are the Venerable Twin Engines That Will Make Your Personal Prosperity Take Off Like a Rocket Ship to Mars!

These are the two essential ingredients necessary for gaining the kind of prosperity that can sustain you for the rest of your life and the lifetime of your heirs. They are the **twin engines** that will propel your prosperity rocket ship.

1. **<u>REAL ESTATE INVESTMENTS</u>** – Using your discretionary income and capital in real estate investment properties can produce a lifelong income stream that can become a part of your personal legacy.
2. **<u>ENTREPRENEURIAL BUSINESS OWNERSHIP</u>** – Creating, building, developing, and owning an entrepreneurial business that is involved a product/service that is unique and marketable will contribute to *a cash machine income stream.*

Learning Lesson:

The above two investments also help feed other profitable investments, such as those in the stock market, securities, and other paper investments.

Exactly What Is Financial Security?

The ultimate source of financial security in life is self. It is *not* in financial institutions, your employer, your job, the government, or even your current earnings or income. It is not the result of *any* external source. No one is responsible for your long-term financial security, except you yourself. The entitlement mentality that is so popular today focuses *more* on what is expected to be received and *less* on what can be given. People who subscribe to this view and attitude are only concerned about what they can *get* from others and not what they can *give.*

Placing our faith in false security can rob you of many of the life opportunities that come along only ever so often. Without the necessary training and education, you will fail to recognize them, much less be able to take full advantage of them. Chance is a factor in prosperity, but so too is preparation and planning.

Many highly prosperous and successful people all share the following traits and characteristics:

- *They are focused and persistent.*
- *They are patient and understanding.*
- *They are willing to do the things that others will not do.*
- *They are common sense-oriented.*
- *They are constantly reading, studying, and learning new ways to improve themselves.*

By comparison, many of them make a smaller amount of money from their financial investments than they do as a result of the continual performance of their passionate pursuits in life. It is that work that ultimately makes them prosperous. It seems that investing in yourself is the best investment that you can make and is one of the most important factors in creating personal prosperity and financial freedom in your life. It appears that the more we are self-reliant, the more that we can begin to realize how important *we are* to our ultimate prosperity achievements. Taking personal control of our future prosperity is an effective success strategy.

In the end, you need to ask yourself the important question:

"Am I a producer who produces maximum value in life?

or

Am I a consumer who relies and depends on external factors and

opportunities that come along in my life?"

Ask Yourself the Following Question:

Am I a Producer or a Consumer When It Comes to Creating Extraordinary Income?

If you or someone you know experienced the Great Depression that started in 1929 and ended in the mid-thirties, you might be familiar with the term "the forgotten man" that was used to describe the countless number of people who were thrown out of work during that period in our nation's history.

A popular depression-era song that was created during that period gave great realistic meaning to their financial plight:

> *"They used to tell me I was building a dream,*
> *With peace and glory ahead.*
> *Why should I now be standing in line?*
> *Just waiting for my bread?*
>
> *Once I built a railroad, I made it run,*
> *Made it race against time.*
> *Once I built a railroad; now it's done.*
> *Brother can you spare a dime?"*

These lyrics remind us about the economic downturn that many experienced in 2008 when many lost their jobs, their homes, their vehicles, their pride, and even their future. As a nation, we very nearly lost our entire banking system. Although a dime doesn't have the same value now as it did then, the important point is that without sufficient money resources, we will suffer as a result of not having enough resources to pay for such necessities as shelter, transportation, and food. Many younger people today have never even known hard times in their lives and have only experienced abundance in everything and anything that their hearts desired.

The issue of depression, recession, and economic downtimes serves to emphasize the need for old-fashioned personal money management, especially savings, so that you have the appropriate "safety values" in place to help ease your financial condition. Those, it seems, who were hardest hit during this time were the ones least prepared, the classic, fabled "grasshoppers," while many of those who survived (and even thrived) were the "ants," who had learned to put some of their hard-earned money aside for just such a time. Sound prosperity planning teaches us the necessary financial preparation that must be a part of every individual's long-term prosperity-building strategy. It is at the very core of successful prosperity creation. Although it will not prevent negative economic and financial calamities from occurring, it will significantly help offset the effects of it.

Consider the Hardworking Ant

Go to the ant, you sluggard;
Consider its ways and be wise.
It has no commander, no overseer or ruler,
Yet it stores its provisions in summer,
And gathers its food at harvest.

How long will you sleep, you sluggard?
When will you get up from your sleep?
A little sleep, a little slumber,
A little folding of the hands to rest—
And poverty will come on you like a bandit
And scarcity like an armed man.

—Proverbs 6:6–11

Question:

Are You a Grasshopper or an Ant?

Morale:

Ants are diligent and resourceful in their work and efforts. In addition, they know what teamwork is all about. The more that you put into something, the more results you will receive from it.

How to Financially Succeed in Your Life and Career

<< Fifteen Proven Strategies That Will Achieve Results >>

1. *Work Is a Verb, Not a Noun*
2. *It Is Not All About You*
3. *Be Reasonable; Do Not Be a Jerk*
4. *Listen More Than You Talk*
5. *Every Job Involves Sales*
6. *Simple Is Better Than Complicated*
7. *Less Is Usually More*
8. *Say What You Mean and Mean What You Say*
9. *The Most Powerful Weapon Is Honesty*
10. *Open Your Mind and Imagination*
11. *Deal with the Reality of Life*
12. *Do Not Keep Score of Issues*
13. *The Best Advantage Is Energy*
14. *Imagine You Met or Worked for You*
15. *Take a Realistic Inventory of Yourself*

Important Success Qualities

In his book *Talent Is Never Enough*, author and motivational speaker John C. Maxwell makes many success affirmations that can apply to anyone in their life and career. Among the most important of them are the following:

If you cannot be teachable, having talent won't help you.

If you cannot be flexible, having a goal won't help you.

If you cannot be grateful, having abundance won't help you.

If you cannot be sustainable, having a plan and preparing won't help you.

If you can't be reachable, having success in your life and career won't help you.

Learning Lesson #1:

Don't let your talent get in the way of your success.

Learning Lesson #2:

The most important thing in life to remember is not to only attempt to capitalize on our gains. Anybody can do that. To be able to achieve more requires us to profit from our mistakes, failures, losses, flaws, and shortcomings.

Bettering Our Self-Assessments

Research shows that very few of us are very good at critical self-assessments. Because most of us generally don't have a good idea of how we think and why we act in certain ways, we simply don't do as well at some activities in life as we could. Anything that can help us understand ourselves better will also serve to improve our long-term performance over time. In the end, doesn't it make good sense to pursue a career field that takes advantage of your natural abilities and strengths as opposed to putting yourself into mold that is ill-suited for your talents and abilities?

There have been a countless number of books written by highly intelligent people concerning this subject, but essentially, what it comes down to are three (3) distinct factors in making this determination. Each of them is important and key in our long-term career success:

1. **HOW YOU WERE RAISED** – Your upbringing, it seems, has a whole lot to do with your ability to make critical self-assessments and factors in issues of self-esteem and confidence, depending on whether you were encouraged as a youngster to pursue your passionate pursuit or, instead, told to follow a more secure path.
2. **YOUR VARIOUS LIFE EXPERIENCES** – It seems like the School of Hard Knocks is another critical factor in this process, and many of your previous trials and tribulations have a huge impact on your abilities to assess yourself.
3. **YOUR GENETIC MAKEUP** – It should not be surprising to learn that genetics play a highly important role in our ability to look at ourselves in the looking glass and determine where we might be able to improve for maximum benefit.

This process that many call introspection comes at a price, however. Once you have identified a specific behavior in your life or career that you have determined needs to be improved, it becomes your responsibility to do something about it. Taking a class; studying a self-improvement book; seeking the counsel of a trusted friend, mentor, or coach; or creating an effective strategy to overcome the challenge are all extremely useful methods to accomplish this. Those who desire higher and higher levels of self-betterment know that isolating a certain behavior is only the first step. From there, you must take action and do something about it.

Fifteen Master Strategies for Personal Achievement

In the book *Mentored by a Millionaire* (2004 by John Wiley & Sons Publishers), author Steven K. Scott created a list of fifteen master strategies in seeking to create personal success in life and career. They are a captivating and engaging look at what's necessary to achieve it in your personal life and career.

1. **REPROGRAMMING YOUR MIND AND ATTITUDE TO ACHIEVE EXTRAORDINARY OUTCOMES** – This involves creating a virtual new software package for your brain as it applies to the undertaking involved.

2. **PLAYING TO YOUR STRENGTHS, STRENGTHENING YOUR WEAKNESSES, AND PREPARING TO PARTNER** – Discover your personality type and use it to your advantage. Know when to team up with others to achieve a successful result.

3. **POWER PASSING YOUR LACK OF KNOW-HOW** – No time, no talent, no money, no problem. It can be done even though you lack some of the knowledge in doing it.

4. **REMOVING THE LIMITS OF YOUR LIMITED RESOURCES** – Access your resources, allocate them, and learn how to effectively expand them.

5. **IDENTIFYING, RECRUITING, AND EFFECTIVELY UTILIZING PARTNERS** – Increase your current level of success by effectively using necessary partners in areas where you don't have the expertise.

6. **BECOMING AN EFFECTIVE AND PERSUASIVE COMMUNICATOR** – What you say and how you say it changes everything.

7. **GAINING A CLEAR AND PRECISE VISION OF WHAT YOU WANT TO ACHIEVE** – A vision without a map is worthless and cannot be achieved.

8. **SETTING AND ACHIEVING THE NECESSARY GOALS** – With this technique, you'll super achieve; without it, you won't.

9. **DREAMING BIGGER THAN YOU CAN POSSIBLY ACHIEVE** – The secret strategy of the world's most successful achievers is this.

10. **USING BREAKTHROUGH TECHNIQUES FOR "CREATIVE PERSISTENCE"** – The reason that many successful people achieve results time after time is that they have the creativity, imagination, and ideas to do so.

11. **OVERCOMING YOUR SUBCONSCIOUS AND CONSCIOUS FEARS OF FAILURE** – This removes the single greatest roadblock to achieving your dreams and ambitions.

12. **OVERCOMING YOUR AVOIDANCE OF CRITICISM** – Bring on the critics and beat them!

13. **TAKING CONTROL OF YOUR LIFE ONE DAY AT A TIME** – Take firm control of your life and your future and keep it.

14. **ACQUIRING A POSITIVE PERSONALITY** – It's easy to become positively amazing.

15. **GAINING PASSION FOR YOUR DREAMS** – This is the high-octane fuel of the world's most successful people.

The Twenty Laws of Extraordinary Success

The following are the twenty extraordinary laws of success. They apply to anyone's job, career, and life. They serve to highlight the efforts that are necessary in one's ability to be able to achieve any significant accomplishment and the efforts necessary to achieve it.

FIRST LAW – Ordinary people achieve ordinary incomes by using conventional approaches taught in schools. Superachievers use a different set of master strategies virtually unknown to the masses.

SECOND LAW – Superachievers learn these techniques and master strategies from mentors and coaches and not through the agonizing process of trial and error.

THIRD LAW – Anyone can reprogram their brain for extraordinary outcomes. All that is necessary is the right combination of "software," commitment, and discipline to do it.

FOURTH LAW – A lack of know-how serves as the springboard to extraordinary achievement.

FIFTH LAW – Superachievers accurately access their resources, wisely allocate them, and expand them by recruiting and networking with outside resources instead of trying to do everything by themselves.

SIXTH LAW – It is impossible to achieve extraordinary success in your career without the use of effective partnering.

SEVENTH LAW – Using effective partnering raises and accelerates success and enormously reduces personal risk.

EIGHTH LAW – Achievement is accelerated by use of good communications and effective persuasion skills and is retarded by the lack of those skills.

NINTH LAW – It is the speaker's responsibilities to grab the listener's undivided attention, impart a clear understanding of what's being said, and implant it within the listener's emotions.

TENTH LAW – Extraordinary achievement is literally impossible to attain without a clear and precise visionary map and a detailed plan to achieve that vision and result.

ELEVENTH LAW – The use of vision infuses life into any project or endeavor, and the lack of vision infuses the dying and failure process.

TWELFTH LAW – Ideas and dreams without clearly defined goals and goals without clearly defined steps to achieve them will never be attained or rarely be achieved.

THIRTEENTH LAW – No one has ever achieved extraordinary success without shooting for the stars. Anyone who has ever achieved their impossible dreams has done so by shooting for the stars.

FOURTEENTH LAW – Extraordinary success can never be achieved without encountering hurdles, roadblocks, setbacks, and failures. These can only be overcome through creative persistence.

FIFTEENTH LAW – Fear of failure blinds one's vision to opportunities.

SIXTEENTH LAW – Failure, when revisited, will rarely be relived. Failure, when analyzed, will provide the building blocks for future successes that will be far greater than the failure itself.

SEVENTEENTH LAW – Conscious or subconscious avoidance of criticisms will short-circuit the ability to achieve extraordinary success and long-term happiness.

EIGHTEENTH LAW – You will not be able to achieve extraordinary success if you cannot control your time and priorities.

NINETEENTH LAW – You will not achieve much success in life until you become a positive person.

TWENTIETH LAW – Without developing a passion, extraordinary success is impossible.

The Prosperity Success Formula That Will Not Fail

As with many things in the rest of our lives, there is a ubiquitous formula for ultimate success accomplishment.

The following is the one that has worked time after time without fail and has helped thousands of people to reach a high level of success by following it:

1. <u>MOTIVATION</u>

This is the drive, the inspiration, the inner urge, the go power, and the call to action to accomplish one's goals.

2. <u>KNOWLEDGE</u>

This is the information, both formal and informal, that is obtained by reading and studying books, materials, and other sources of information, including social networks and media, and in one's dealing with others.

3. <u>KNOW-HOW</u>

This skill is acquired by doing things and accumulating knowledge and wisdom and is the ability to be able to do things effectively based on experience.

Remember that the above formula is a trio *of related components and that you cannot succeed if even one of them is missing.* In addition, *you cannot succeed if you don't even begin the journey!*

Adapted from the book *The Success System That Never Fails* by W. Clement Stone (1962, Prentice-Hall Publishers).

Inventing Your Personal Success Style Formula

When closely examining your potential and opportunity for high levels of accomplishment in your life and career, it is helpful to take a hard look at many of the qualities that compose a successful achiever. The following is designed to help you take a careful look at many of the tried-and-true components that will help you in this process. Ask yourself in which class do you belong:

1. **<u>INITIATIVE TAKER</u>** – Do you need to be *invited* to participate, or do you take the proverbial bull by the horns and jump in as the opportunities occur?

2. **<u>DEFINED PURPOSE</u>** – Are you focused and intense in your pursuit of your goal? Do you have a clear image of what it is that you wish to achieve?

3. **<u>SELF-CONFIDENCE</u>** – Do you believe in yourself first? Do you have a belief in self that makes it easier to convince others?

4. **<u>ORGANIZED EFFORT</u>** – Are you a capable and able planner, preparer, and organizer, or are your efforts mired in chaos and disorganization?

5. **<u>APPLIER</u>** – Can you learn and apply knowledge that you learn as a result of your efforts, research, study, and experience?

6. **<u>LEADERSHIP</u>** – Can you forge a path that others will willingly follow? Are you an Abraham Lincoln or Napoleon Bonaparte style leader?

7. **<u>RESEARCHER</u>** – Do you study and research before making important decisions, or do you shoot from the hip?

8. **ADVISORS** – Do you have an ally advisory team in place that will advise, guide, and direct you in your efforts or when you incur a problem or serious issue?

9. **NETWORKING** – Do you know how to network with others and create a combined effort to accomplish important goals?

10. **MOTIVATOR** – Do you have the proper incentive, and are you properly inspired?

11. **CREATIVITY** – Do you have an imaginative mind that helps you makes your dreams come true?

12. **SPIRIT OF CHEERFULNESS** – Do you really enjoy what you are doing, and are you happy doing it?

13. **SERVICE RENDERING** – Are you willing to take on a responsibility for less-than-market compensation for the purpose of learning how to do it better, or are you instead more income-oriented?

14. **SELF-DETERMINATION** – Do you have the necessary resolve and perseverance to accomplish your goals and objectives?

15. **COOPERATIVE EFFORT** – Do you have a spirit and willingness to work together with others who avoid dissention?

It is these as well as other leadership qualities that will help you accomplish your long-term efforts in building your success. When you closely examine all high-level leaders in government, business, and private endeavors, you will see that each of them closely maintained the above factors that helped them achieve their success results. It is not easy to do it and takes a great deal of conscious effort, but creating your own leadership success formula will undoubtedly include each of these—and more.

ORGANIZATION: the Very Core of All Successful Achievement

<< What Do You Do with All Your Stuff? >>

How well organized are you? How efficient are your categorizing, cataloging, and assembling efforts? Can you find and locate information when needed? Do you have a useful system of administration and orderliness that can be used for your short- and long-term planning and preparation?

Effective and efficient organization is highly important to your success planning in life and career. By collectively organizing your thoughts and ideas, it will allow you to document your thoughts, ideas, plans, and strategies to better able create bigger and better achievements. It also will help you in many ways to be able to measure your existing successful accomplishments and those that you may need to work on.

A Place for Everything and Everything in Its Place

What are the most important areas of organization? How do you even go about deciding where to start? What system should you use? Among the documentation that is most needed includes the following:

1. **GOALS, AMBITIONS, AND OBJECTIVES** – Effective organization begins with a description of where you want to go in your career and life. Without special ones, you subject yourself to a haphazard method of wanderings in this very important process, which leads to lukewarm success or, worse, failure.

2. **NUMERICAL VALUES** – To make each of your goals realistic, it's necessary to place a value on many of them. Not only does this have the effect of making this more specific, but it also personalizes each of them so that you know if they are ultimately achievable in the long run or not.

3. **ACTION STEPS** – You can put teeth into your organization by creating a series of action steps on paper that will be necessary to achieve the desired results. This important step provides the ability to document the exact effort necessary for the successful accomplishment of your planning and serves to allow you to determine the effort that will be necessary to achieve it.

4. **MEASURING SYSTEM** – No organization is complete without an effective system of measurement. This is the only way to know how effective the results of your actions will be. Without a method to view your progress, it's difficult that you will stay on track with your planning.

5. **TIMELINE** – Effective organization includes the use of a timeline in determining the time element in achieving each of your objectives. This is one of the most important tools in developing the right planning techniques and one that should not be overlooked. When do you want to see the results?

6. **PROPORTIONAL ELEMENTS** – Your organizational plan should contain many other essential elements, including income, education, use of debt, investing options, family and relationship considerations, and the ultimate measurement factor—happiness and joy. As a result, each of these needs to be kept in proportion to one another to avoid having a lopsided plan.

You can, indeed, accomplish far more with an effective system of organization and be able to do it with less stress and anxiety than without one. If you find yourself spending a lot of time looking for information, searching through files, asking others what you did with certain key documents, and becoming frustrated when you can't find them, you might need to create a better organizational system.

Intelligently Failing

Is *intelligently failing* something that is possible to accomplish, or is it more of an oxymoron?

When you carefully analyze failure, it is really an MBA on the "how to" experience of learning how to do it better the next time. This is especially true when it comes to building your career and relationships or creating an entrepreneurial business. Failure, it must be remembered, doesn't lead to success; it does lead to knowledge, understanding of what went wrong, and the critical information that does lead to success.

Learn from your failures. If you really want to ensure your overall success rate, double or even triple your failure rate because it is often within the experience of deficiency that successful achievement is often accomplished, which does lead to eventual success. Without a certain number of defeats, the best and most efficient method to attain results will never be effected.

It should be remembered that the average entrepreneur fails three to eight times before finally achieving ultimate success. Obviously, they learn something in those "busts" that lead to their final achievable success, yet what is it that makes them continue to strive for the *golden ring*? Many would argue that it is an entirely monetary issue; those who would try so hard, it is argued, must be seeking the entrepreneurial *treasure chest*.

Others, however, feel that the motivation to succeed in this highly complicated endeavor do so to somehow fulfill a more basic need to succeed for any number of other reasons, including independence, desire to be their own boss, being able to have more input as to the outcome of various projects, the ability to "make it happen" in their respective venture building, and even the sense of satisfaction and appreciation of actually being able to do it.

It seems that failure is not the opposite of success after all. It appears that it may be just one of the steps in creating the final result. Without occasional failures, it might be that we would not be able to chart the eventual course of the consequence. Call it a flop, a fiasco, a disaster, a defeat, a washout, a snafu, a clinker, a dud, or a no-go, failure, by any other name, is still a learning lesson that tells you what didn't work and a step closer to what does.

It should be remembered that Thomas Edison called himself the biggest failure of all time. His efforts in inventing the lightbulb failed over ten thousand times, yet today he is known as a creative genius! History is replete with many other examples of failure that turned out to be success pulled inside out.

Setting Yourself Free from Your Fear

<< *What Are You Scared Of?* >>

What is it that you are really afraid of? What do your personal fears consist of? What is it that keeps you up at night and causes you anxiety and stress? Many fears are vague, imprecise, and even hard to understand and comprehend. You may have a sense that you are afraid of something, but you're not really sure of exactly what it is, or perhaps it's difficult to fully describe it. On the other hand, there are fears that are compellingly specific—fear of starting a business, fear of losing a relationship, fear of dying, fear of spiders, fear of losing your job, fear of the future, and fear of not having enough money when it comes to retirement. Fear makes you anxious and worried. It saps your strength and eventually robs you of all the joy of living a better and more productive and comfortable life. If only you could learn to live your life unafraid.

In some ways, fear is a good thing. It stimulates you to take defensive measures when you confront or perceive a threat. Fear can be a wake-up call that alerts you to your lack of knowledge and can steer you back on the road to successful achievement. *In* some cases, it can even be a helpful, healthy emotion that produces a positive and desired result. Many of your fears are unfounded, however. They are a result of the failure to understand and apply many of the highly useful and effective steps needed to achieve the highest levels of prosperity personal achievement. By more fully understanding each of them better, it is possible to come to grips with your fears.

The best way to set you free from the shackles of fear is through knowledge, learning, and education. By understanding your fears, you will be able to build a carefully constructed, step-by-step prosperity future through a system of effective techniques and strategies that will help you achieve the desired results. It is also achieved through planning and preparation that identifies each of the moves that will help achieve the desired results. You will often be surprised that our view of fear can be summed up just like the immortal words of Pres. Franklin D. Roosevelt that was spoken during the Great Depression of the 1930s: "The only thing we have to fear is fear itself." Often, overcoming your personal fears is as simple as understanding how to go about doing it and who can help you through it.

Conquering Our Demons

Even people who appear supremely successful, extremely organized, and hyperefficient are sometimes saddled with debilitating doubts, self-criticism, and fears. Most people put on a good front, but the reality shows another side.

There's often a big divide between our external image and what's going on inside us.

Being able to conquer self-doubts can be effectively done in several ways: either by changing the behaviors itself that go along with it (I can't figure this out. I must be too dumb to do it.), by challenging the thoughts and beliefs (I'm only thirty years old and don't yet have the life experiences to understand this. It will take time. I must be more patient.), or by training our subconscious thoughts into not judging them, which can result in a far better and more effective way to manage them rather than pressuring yourself to change or denying their existence. In the end, it is the same type of action used to train an animal or pet and coaxing yourself to deal with the feeling. It should always be remembered that there are always choices to be made in how we react to situations and issues. Accepting the fact that there are always some doubts can be key in helping to overcome them. The idea seems to be that these feelings are frequently and eventually going to come, so what are you going to do about them? Sometimes it seems that you don't have to react to them whatsoever and just allow yourself to let it pass by acknowledging that they exist, and it somehow can take away their power. By giving yourself some compassion, you can avoid beating yourself up and give yourself a needed break and be able to interact better with the world and your work. In addition, accepting nonjudgmental, your behavior does not necessarily mean accepting or settling for the status quo. You can opt to change your situation by temporarily changing your environment and return with a clearer set of reality options.

In the end, mindfully accepting their thoughts and feelings as opposed to rationally dealing with them is always an option, but accepting that there are other ways that can be applied in dealing with your fears can become a significant step in conquering your fears.

The Key to Overcoming Fear

CONFRONTING IT!

There have been many books and articles written on the subject of overcoming fear. Fear, when not handled in the right way, can become larger than life and a literal nightmare if left unresolved. When it all boils down, the best and most effective method of overcoming personal fear comes down to actually confronting it and not sticking your head in the sand, avoiding it, or making "temporary repairs." By using this strategy and doing this, you are empowering yourself by being able to look your fear in the eye, which will become the first step in solving it.

Failure to do this can often result in building up the fear, problem, or issue larger in your subconscious mind than maybe it actually is. The most common mistake many people make is that they attempt to dodge or sweep fears and problems away and avoid dealing with them at all. This method simply does not work as a short- or long-term strategy as it will only loom its ugly head once again in the future and be more apt to become a larger and more complex and complicated problem later on. *Some useful techniques in resolving fear are as follows:*

1. **<u>IDENTIFICATION</u>** – What exactly is it that you are afraid of? Can you isolate and identify specifically what it is that you fear? One useful technique is to sit down with paper and pen and write down exactly what the fear you are facing is and be as detailed as possible.

2. **<u>DESCRIPTION</u>** – Can you fully describe the fear? Can you list the reasons why it is such a concern to you? Again, writing down the particulars of your fear, issue, or problem can serve as a useful method in resolving it.

3. **<u>RELEVANCE</u>** – What are the relevant factors of the fear? Is it a result of other issues, or does it stand on its own? Is it an issue that needs to be dealt with right away, or can it be postponed until later?

4. **<u>STRATEGY</u>** – What will be your strategy in resolving your fear? Will you need the help of a trusted advisor, relative, spouse, or friend? Is it a simple solution or a more complicated one? Again, writing down your key points in overcoming it can prove to be a useful technique in solving your fear.

5. **<u>TIMETABLE</u>** – Unfortunately, not all fears can be swept away in a single day. Some of the bigger ones involve a step-by-step and move-by-move process that can achieve successful results. Regardless of the strategy that you use in overcoming your fear, make sure that you stick to a strict timetable in finding a solution to your fear.

6. **<u>REFLECTION</u>** – Believe it or not, many problems are sorted out by using reflection and contemplation instead of trying to force an answer. Our subconscious mind is a remarkable work of nature when it comes to finding creative solutions to vexing fears and problems, and frequently, it offers an assortment of possible solutions but only if we listen to it.

7. **<u>OPTIONS</u>** – Like many things in life, there are usually more than one solution per fear. Obviously, some are easier to apply than others; but in the end, there is often more than one of them to consider.

8. **<u>APPLICATION</u>** – Every fear needs to ultimately become addressed, and your strategy needs to be applied. It may take a while, or you might have to make more than one "application," but if you have chosen the best one, it can eventually provide success.

Fear can be a crippling, paralyzing, and painful experience for each of us. We all have aversions, phobias, trepidations, and anxieties in our lives; so it should not come as a surprise that they exist. Knowing how to deal with fears as they occur in our lives is the first step in finding effective solutions to resolving them regardless of the type of fear.

Your Personal Mission Statement

Many wonder why some people in life become financially independent in their lifetime and others do not. In the end, it comes down to a personal mind-set as opposed to a unique set of circumstances or a select environment. The most successful among us have a carefully conceived and documented perspective of what they want to do with their life and career. They take this into consideration with virtually every decision they make as they progress through life. In the book *Launching a Leadership Revolution,* authors Orrin Woodward and Chris Brady state that the cycle of personal achievement begins with vision, which is another way of saying that ideas and dreams will become realities if they are identified and then acted on.

One of the first steps in this process is to define your personal mission statement. Do you have a vision of where you are going in your life? Is it a haphazard wandering or a specific direction that you are headed? Do you have a purpose and defined goals? A personal mission statement that is created with careful thought and deliberation can set a valuable course for you in your life and career. It will help you recognize who you are and what you are all about. It will serve to help you make the critical decisions in your future that will guide you when you are off course and serve to help you get back on track. People who have never completed a personal mission statement don't realize that it is a very simple process that can change your life forever. Once you have created it, you can use it to guide and measure you in both the short and long term by identifying your priorities. As Peter Drucker once said, "Efficiency is doing things right, but effectiveness is doing the right things." How many times in your life have you made the decision to do something that was important only to discover that you were not motivated to accomplish it?

Learning how to recognize the difference between urgent and important is a habit that can assist you in this process. Stephen Covey in his book *The 7 Habits of Highly Effective People* says that the trick for most people is to stay focused on completing the items that are important and nonurgent over the ones that are urgent and nonimportant. By creating a personal mission statement, you will be able to set your priorities and develop a lifelong formula for personal success. You might want to look at it as a personal business plan, just like the one you will create for your entrepreneurial business. For additional assistance in writing your PMS, you can access the following website:

http://www.revolutionhealth.com/healthy-living/
relationships/time/time-savers/life-goals

In fifty words or less, describe your personal mission statement _____

-------------------------------- --------------------------------
----

CHAPTER 6

Necessary Planning and Preparation

Right Now Could Be the
Prosperity Pivotal Point in Your Life

Years from now, you might look back and recognize that *now* is the exact time that you were glad that you started working on your prosperity preparation and planning. As the well-known, familiar saying goes, "There's no time like the present to do it." This is especially true when it comes to building your long-term prosperity plan. Procrastination and putting it off simply doesn't strategically work well in creating and building your prosperity-building achievements simply because T-I-M-E is one of the essential elements in accomplishing its success.

Fast forward your life to five, ten, or even fifteen years from now and you will see how your discipline and commitment in building your prosperity plan will grow with only a modest amount of investment money plus the learning and education that you will realize as a result of making this a priority in your life. It will dramatically and forever pay off for you as it builds like a snowball. Once it gets started rolling, it will begin hurling downhill, gathering momentum, and will really begin to take off.

It is also important to remember the value of compounding in your S & I program (savings and investing). This is yet another reason why getting started *now* is so very important in building your prosperity plan. Applying each of the strategies and techniques in this book to your personal situation will help you establish a highly creative, effective, and unique formula for every reader and participant in our prosperity training and education.

Arm Yourself with Information

Preparation is the key

The overlooked part of many a long journey is the *necessary planning and preparation* for the successful outcome. This is true of any task worth completing and applies in particular now with the complex and complicated world that we live in today. The very process of *P & P* will ensure that you will arrive intact, well sustained, and on time. Those who fail to recognize the importance of this are doomed, like the ancient Israelis, to wander about in the desert of opportunity and seldom, if ever, arrive at the desired destination.

Ask yourself how much planning and preparation did you experience on the last long vacation that you took. If it turned out well, it is understood that you underwent an ample amount of work to create the right kind of result. Essentially, this is the single biggest reason to undergo plenty of planning and preparation, to make sure that you end up where you want to be and can enjoy the journey.

How You Can Go About Doing It

How does one create the necessary P & P, you ask? It all starts with *researching the subject*. This is not to be confused with merely reading a single article. It can be achieved via the Internet, through study of books and related materials, and by building a database of relevant information that will guide and assist you with making the critical moves that will provide the successful conclusion. Another needed step is to *network with others* who have or are pursuing a similar path and exchanging views and opinions with them regarding the chosen work. This can greatly assist you in evaluating many of the right moves to make and, just as importantly, avoiding the blunders that are always a part of any extraordinary undertaking. Another step is in *taking a formal class or course* concerning the work being considered. This can create an unlimited amount of practical knowledge and information that can answer many of your personal questions concerning your interest. Many of these are available in a wide variety of subjects, and regularly attending such classes can help you further network with others who have the same passionate pursuit. Finally, finding a mentor or coach to personally guide and assist you can help you immensely in overcoming the stumbling blocks, hurdles, and diversions that prevent many from ultimate success and achievement in their life.

Creating an Inner Circle of Supporters

Establishing your *inner circle* of positive relationships with those who have a similar interest can provide a substantial opportunity to cultivate mutual education and knowledge and is always a win-win. Every so often, some of these relationships can go from a structured or secure relationship to one of a solid or significant one that can become a defining period in your life. It's impossible to create these types of relationships. They just seem to happen. They affect each of you in a major and compelling way.

Often, these are the people who lift you in many ways, personally and professionally; and if you manage to develop one of these special relationships, don't ignore it. Show your gratitude often and fight to preserve it. Make sure that it is reciprocal and not merely one-sided. It's also important to not let success of life prevent you from creating and developing those relationships or keep you from maintaining or losing track of them. Many of these inner circle friendships are based on the following:

- **Shared Experiences** – Positive and negative experiences both help create a mutual bond between people.
- **Mutual Enjoyment** – Enjoyment of spending quality time with one another assists the relationship among people.

- **Mutual Respect** – It often helps to remember that issues and events are not more important than the relationship itself.
- **Trust** – This is the very foundation of every good friendship, personally or professionally.
- **Reciprocal Relationships** – One-sided relationships will not last if they are out of balance and more taking than giving.

In the end, all enduring good relationships, personal and professional, are very much like maintaining a bank or other personal financial account. You must exercise care to not make more withdrawals than deposits to keep the account from becoming "overdrawn" or in jeopardy of being "closed out." By ignoring this rule, you will not be able to sustain or maintain them. The same is true of meaningful relationships, especially in your inner circle of friends and professional advisors. The most successful achievers are those who recognize this and work hard to maintain balanced relationships that provide equal advantages for both parties.

Creating a Solid Prosperity Plan That Really Works

> *Dear God, I pray for patience and I want it right now!*
>
> —The Prayer of the Modern American

We live today in an "instant" culture that prides itself on having an easy, quick fix for virtually anything in our lives. Not surprisingly, this is also reflective in our approach to prosperity building. Too often, we choose to reward ourselves with short-term, patchwork wealth-building strategies that frequently create more money problems than they actually solve. As many know, the future belongs to those who prepare for it. Remember the Boy Scout motto? "Be prepared." Our microwave instant-gratification culture has created a hedonistic myth that says tomorrow will somehow mysteriously always take care of itself.

The old fable of the ant and the grasshopper comes to mind when contemplating this attitude:

"The ant worked hard all summer and harvested in the fall. Meanwhile, the grasshopper played and enjoyed himself. As a result, when the cold winter arrived, the grasshopper was left with neither food nor shelter, while the ant remained warm and secure."

Solid solutions to our lives take responsibility, time, foresight, patience, discipline, commitment, and sacrifice; yet they also have long-term payoffs for those who are willing to do them. The basic and fundamental difference in preparation and the live-for-today philosophies common today is the difference between investing in your future and mortgaging it. Now let us develop a rock-solid personal prosperity strategy that really works and will significantly help you build it each step of the way to achieve the most desirable long-term results.

Are you managing tomorrow as if it really mattered?

Your Prosperity-Building Plan: a Lifelong Journey

Prosperity preparation and planning should not be approached or viewed like an engineering problem. Instead, it is a lifelong process as opposed to a singular life event experience. It will change frequently as your life events evolve over the course of your lifetime. One of the reasons for this change is that most changes that affect your prosperity are the direct result of internal personal life variations and changes, such as birth, death, sickness, marriage, divorce, income, and career changes, along with other dramatic personal events in your life. They are not so often the external factors, such as inflation, stock market results, global conflicts, deflation, or national or international economic issues. It is a good idea to remember this in your prosperity planning and preparation.

Therefore, a good lifelong prosperity plan strategy should be to *annually review your plan* and update it to make key and important specific adjustments for new and changing circumstances in your personal life, career, business, family, and other situations. A good time to do this is during the Christmas holidays when most people have the time and the inclination to reflect over the past year's changes as well as to look into the coming New Year. Designing a prosperity-building plan based on static assumptions and one-time events is frequently meaningless over the long term and may even prove to be a mistake. The best and most effective prosperity-building plans are those that take these important life factors into account and then include them in the plan during the annual review.

Steering Around Life's Financial Hazards

Each of us makes personal finance decisions in our lives—some good, some bad, and some that have little consequence. They range in size and magnitude from the not so grand all the way up to the tumultuous life-changing ones that affect our lives forever. Unless they are averted, sidestepped, and maneuvered around, they can create delays, barriers, and booby traps that will hinder your prosperity building. Despite all the strategies, techniques, planning, and preparation that you make to ensure your prosperity in the future, you will undoubtedly experience many *life* challenges that frequently happen to each of us, often, far more than we care to even think about or admit. No one gets through their life without an occasional mishap caused by a financial mistake, error, or bad judgment call. Often, these hazards may not even be our own fault. Many times, you don't even have to be the one who *caused* the problem. These hazards may be caused by bad luck, accidents, incidents, or as a victim of someone else's actions. Whatever the reason, it is sure to affect your personal finances. Experts all agree that many of life's hazards fall into many various categories that each require a proportionate personal finance response to the level of hazard (and usually the solution is monetary). This article discusses four of the most common hazards we can encounter in our lives:

1. **FINANCIAL "ISSUES"**

   These are the most common and minor of all of them and frequently can easily be rectified. The cost is typically under several hundred dollars. Some examples of these "issues" are overdrawn checking accounts, a sudden unexpected school- or work-related expense, a minor vehicle repair, or other headache. While always annoying, "financial issues" require an infusion of cash from somewhere and always negatively affect your budget.

2. **FINANCIAL "PROBLEMS"**

   Financial hazards that fall into this category are slightly higher in degree and amount and, as a result, take more money to resolve. These are expenses that run up into the $1,000 plus or minus category and require much more needed financial help in resolving. Frequently, these are unanticipated expenses, such as deductibles on insurance claims, unexpected home repairs, appliance replacement, and similar expenses.

3. **FINANCIAL "CATASTROPHIES"**

   The third category of life's financial hazards is aptly termed "catastrophe" since it involves significantly more money, often from $1,000 to several thousands of dollars or more. These catastrophic expenses can wreak havoc in any family's household budget, and the solution usually results in borrowing money in some form of consumer loan, equity load, or use of a credit card. Examples of these catastrophes are personal accidents or injuries, property accidents where no insurance coverage is in effect (or coverage is denied for some reason or other), major replacement of a home's internal systems, unexpected replacements of major appliances, or the result of robbery, fraud, or other types of crime.

4.   **FINANCIAL "DISASTERS"**

This is the most expensive form of life financial hazard that usually involves a substantial amount of money, typically over $10,000 or more, which is commonly a result of divorce, death, major illness, lawsuit, uninsured liability, incarceration, or other emergencies that suddenly and violently enter your life and send your personal finances into a tsunami-style tidal wave that may take many years to recover. Sadly, you may never recover from it and keep paying the price for its effect forever.

Summary

Do any of these sound familiar? Have they ever occurred in your life or in your families, your friends, or your coworkers' lives? If so, you know clearly how damaging financial hazards can be to your personal finances, much less to your prosperity-building plan.

Successful Strategies to Consider

There are many ways to offset these financial life hazards. We have carefully chosen a number of techniques that you can consider using to sidestep each of them. Some of the ways to handle hazards are the following:

1.   **First, let's start with the simplest one: *financial issues*. These are neither gut-wrenching experiences nor full-fledged calamities yet *do affect* your personal finances from time to time.**

The best and most effective strategy is to always live within your means and to anticipate these potential issues and set aside a few dollars from each paycheck somewhere where you can access it quickly (in my growing-up years, my parents used a cookie jar on top of the refrigerator to keep a few excess dollars. Later, as an adult, my choice was to use a bank depository bag, which I kept in my desk at home and deposit a couple of hundred dollars in it for emergencies). Whatever method you choose to use is not important. The key is to *have* a suitable system or technique that swerves to *prevent* financial "issues" as much as possible and helps *solve* them when they invariably pop up. Without such a strategy, your issues will quickly snowball into the next category: *financial problems*.

2.   **The second set of personal financial hazards is *financial problems*. These are larger in size and scope and, as a direct result, are more costly to deal with and solve.**

These are not the type of problems that a little "mad money" will fix and require more strategic thinking to resolve. Enter the *emergency fund* (or other commonly known as the rainy day fund). We have all heard about these in the past. We know we should create one at our local bank in the form of a savings account or money market account to keep it fully liquid, but how many people actually have a fund? Ideally, it should consist of three to six months of net earnings (take-home pay). Even if you cannot fully fund that amount, you should still have several thousand dollars tucked away (maybe $50 per paycheck until this goal is achieved) to be able to sidestep these expenses that come up from time to time in your life. These expenses are larger in scope and therefore need a larger solution. By having an emergency or rainy day fund available, you can recover from the financial episode intact without having to borrow money or through the use of a credit card. One of the keys is to not use this fund for *anything else*, including vacations, clothes, gifts, or other purposes, only for *legitimate* emergencies. Once used, it is important to rebuild the account so that it is available for the next time you may need it.

3. **The next category, *financial catastrophe*, is a much deeper personal finance problem than either of those previously covered. By nature of the term, a heightened state of impending loss is recognized in a catastrophe that has developed, and it results in several thousands of dollars needing to be quickly located.**

The best and most familiar strategy to implement is through the use of obtaining insurance that protects your large personal assets as a fundamental part of your prosperity planning *before* the catastrophe strikes. There are many types of coverage for many categories of catastrophes, and you should be aware that some of them are expensive and useless. This is an area of personal finance where too much of it can be as economically draining to your finances as too little of it. You can find insurance for literally almost anything today. The best technique is the traditional insured approach. Make sure to insure your home (and contents), your vehicle, and your family members but keep the expenses of insurance as reasonable as possible through the use of higher deductibles and knowledge of particular insurance coverage and types of coverage. Make sure that you have enough coverage to sidestep a major catastrophe but keep the expenses affordable. For example, a $500 to $1,000 deductible on your homeowner's policy will produce a significantly lesser premium than a $250 deductible. Yes, you will have to pay more in the event of an accident, but the savings that you will experience in the cost of insurance plus the use of your rainy day fund will help you to be able to afford to do it. *Having adequate insurance coverage is a fundamentally sound prosperity planning tool that should be used by everyone.*

4.   The last category of personal finance hazards deals with the
     worst nightmare of all: a *financial disaster*. This category is a huge
     personal expense that is a result of an unfortunate event in life and
     can be minimized by plenty of advanced thinking, planning, and
     preparation.

One of the best strategies to employ is to make sure that you have will
or estate plan already in place well in advance. Financial disasters typically
involve legal action; and you can limit your exposure to the disaster if you have
a carefully thought-out plan, including legal entities, such as limited liability
organizations, family limited partnerships, trusts, and even foundations
included in your estate planning documents that limit your personal exposure
and liability. The rest of your existing liability exposures can be handled by
insurance that you have in place. This is an example of the proven techniques
that virtually all prosperous people use to offset their personal exposure to
large assets regardless of the type. Another suitable option and alternative is to
purchase a large ($1–$5 million) umbrella liability insurance policy through
your insurance agent that can be added to your homeowner's policy coverage.
This can be done for a reasonable cost and will cover you in the event in a major
lawsuit. Even though the umbrella coverage *will not cover* every conceivable
incident or exposure that could happen to you in your life, it does offer large
protection and will also include defense attorney expenses. There is no amount
of planning or insurance that can offer you 100 percent protection from all
of life's hazards. And even if there were, you would probably not be able to
afford the cost of having it. The best strategy to consider is to use a cautious
consideration of each of these hazards to see how prepared you are to offset
each of them.

*Just how prepared are you to deal with each of the financial hazards? List your
defensive action plan to each of the outlined categories in the corresponding section
of the workbook. Even though the personal prosperity plan focuses on many of the
positive wealth-building aspects of creating and building your prosperity on a long-
term basis, it makes a lot of sense to look at financial hazards that each of us encounter
in our lives and create a venerable moat around those people and assets that mean the
most to us. It is this wise planning and preparation that will often make the difference
between merely a financial issue and cataclysmic financial disaster in your life.*

Life's Necessary Planning and Preparation

< Creating a Personal Emergency Fund >

Planning an eventful trip takes a lot of research—finding and exploring
places and events to visit, reserving lodging, having someone stop by to

watch your home while you are gone, boarding the pets, holding the mail and newspapers, and carefully and prudently budgeting all the expenses for the journey weeks and months in advance. Indeed, making plans and preparing for the trip help to make it go much smoother and usually results in fewer unforeseen circumstances. Yet unlikely events do happen that produce unanticipated results in our vacations, trips, and adventures. Detours, slowdowns, and unwelcome delays are often a part of the total travel experience. Making the necessary plans and preparations (and even backup plans) greatly help the process of traveling. We all would agree that unwelcome occurrences in our plans do not create any added sense of adventure in our journeys.

Ideally, we should also try to plan our lives so that our future unfolds into many months and years where life's security is systematically laid out and followed. However, we should also realize as we become older and wiser that life's "detours" are an inevitable fact of life. No one gets through their life without experiencing their share of troubles, turmoil, and tribulations. Frequently, they are defined by a proportionate share of numerous dollar signs and expenses. More specifically, it usually results in a lack of enough money to handle the emergency or event.

The unknown is always frightening, but there is no reason why we cannot better prepare for the unknown a little at a time by carefully setting aside a few dollars each payday into an emergency or rainy day fund that will benefit us when those situations occur. Life is full of delays, detours, and disasters; and we unfortunately don't always know how our long-term plans will unfold and how these unforeseen circumstances will affect and interrupt our lives. All too often, they occur at the worst possible times. Will they inevitably cause sorrow, heartache, fear, as well as money anxiety? Some of the events in life are not solved by money alone, but *it is possible* to deal with many of life's conundrums easier and better if you have judiciously funded such a savings or money market account and earmarked it as an emergency or rainy day fund to be able to better cope with them.

Creating Your Personal Finance Prosperity "Dashboard"

What exactly does a "financial dashboard" consist of? What is it? How is it used? How do you go about creating it? Where do you find it? How expensive is it? A useful and effective dashboard includes many "instruments" that can help you personally monitor your personal finances and prosperity building and help to keep you "on the road" and will prevent you from making one of more wrong turns, getting lost, breaking down, getting in an accident, and allowing you to arrive at your financial destination on time and intact. Similar to your vehicle dashboard controls, your financial dashboard can also alert you of danger.

Some of the monitoring tools consist of each of the following "gauges":

- **SPEEDOMETER/ODOMETER** – This is your system of determining the "speed" in which you are achieving your financial goal, objectives, and ambitions and the length of distance you have traveled in achieving it. Some of the factors that play a part in this are interest rates, yields, and long-term effects of compounding.
- **TACHOMETER** – This is the RPMs that your prosperity plan is operating and determines if your plan is finely tuned or is about to "red zone" and ready to crash and burn. An example of this is annual portfolio balancing that allows you to rebalance all your investments once a year to match your objectives.
- **OIL PRESSURE READING** – This is the intensity of your prosperity program and if it is working on all cylinders or not. An example of this is the right mix of investments relative to your age, income, and goals.
- **CLOCK** – This is the time factor that is used in determining your overall prosperity-building timetable. It serves as a guide in determining how much of it you have remaining and how much you have used up. Some of the key financial factors that play an integral part in this relative to prosperity planning are age, overall health, and length of time before retirement.
- **GPS SYSTEM** – This is a navigational tool that shows you how to stay on course or how to get back on course if you become lost. Some of the personal financial factors involved in this include some tools as your personal financial statement, Personal Prosperity Success Plan Paradigm®, and unique and specific prosperity plan that is customized for your use.
- **TEMPERATURE GAUGE** – This gauge represents how "boiling hot," "moderately warm," or "ice-cold" your personal prosperity plan is performing. Some financial examples of this include your type of investments, mix of assets, and rates of return.
- **VOLTAGE METER** – This is the instrument that shows the degree of polarity in your financial vehicle's electrical system and is either "negative" or "positive." An illustration of this includes high-risk (positive) investments or negative (low-risk) ones. A proper blend of all of them is the "midpoint" range reading.
- **FUEL INDICATOR** – This is one of the most important and most "looked at" gauges on your financial vehicle and probably monitored more than any of them because it determines how much "fuel" you have in your prosperity-building tank. Factors in your personal prosperity plan include the overall value of your prosperity plan, your net worth, and the value of your other portfolio investments.

- **HORN** – A financial horn on your financial vehicle can be used to sound an alarm when you are too close to an accident or disaster. Some examples of this include downturns in the economy, global disasters, or even cataclysmic and severe weather conditions.

- **STEERING WHEEL** – This is the virtual "rudder" of your prosperity vehicle that allows you to direct it exactly where you want it to go. The best example of this is the literal "hands-on" attention that you give to your own investing and personal prosperity planning.

- **RADIO/CD/SOUND SYSTEM** – This is the communications system that is used to receive updated new, information and broadcasts that allow the driver (investor) to steer the vehicle on the journey. A good example of this is the advice that you receive on a regular and consistent basis from your trusted personal financial prosperity team of professionals.

- **COMFORT SYSTEM CONTROLS** – This is the level of interior comfort that you experience in your unique and individual prosperity plan. It includes the extremes of heat and cold as well moderate inside temperature. Examples in your personal prosperity plan include embracing high-risks (hot), medium-risks (moderate), and low-risks (cold) investment choices.

- **CRUISE CONTROL** – This is a feature in your prosperity vehicle that needs to be unhooked or dismantled. Many well-intended and potentially great personal prosperity plans have nose-dived because the investors felt they could put their plan on "autopilot" and forget about it. When they eventually examined the distance traveled and looked at the overall results, they were very disappointed with the long-term results. Prosperity building is not something that you can ever forget about for a long period without disastrous results. It is further a reason to have a "financial dashboard" actively in place.

- As you can easily see, not having a "financial dashboard" consisting of each of the above gauges to measure how your prosperity vehicle is working to take you on your asset-building journey would be like getting into your transportation vehicle blindfolded and expecting to be able to steer it down the road without getting into an accident or causing injury to someone (including the driver and passengers). The specific system that you choose is unique to your goals and objectives and results from a carefully and detailed process of selecting from many choices that are available to you. Unlike a transportation vehicle, you cannot merely order a "financial dashboard" from the manufacturer. These have to be cautiously created one at a time, step by step, and move by move to have one that is personalized and unique to you.

- The *best method* to use in achieving a spectacular result that will allow you to travel along the prosperity highway at maximum speed with the top down and the wind blowing through your hair is through a proven process called

E - D - U - C - A - T - I - O - N

A Prosperity Warning Light

We are all guilty of this. You didn't think that the hesitation in your "prosperity engine" and that pesky little yellow "check engine" indicator lights on your financial dashboard really needed your immediate attention. You rationalized it away, saying that you would get at it soon, maybe even in the next few days or weeks or when you had time to do it. However, very soon, when you turned on the key to start the engine, it wouldn't start. Worse, it had now left you stranded in an undesirable location, and you couldn't go *anywhere* now, much less anywhere you *needed* to go. Your first reaction was that of frustration, maybe even anger. Why didn't you do something about it when the warning light came on? Now it will cost you even more money, time, energy, inconvenience, and maybe even some lost opportunities.

Your second thought (hopefully anyway) was more of a personal resolution: you now realize that you need to pay close attention to the prosperity dashboard "warning lights" that are trying to get your attention, including such issues as too much personal debt; higher and higher levels on credit cards and consumer equity loans; not following that spending plan; taking a pass on a good, sound, long-term real estate investment; getting behind on some of your payments; living too "paycheck to paycheck"; and so forth. They can each mean that something is, indeed, wrong with your prosperity engine; and it needs to be closely examined, looked at, and looked over. You need to pay close attention to the warning light on your prosperity dashboard. What warning lights are flashing in your prosperity life now? What needs to be tuned up, replaced, or repaired through better planning and preparation? What can you do to get more MPG (more prosperity gains) from your existing plan? Just like the vehicle that you depend on to get you to or from work, the grocery store, vacation trips, and church, your prosperity engine needs to be well maintained too.

Prosperity Planning Can Answer Many of the Personal "What-Ifs" in Life

"Avoiding the Coulda, Woulda, Shouldas in Prosperity Investing"

The debates take place at dinner with your family, at work with coworkers, on the golf course or fishing boat with friends, over coffee with a buddy, over drinks with a trusted relative, or during those quiet moments in the early morning or late evening with your spouse. They can often evolve into a compelling and engaging look at "I wonder what would happen if we . . ." Such "what if" moments can serve to answer a wide range of hypothetical questions from "What would happen if we could set aside another $100–$150 per month into our investment portfolio?" all the way to "What would happen if we purchased that lakefront property foreclosure and leased it out in the summer?" or even "What could we do if we reduced our credit card balances and consumed debts and invested the new discretionary income into that small business enterprise that we have been thinking about the last few years?"

Some of these inquiries are derived from statistical options that have become available as a result of the number-crunching capabilities that are created from today's sophisticated computer software programs. They have helped to better define and explain how those future possibilities can compare to the present and greatly help to extrapolate the figures into endless possibilities. Even though they are still only speculation and assumptions and are far from perfect, they are certainly much better than simple guesswork. Used properly, they can greatly help determine the probability factor to estimate and forecast how each financial prosperity decision will impact the overall long-term result. They can each be used to apply to scenarios that were previously never even considered, much less acted upon.

Many of these are available from various software programs, such as Microsoft, Excel, Quicken, Microsoft Money, and other custom programs. Being able to bridge the gap from the present investment model to an exaggerated, even far-flung possibility is at the very core of these statistical "what if" options. The results for many are striking reminders of how certain options can justify serious investments to achieve greater prosperity successes. In the past, these calculations and forecasts may have taken literally weeks or months to accomplish, but they can now be done in a few simple key strokes via an applicable software program. By doing this, it is possible now to engineer a personal financial "scoring system" that can help you to better achieve an ideological method of tracking subtle and even not-so-subtle changes in your long-term prosperity investment philosophy and closely examine the overall results. Although many of these analysis are far from perfect, they do offer a closer glimpse of many of the "what if" factors that can significantly benefit from Personal Prosperity-Building Success Paradigm®.

This careful financial engineering can also provide many strong clues on how slight adjustments can or should be considered and perhaps even taken in key areas and at critical and optimum periods in the national and regional economy to take full advantage of each of the ups and downs that will provide higher success-building achievements.

Pearl of Wisdom: *Let Your Plan Stand Out, Not Stand Still*

Six Key Factors That Will Improve Your Prosperity Success

< Redirecting Your Focus >

1. **IDENTIFYING YOUR FINANCIAL PERSONALITY.** Each of us has a unique, individual money personality that greatly determines how we perceive it and how it is used in our life. Being able to understand yours is extremely important to understand and interpret your personal relationship to money and to achieve your long-term prosperity success.

2. **CREATING GOALS AND OBJECTIVES.** You cannot hit a mark if you do not know what it is or have a clear method of being able to track and achieve it. Designing your individual goals and objectives is critical and important. Otherwise, how do you know if you are making any progress? Creating finely tuned goals and ambitions is a critical necessity.

3. **RELYING ON FACTORS OUTSIDE YOUR CONTROLS.** Learn to change your *internal* self (earning, saving, spending, investing, debt) as opposed to *external* factors (interest rates, wars, energy prices, global economics). The former are things that you can change and influence. The latter is beyond your control. Once you begin doing this, your financial future will start to change and improve.

4. **EDUCATING THYSELF.** Your long-term prosperity program all begins with knowing and understanding the basic core foundational block principles. The method to do this is via education (classes, courses, workshops, and seminars) and by reading and studying the proven asset-building techniques and strategies that have been successfully used by others over time.

5. **LEARNING TO USE THE FINANCIAL TOOLS AVAILABLE TODAY.** The ability to measure accomplishments is critical to keep prosperity seekers motivated. There are many, many of these financial tools available to do this today, ranging from the Internet, PCs, and laptops all the way to complex software programs, financial calculators, and even investment mentors, coaches, and advisors.

6. **DEVELOP A CAREFULLY WRITTEN PROSPERITY-BUILDING PLAN.** Dreams and desires are good. However, written and

documented plans are even better. Writing a prosperity plan takes a great deal of time and is not simply a weekend exercise. It takes a great deal of thought and examination of many personal factors to create a good one. Working with a professional who can help you develop an individual prosperity plan is an excellent and functional strategy in building, engineering, and finally achieving it.

The secret is to know **how** *to use and apply each of them to your unique personal situation. Without using these tools, you can quickly wander off course. It is more important to understand how to use your existing tools than to have them merely because they are high-tech or expensive.*

Learning to Somehow Avoid Financial Incompetence

Be very careful who you listen to when it comes to your personal finances and prosperity building. There are many so-called experts or professionals in the financial world who are anxious, clever, and very willing to give you their advice but are perhaps more concerned about making their sales goals and commissions than they are about helping you achieve *your* goals and objectives. The truth is that much of what these individuals *say* passes for good theory in many cases yet isn't. This is also true in other phases of financial products and services, including insurance providers, mutual funds, brokers of all types, informational organizations, and even others, including financial advisors and planners, who can be motivated by portfolio fees and commissions. Many of these do not always have your personal objectives in mind as much as their own. It is important to always ask a lot of questions and even seek second opinions when it comes to building your long-term prosperity program and to recognize that there is a lot of marketing that exists.

On the other hand, you might just have more control than you think in many areas of your prosperity plan, including taxes, investment diversification and resourcefulness of money management, earnings, percentage of income devoted to savings and investing, and other areas. The secret is to be *proactive* rather than *reactive* in the process of each one of these. Select the right investments that will boost your overall prosperity building over time and not attempt to do it quickly or overnight by accepting only the advice of experts and financial marketers.

Your Personal Prosperity Success-Building Paradigm® is not realistic, functional, or complete unless it addresses each of these critical factors:

1. **A DIVERSIFIED ASSET-CLASS BASE** – A mixture of several different investment categories is always recommended.

2. **AN ELEMENT OF REAL ESTATE** – Property investing is still one of the best long-term investments for virtually any portfolio and any investor.

3. **THE IMPACT OF TAXES** – Taxes are one of your biggest expenses in life and play a significant role in prosperity building. If there is not an effective strategy in place to keep them proportionate, you could be paying more than your share of taxes.

4. **THE DIMENSION OF LIQUIDITY OF SOME ASSETS** – You need a certain amount of access to cash and cannot have everything tied up in long-term investments.

5. **THE NECESSARY FLEXIBILITY OF THE INEVITABLE IN LIFE** – Birth, death, marriage, divorce, accidents, sickness, challenges, and opportunities are all part of life.

6. **AN EMPHASIS ON FINANCIAL LITERACY EDUCATION** – If you are going to succeed, you need to know how to play the game. It all begins and ends with a good understanding of the "rules."

The learning lesson here is that personal prosperity planning is a *highly personal* experience and needs to be addressed in that manner. All the sophisticated computer printouts, charts, graphs, and statistics in the world *do not* represent your unique, individual, and personal life situation. It is the same difference between finely crafted heirloom furniture and the off-the-shelf varieties sold in countless home improvement stores by the thousands. Ask yourself which is more valuable: custom-created personal planning or boilerplate ones? The evidence shows that boilerplate financial advice is simply not very effective for most prosperity seekers. It is absolutely amazing how much advertising gets passed off for insightful financial advice in magazines and investment programs in the media today. The conflicts of interest, abusive marketing practices, and self-dealing in financial markets are alarming to witness.

In addition, it is a myth to think that there is any single person, group of people, or even financial institution that can accurately predict what is going to happen next in the financial markets (arguably, they have enough of a challenge in even deciphering what happened in yesterday's results, so how could they accurately predict tomorrows?). If there were, indeed, a really hidden investment opportunity out there, what makes investors think that they would be even inclined to share it with others? In truth, the odds of predicting the next hot investment opportunity are not necessarily a result of keen analysis, insight, or psychic capability and more commonly known by many economists as the theory of large numbers (i.e., at best, there is only a fifty-fifty guesstimate probability). Even if correctly selected, luck promises to run out eventually. In the end, investment advice frequently comes down to sophisticated marketing more than a solid investment possibility or opportunity. The solution to this financial investment conundrum is that your ultimate financial prosperity building lies where it should be—squarely on your shoulders and within your prosperity map plan that has been carefully prepared through the input of others but recognized as being your own.

It is your plan after all, and you are the one who will benefit from it or not. Know what it takes to create it and follow the steps that will take you where you want to go.

Seven Categories That Must Be Carefully Considered for a Successful Retirement

The following is a list of seven fundamentals that must be carefully considered to achieve a long and successful retirement:

1. **FINANCES** – Even though some regular living expenses will be reduced at retirement, they will not go down as much as you might think, perhaps only 10 to 20 percent in most cases. As a result, you must ensure that your income and expenses are carefully studied and planned so that you can maintain your current standard of living.

2. **WORK** – Postretirement work is more about emotional and mental well-being than it is about earnings or income. This may well be the time to discover a new hobby or passion unrelated to previous career work, which may involve some additional formal training or schooling.

3. **RELATIONSHIP WITH SPOUSE** – If you are married or have a life partner, you must consider their needs too. When discussing retirement plans, you should think about those activities that you can do together and separately. You should each have your personal pursuits and also those that you do together for maximum happiness.

4. **PERSONAL AND PROFESSIONAL INVOLVEMENTS** – Where will your new personal and professional image come from in retirement? Your newfound time and involvements need to be carefully considered in the retirement phase of life, including volunteer work, social interaction, passionate pursuits, and other involvements.

5. **NEW IDENTITY** – Creating a positive new self-image is important to you in retirement. Although your working career probably did a lot to define your identity, this new period will be a time where your new identity can be shaped and formed based on many of your new interests.

6. **LEISURE AND PLAY** – Your leisure activities at retirement can be expanded and developed or perhaps even combined with others, such as traveling, studying, and socializing. They can even result in new

discoveries since you now have the capabilities of time to enjoy them better. The pursuit of play is important at this stage of life.

7. **FRIENDS, FAMILY, AND SOCIAL RELATIONSHIPS** – Retirement is the perfect time to bond (and even re-bond) with friends, family, and other relationships that might have been distanced because of career work. Having solid social relationships is very important in this phase of life.

Fast Versus Best in Your Prosperity Planning

Many people believe that "fast" beats "best" in their prosperity planning and preparation. They seem to be obsessed with speed, yet this "fast craze" does not really get you anywhere when it comes to building a good, effective plan. When closely examined, a slower, more deliberate method appears to be a much better strategy in building a successful plan. Things that often go up quickly can also come down just a quickly. Speed in building your prosperity plan is not always the best policy. Using patience and a thorough understanding of the process is preferable to quickness in building your future, one of the most important areas of your life. A slower, more painstaking method will usually result in something that will benefit you for many, many years in the future. Remember the story of the tortoise and the hare? At the end of the race, the tortoise won as a result of using a better strategy: slow and steady was his technique as opposed to the hare's short bursts of speed and then rest. It also is important to remember that the prosperity journey is not a sprint but a long marathon that requires conditioning as well as an effective plan of how to successfully build for your retirement.

Finally, in creating your plan, you must also take into consideration many of the events that change or alter your life and those close to you. Allowing some level of flexibility to achieve each of your goals and objectives is also a wise strategy to employ. In the end, your very existence, it seems, is a series of actions and events that together make up this thing called L-I-F-E; and it is best enjoyed and accomplished with an adequate and well thought-out prosperity plan.

Use of Financial Protection

< How to Keep Your Finances Safe from Predators >

It is an unfortunate reality today that building your overall prosperity is hard work, yet holding onto it and keeping it safe from predators is even harder. There is a vast number of schemers, scammers, thieves, and fast-buck artists who prey on the unsuspecting and lure you into their web of deceit. In addition, there are many who engage in identity theft, a serious and multibillion-dollar problem that didn't even exist twenty years ago before the proliferation of computer and software that made your information available to people throughout the entire world.

Identity theft has topped the FTC's list of consumer complaints for the past eight years in a row. A new survey shows a record that 9.9 million Americans were victims of identity theft last year. It is a big business, and everyone needs to take steps to protect themselves:

- *Many of the victims of identity theft know the person who stole their identity. Called friendly frauds, these perpetrators were well known to the victims.*
- *New-account theft is one of the most difficult areas to detect and occurs when thieves open a new account and lines of credit using stolen identities.*
- *Even minors and unborn children are at risk and ripe targets for thieves who know that it can take years before a child's identity theft can be discovered. By then, the damage is long since done and can often ruin a young person's life and credit history for many years to come. A recent law requiring a parent's signature for a minor under eighteen years of age to have a credit card may help this situation, but the perpetrators will find a way around these laws too.*
- *How many of you have been subjected to identity theft in one form or another in your life? How many of you have known someone who has been a victim of identity theft through a lost or stolen purse or wallet?*
- *Those of you who have been on a computer and gotten an e-mail from the infamous Nigerian who promises a "sizeable return" if you can only send him $5,000. He promises to double your money in just two weeks! This is just one example of the types of computer fraud that is so rampant today via the Internet. There are thousands of others ready to prey on those who have not made the necessary preparations to keep it from happening to them.*
- *Preparing yourself for a potential financial fraud all the way from losing your wallet to outright identity theft has become a real issue for each of us in personal money management today. It is reported that there is more than ten identity thefts every single minute in America today, and the trend is growing rapidly.*

What's in Your Wallet?

Let's borrow a popular bank's credit card advertising slogan for a moment: "What's in your wallet?" Each of us carries some sort of method to carry our personal finances around with us whether it is a billfold, money clip, wallet, purse, pocket secretary, coin purse, checkbook, pocket organizer, or other device. Let's take a few minutes to list the "stuff" that you carry in your preferred method.

Take a few minutes to write down everything that you carry with you in your carrier (examples: money, photos, driver's license, Social Security card, health insurance card, ATM or debit card, gas card, auto insurance cards, library card, movie rental card, lucky four-leaf clover, etc.). Your list may also include such things as your sensitive PIN number and other sensitive data (never a good idea).

- *Now imagine what would happen if you lost your carrier or, even worse, it got stolen by somebody intent on stealing your identity. The very least of your concerns is that your cash, which can be more easily replaced, is gone; but what about the other information that has been taken? How will you get it back, especially if you don't even know it is gone?*

- *It is a fact that today knowledgeable thieves can completely clean you out within twenty-four hours. That includes checking, savings, IRAs, and investment accounts,* everything, *if you haven't taken precautions to prevent it.*

- *Cyber thieves are so adept at doing this from operations around the world that your entire net worth can vanish, and your personal identity can be bought and sold several times within just a few days if you haven't taken precautions to prevent it.* That is what this session is all about.

- *The first step in this process is to maintain an inventory of everything that you keep in your wallet or purse in a secure place. By doing this, you will at least have an idea of what was actually taken and know who to contact.* Sounds simple, doesn't it? *Yet how many of you have even done this? It is a critical first step in being prepared for such a personal financial disaster and will go a long way in being able to quickly rectify the problem—less cash that you will never recover.*

- *Exactly where do you keep this register? Obviously,* not in your wallet or purse *or on your computer! That would defeat the purpose of having the inventory. Keep it in a safe place in your home or in a safe-deposit box at your bank. Home is preferable since you can access it 24/7/365 in the event of a theft. Don't keep it in your sock drawer either. That is the first place that break-in thieves will look. Remember, it contains a* lot of sensitive information.

- *Nest, you need to make out a list of important contacts called a* personal finance information register, *which includes the name of the financial institution, the account number, the account type, the website address as well as the log in and password, the phone number to call, and where the specific documents for checking, savings, brokerage, IRA, retirement, investing, and insurance policies are kept.*

- *Just as with your wallet registry, an inventory of your other financial documents is a highly useful idea too. If you have a CD, IRA, brokerage, checking, savings, or other financial accounts, it is important to keep track of those as well. Having in an easily accessible location, along with your wallet/purse inventory, will allow you to put a hold on each of your accounts within a few minutes of a theft.*

- *In your absence, be sure to let your spouse or other responsible family member know where this information is kept in case you are away on a trip or even out of the country. Common sense is key in accomplishing this security.*

- *Don't keep this information in a computer, especially a laptop or a PDA, or even a cell phone. These are all places where your sensitive information can be easily compromised today. Instead, place a hard copy in a secure place in your home or in a safe-deposit box in a bank.* Be creative where you store it.

- *Another valuable record is a location for all your key and important family documents. Every one of us has critical and valuable family papers that are not easily reproduced and yet are of utmost value to you and your family. It makes sense to have a* document locator *that you can use to access these documents quickly and in case of an emergency.*

- *The use of all these documents is one of the critical elements of organization. It doesn't require a lot of cost to produce this personal money management and security system, just a fair amount of effort in preparing it. After that has been accomplished, a yearly update (on your birthday, for example) is all that is required, and you will be able to sleep more soundly.*

- *Another viable option is to scan the documents, one at a time, to a CD, disk, or even a flash drive. This allows you to have an exact copy of each one of the documents in a convenience device. The problem, however, is that you have created a condensed version of all your most important personal financial information for a would-be thief if you fail to store it in a secure place.*

THE SILENT ROBBERY: Identity Theft

Identity theft today is not limited to only credit cards and Social Security accounts. It is an epidemic problem that affects health-care accounts, insurance, investments, even deeds to properties, as well as all financial accounts, including retirement. It is one of those events that will substantially change your life forever if you are not prepared.

Taking the time to prepare for such an emergency cannot prevent the event, but it can minimize the long-term effects. Those who take the time to create and maintain these organizational inventories, registers, and locators will suffer only minimal damages.

Here are some other useful suggestions:

- *Invest in a crisscross paper shredder and use it to destroy all your old statements, old policies, records, credit card offers you receive in the mail, and other sensitive data and information.*
- *Use caution in responding to questionable e-mails and offers. Install a virus and spam protection program on your computer.*
- *Never purchase anything online from someone where you didn't make the initial contact.*
- *Avoid downloading information from sites that are not secure.*
- *Contact your account issuers immediately if you suspect fraudulent activity or, better yet, have them contact you if your account is being used in a manner that is not normal for that account.*
- *Monitor your financial statements each month on receipt for suspicious activity.*
- *Be vigilant in your dealings with those who have access to your accounts.*
- *Never loan your credit cards, ATM cards, or debit cards to anyone or let them out of your sight at retail stores.*

Don't underestimate cyber theft. It can happen to anyone, at any time, for any reason. It is a problem that affects potentially everyone and runs into tens of billions of dollars worldwide. These suggestions are an example of the old adage that your grandmother probably used: "An ounce of prevention is, indeed, worth a pound of cure."

Personal Finance Planning

< Learning to Prepare Yourself Financially >

When you get ready to prepare for a trip, what is the first thing that you reach for? A map (or maybe your GPS)! Studying a map allows you to gauge and measure the length of a trip, the probable duration, the geographic terrain, and even the anticipated weather and climate. It is the logical method of determining the who, what, when, where, and how so you can arrive at your destination intact, safe, and sound. It is the same way with achieving personal finance prosperity in your life. Without planning, you may very well end up in the wrong place, possibly broke down in some remote location, or maybe running out of fuel and, because of all this, never making it to your final destination.

In the 1970s, I worked for a major national trucking company called TransCon Lines based in Los Angeles, California, whose slogan was "Planning is essential to progress." It is doubtful that they applied that slogan because when deregulation occurred in 1980 and created the opportunity for many others to start trucking businesses, they went bankrupt. The same is true with personal financial planning. The failure to plan can have major effects on your long-term prosperity planning. One of the ways to create long-term financial planning is to create a benchmark of where you are currently, which will give you an idea of where you are headed and how quickly you are moving toward your objectives.

Your Personal Life Timeline

Set up a timeline in ten-year increments from ages twenty through eighty. Go over each increment, along with the typical events experienced in each of them as follows:

Twenties (Getting Started Stage) – Here, your formal education ends, and you begin the process of starting your first job or career employment. It is also a period of discovery of many of your individual likes and dislikes, including personal and romantic relationships as well as hobbies and other interests. It is a time that many people begin becoming their own person, and their individuality starts showing through. Sadly, however, it is often a period of financial irresponsibility.

Thirties (Getting Serious Stage) – At this stage, people start "coupling," getting married, getting divorced, and starting to have children. It is a time that life's reality begins to form and the need to earn a better income because of the expenses of buying a home, vehicles, and a life with children and a spouse. At this stage, people become firmly established in work and career. Long-term finances are often neglected because of the month-to-month realities of child rearing.

Forties (The Midlife Stage) – This is a period where children are starting to become more independent, but there are college education expenses to consider. Instead of being a time to catch your breath, it is a time to wrestle with other life expenses. It is when career and families can come together, and your dreams are now starting to become possibilities. It is also when you can pause, financially, to see where you are now and where you need to be down the road. Few people, however, do much more than just think about it.

Fifties (The Preretirement Stage) – During this stage, people begin to seriously think about what they need to do and what they have not yet done for their post-working life. By this time, your kids have left the nest and started their own lives and careers. You can seriously take the time to assess your income needs. If you have not set aside a percentage of your income over the past thirty years, you realize that you have a lot of serious catching up to do!

Sixties (The Full Retirement Stage) – As you enter this period, people begin to actively calculate their personal financial position and to assess whether they are in a position to even think about leaving their job and not work any longer. For many, panic begins to set in as they discover that there is no way they can get by without working, even part time, because they need the income to live.

Seventies (The Kick Back Stage) – Life in your seventies has a major element of personal independence to it. The biggest consideration is health-related issues. Those who are fortunate to be in good health and who have *carefully planned* their retirement years can now enjoy a decade or more of financial independence, relaxation, leisure, travel, participation in hobbies, and fun. Those who have failed to plan will be destined to scrape by waiting for the Social Security check to arrive at the first of every month.

Eighties (The Health-Care Challenge Stage) – Despite the fact that the median age for both men and women today is in the mid-eighties, it is also destined to be a period of your life when health issues arrive on a more frequent basis. Studies have shown that over 90 percent of your total life expenses relative to health care occur during this period. Those who have carefully planned and prepared for this stage financially will be able to afford these health-care expenses while still able to enjoy a satisfying lifestyle. Those who did not plan well will not fare nearly as well.

> *The question is where do you see yourself in each of these decades? Are you planning and preparing or just getting by and having fun through each of these stages? Your retirement years will get here faster than you will ever think. Just remember how quickly your kids are growing up. The key is to plan and prepare for retirement a little bit each year. This is what we are going to cover in detail in the pages to come.*

Your long-term financial success and prosperity comes about as a result of careful, detailed, and prudent planning and preparation and not a result of some mysterious form of hocus-pocus. It does not just somehow fall from the sky. Investing, retiring, buying a house, and taking a dream vacation are all the result of the necessary efforts that are provided by planning and preparation. Having the right goals, objectives, and priorities over a period not only makes sense, but *it really works* too! Yet it doesn't happen over a weekend. The other technique that works well in planning is a good dose of old-fashioned patience. Consider that today many people live well into their eighties, and you will realize that planning for a secure retirement, often lasting twenty to twenty-five years of post-work, is a relatively long period to go without enough income. That is why it is necessary to plan well for that final stage of your life beginning when you first start out in life. If you start early, that little bit of money set aside regularly and consistently can provide major benefits in your senior years. It is important not to leave your retirement future to mere chance. Other large expenses, such as a college education for your children and even a vacation home as well as starting a small business, are things to consider in your financial planning also.

Retirement funding is by far the most important goal in your life. Social Security just is not enough to make your future retirement affordable, and there is no better time to supplement Social Security than *now*. Retirement and your golden year's nest egg cannot be financed like a college education. There are not retirement loans, grants, and scholarships. In retirement, the total of a pension, Social Security, savings, cash, home equity, and a few carefully chosen investments can create the monthly income that will sustain you and your spouse for many, many years. The reality, however, is that it all starts with proper planning.

Calculating Your Net Worth

Your total assets less your total liabilities equal your net worth. Sounds simple, doesn't it? It is the virtual barometer of your personal finances at a given point and time in your life. It is the information necessary for you to calculate just how much money you have (assets less liabilities) to determine how much you will have to save or invest for your retirement. Net worth is a key and important measurement tool in realizing where you are financially versus where you want or need to be to enjoy a comfortable and lengthy retirement. Banks, insurance companies, investment brokers, financial planners, tax advisors, and many others need to know this information to create a benchmark measurement of exactly where you are; and you need to know this as well to see if you are staying on the right track.

You should ideally revise your personal net worth statement once a year. A good time to do this is either at the end of the year or shortly after the first of the year when you are receiving all your year-end statements. If you do not know where you are, you will never be able to arrive at the proper destination. By reviewing your net worth once a year, you are also able to see your progress and if you are steadily moving toward your financial goals or getting behind in them. Your net worth is a snapshot of the reality of your current financial life. Know that number is important because it forces you to come to grips with where you are and the direction that you are headed. Once you know where you are at, you can start the process of planning your future whether you are twenty-five or fifty-two.

PRACTICAL EXERCISE: "Figuring Your Net Worth"

Let's take a few minutes to attempt to determine your personal net worth. Using the template form, list each of your personal assets on one side of the form and your liabilities on the other side of the form. Then subtract what you owe from what you own to determine your net worth. Please note that this exercise has nothing to do with monthly income and expenses. That is your *cash flow*. Net worth is all about what you *owe* and what you *own*.

How Much Is Enough?

How much money do you need to be able to supplement your retirement income? Financial planning as you have already learned is not a one-size-fits-all exercise and varies among everybody. The average retirement today is based on a total asset value from $300,000 to $600,000 based strictly on your standard of living and lifestyle considerations. There are also a number of other factors that have a place in the overall size of your nest egg, such as the following:

- *Are your mortgage and vehicles paid off?*
- *Do you have dependants living with you yet?*
- *Are you in overall good health?*
- *Do you have only a modest amount of credit card and consumer debt?*
- *Do you live consistently within your means?*
- *Do you reside in a reasonably low-cost geographic area?*

Some of the factors outside your control include the following:

- *The annual rate of inflation*
- *The shape of the national and global economy*
- *The prevailing interest rate on loans and investments*
- *The conditions of your future health*
- *The cost-of-living index in the future*
- *The overall yields and mix of your investments*

The process of personal finance planning is a reflective exercise that many people tend to put off usually because they have failed to save and invest enough money during their life and are beginning to realize that fact. However, just like any other critical issue in life, is it not better to know the *bad news* early enough to be able to react to it while there is still enough time? The actions of "see no evil, hear no evil, speak no evil" do not work effectively with personal financial planning. Through the power of planning and preparing, with a good dose of compounding of your money resources, a little money set aside each month now can reap *large rewards* in just a few years. Left alone, it will be a significant start to your prosperity map. Working with a qualified financial planner and a good tax planner is another very good option though at a substantial cost. Besides, they cannot tell you what to do with your life. That is your responsibility.

The Effects of Disinformation to Your Short- and Long-Term Prosperity Growth

"All you have to do is . . .," "The best way to accomplish that is . . .," "The only way to figure that out is to . . .," "The solution to that is to . . .," "It is simply a matter of . . ."

If any of the above sounds familiar to you or if any of your professional advisors use these terms frequently, then maybe you are becoming a victim of **disinformation**. This is plainly a result of oversimplifying, misconstruing, and even misaligning various views of what it will take to achieve real results in your planning and endeavors.

If you are hearing the descriptive words "never," "ever," "always," "constantly," and "ceaselessly" used regularly in their dialog, they are sure indicators that the opposing party is maybe trying too hard to "sell you" on their ideas and beliefs that perhaps you should investigate a little more thoroughly. No one has all the answers, and there is literally no such thing as an "expert" in today's environment. There are those who may have a high level of proficiency and expertise in their chosen field, but there is simply too much in the ever-changing informational climate to pin the title of "expert" on anyone in the millennium of worldwide web knowledge.

Those who become successful in their prosperity building today are those who can learn to isolate and digest the important information they need to know and can further separate opinions from the facts to make their own critical decision on important matters that are relative to their prosperity achieving. Often, it is clearly a matter of distinguishing between "guided" and being "lassoed and dragged" to the destination. *Seasoned prosperity achievers know how and when to discern how to separate the "sheep from the goats" in this very important area of know-how and know when they are being "advised" and when they are being "sold."*

CHAPTER 7

How to Build and Improve Your Personal Finance FICO Score Number

In this chapter, you will learn about the following points:

- *Just What Is Credit Anyway?*
- *The Disappointing Adult Report Card*
- *Your Credit Score Is One of the Most Important Numbers in Your Life*
- *Improving Your Financial Creditability*
- *What Is Your Magic Personal Finance Number?*
- *Exactly What Is a Credit Score?*
- *How a FICO Score Is Calculated*
- *Your Credit History*
- *Strategies to Offset Inferior Credit Scores*
- *Other Effective Ways to Improve Your Score*

Just What Is That Thing Called Credit Anyway?

Credit is money that is loaned to you by a lender in exchange for a promise of future repayment. It allows you to secure and pay for goods and services in advance in exchange for your commitment to make regular and timely payments plus interest and other fees. There are many types of credit available today, including the following:

- **INSTALLMENT CREDIT** – These are payments, such as car loans, mortgages, and student loans.
- **REVOLVING CREDIT** – These are credit cards, home equity lines of credit, and store charge cards.
- **OPEN CREDIT** – These are accounts for services, such as electric, gas, and phone.

Your credit history is a verifiable written and documented record of your past use and management of credit in your life over the years. Nearly every personal financial transaction over the past seven to fifteen years is carefully detailed in your credit history. Potential lenders scrutinize and examine this credit history to determine if they will give you credit and at what terms.

On one hand, if you have had a positive credit history and pay your obligations as agreed, you are termed to be a *good credit risk* and qualify for loans with the most favorable terms and interest rates. On the other hand, if you have failed to make your loan payments on time, short paid, or skipped payments, you are deemed to be a *poor credit risk* and subsequently will have to settle for higher interest rates and larger down payments resulting in larger payments, or you might be turned down for loans completely.

Essentially, nothing you will do in your adult life with impact your ability to borrow money more than your credit score. Nothing. For this reason, you are well advised to maintain a good credit history to be able to borrow money at the most favorable terms.

A, B, C, D, or F?

The Disappointing Adult Report Card
FICO Is a Four-Letter Word

You may not have foreseen the poor score glaring up at you from the three FICO reporting agencies, but the comments on the report reveal that you may have maxed out your available credit, may have a disproportionate debt-to-income ratio, might be falling behind in your monthly payments, may have a bankruptcy or foreclosure on your record, might be racking up late penalties and fees, and could otherwise have a troublesome credit history. The way you react to a disappointing credit report card will affect just how well you will be able to adjust and take charge of your important credit history and how well you can improve it. It is important to remember that every grade is a momentary, changeable indicator of your overall personal finance capabilities. The future offers the opportunity for overall improvements and a better score.

Here are some steps you can take to improve it:

1. **TRY NOT TO PANIC** – When you first see a poor credit score, keep calm and focus on solving the problems that resulted in the less-than-desirable score.

2. **TALK TO THE CREDIT AGENCIES** – Verify the information with each of the credit agencies and develop a strategy on how to improve your scoring. They are the best resource for improving your credit score. This is also a method to be able to spot errors and correct mistakes.

3. **DEVELOP BETTER HABITS AND SPENDING ROUTINES** – Old habits can be broken, but it isn't easy, especially if they have occurred for years. You should give yourself plenty of time to slowly create new and better ones.

4. **GET HELP** – If you are really struggling, you may need outside help. A poor credit report is a symptom of missing skills and gaps in achieving better scoring.

5. **CHECK YOUR CREDIT REPORTS REGULARLY** – As you make progress toward rebuilding your credit, make sure to monitor your credit reports every six months or so to view the progress and see how it is improving. This is especially true if you seek to increase your credit card limit or are applying for a new job or taking out a new insurance policy.

6. **EDUCATE YOURSELF IN HOW THE CREDIT BUREAUS WORK** – Know and understand the various events and activities that cause your credit score to go up and go down to continuously hone your score.

One of the secrets to improving your credit report card is to act now to rescue your score, which can give you the confidence and positive attitude that will be necessary to help your next credit score become a really good and improved one.

Your Credit Score Is One of the Most
Important Numbers in Your Life!

Your lender will never ask to see your school grades, academic report card, or graduation diploma even if it is from a prestigious university. They will, however, want to see your credit score as well as your personal financial or net worth statement before giving you an application for a loan or mortgage. What does your grown-up adult report card look like? It has been only the result of the most recent national and international financial crisis that many individuals started paying attention to their personal credit report and FICO score. For many people, it was only after a lifetime of spendthrift behavior did they finally start heeding this well-documented report of their personal financial credibility. When credit was easy to obtain, many of them became careless about how they used credit. They further didn't save for what they really wanted and instead chose to use consumer credit. They simply borrowed through increasing limits on credit cards, through home equity loans, through personal lines of credit, and finally through consumer loans for material possessions that they might not have even needed. Being in debt was no big deal. Many of them had never even experienced a downturn in their income and instead witnessed year after year of growth in their incomes and in their borrowings.

But in the current credit crisis, that is no longer the case. Suddenly and dramatically, having good credit is very important; and for many, it is impossible to quickly improve their lackluster personal credit score. Lenders have significantly stricter guidelines now as well as expensive penalties and other fees that make it much more difficult to get credit and even harder to maintain it. In spite of the media ads touting effective credit repair services, credit repair isn't something that you can buy through an agency or service provider. It is literally something that you have to work very hard to secure. It is the personal finance *fingerprint* of your credit reputation regarding what kind of a responsible borrower you are. It is the documented financial profile concerning how lender institutions view you through a detailed and carefully chosen formula known as your FICO score.

Improving Your Financial Creditability

The word "credibility" has a lot to do with the ability to elicit belief. Your past reputation of repaying borrowed money is closely tied to your personal finance achievement. When you recklessly and ruthlessly abuse credit, it becomes increasingly harder to obtain credit, especially at a good price; and the results are reflected in your credit scoring.

The *best way* to create personal finance credibility is to

a)   *live within your means and income,*

b)   *develop a savings rather than a spending attitude,*

c)   *avoid impulsive and compulsive buying decision,*

d)   *use a sound purchasing strategy when buying big-ticket items,*

e)   *maintain a household budget (spending plan) and learn to follow it,*

f)   *control your consumer spending behaviors, and*

g)   *minimize your use of credit cards and ATM withdrawals.*

Improving your financial scorecard won't happen overnight, but after six to twelve months of practicing these credibility principles, you will start to see your score begin to rise. Once damaged, it can be improved, but it will take discipline and commitment to achieve the results.

What Is Your Magic Personal Finance Number?

Each of us today is inundated with lots of numbers in our daily lives. Phone numbers, identification numbers of all types, password numbers, PIN numbers, account numbers, driver's license numbers, access numbers, credit card numbers, cell phone numbers, address numbers, and the ubiquitous Social Security numbers are just a few examples.

None of these, however, may be more important to you than a three-digit number that was created by the Fair Isaac Company that is commonly known today as your FICO score number. What you pay in finance charges for your mortgage, vehicle loan, and credit card interest rate and terms; and even your insurance premiums are largely based on this highly important personal finance reporting scorecard. For many, it may also even have an effect on your ability to get a good-paying job. We will discuss in this chapter how to document, define, and determine just exactly what a FICO score is, how it is used by lenders, and how it can be improved now and in the future to lower your costs of credit, borrowing, and the interest rates you are charged by a lender.

Lenders use credit scores to determine your level of credit worthiness, and you as a would-be borrower need to make sure that you're doing everything within your power to keep it in the *acceptable or higher* range. It is so often relied on today that it may even affect your ability to rent or lease an apartment and purchase a vehicle and will even affect your future employment. In a nutshell, it largely is a measurement of your overall financial responsibility. Literally, not a day goes by that it does not affect you in one way or another. It is literally *that important to your personal finances*. Therefore, it is critical that you:

1. *know your score,*
2. *know how you can make it work for you, and*
3. *understand how it can be damaged by misuse.*

What Exactly Is a Credit Score?

Your FICO score is the ultimate gauge by your lenders and other creditors as to how you pay your financial obligations and bills. It is also an indication of your character and responsibility. It is the result of a carefully constructed formula that was created by the Fair Isaac Company (i.e., FICO) many years ago. It consists of many factors that are constantly and regularly refined each year to give creditors the very best glimpse of your credit reputation and how you pay your bills.

Together, this information is gleaned and transmitted to the three main credit reporting agencies (see below) and placed in a database that is accessible by both creditors and potential lenders. The higher your score, the better chance that you will be able to qualify for the very best rates and terms when it's time to borrow money from a potential lender.

How a FICO Score Is Calculated

Like other algorithms and formulas used to assess financial risks, your FICO score is largely based on five critical factors that determine your ultimate personal financial risk to lenders as follows:

1. **PAYMENT HISTORY** – How often you pay on time versus late or partial payments. This is 35 percent of the overall score.
2. **TOTAL CREDIT USED** – The higher the debt load, the more negative the total. This accounts to 30 percent of the credit scoring.
3. **LENGTH OF YOUR CREDIT** – The duration of your credit accounts is a key factor. This represents 15 percent of the total score.
4. **NEW CREDIT RECEIVED** – How many new accounts you have opened recently is figured into the formula. This represents 10 percent of the score.

5.   **TYPE OF CREDIT** – The kinds of credit you carry is key with consumer debt scoring very negatively. This represents 10 percent of the total score.

Together, these total 100 percent of the total FICO score. There are, however, some other factors that *do not affect* your overall score, including employment status, income, debit card habits, amount of savings, bounced checks, overdraft fees, utility bills, and late rents. *Ratios of debt to available credit are important as well.* The best scores are those that use *no more than 9 percent of their available credit lines.* If it is more than 50 percent, be prepared to pay higher rates or be turned down.

QUESTION: What is *your available* credit ratio? _____

Your Credit History

Your credit history is important because it is a key part of your personal financial freedom and is critical to everyday money matters. As a borrower, it is important to maintain your credit reputation by evidencing to creditors that you will pay back the money that you are loaned as agreed. It is a measure of the lender's confidence in your ability to repay your debts.

The long-term financial consequences of good credit result in thousands of dollars saved annually as opposed to those with less-than-good credit who will pay higher interest rates and fees. Over time, this can result in a big difference in the amount of money that you pay throughout the course of a loan. It can also have a big impact on your ability to rent an apartment, secure competitively priced insurance, get a car loan, pay reasonable interest rates, what terms you will pay, and even in your efforts to land a job. Lenders tie borrower's loan qualifications to this credit information. There are three separate credit reporting agencies that compile your personal credit information. They are the following:

1.   **Equifax**
2.   **Experian**
3.   **TransUnion**

These reporting agencies operate separately and independent of one another and use a predetermined formula known as the FICO report, which stands for Fair Isaac Company, which is a company based in Minneapolis, Minnesota, that created the formula and updates it periodically. They use and apply the data from your credit history to access a written FICO score for your account. This includes two separate parts as follows:

- **CREDIT REPORT** – This is a written report that includes entries on all your accounts and events as well as other information that affects your credit.
- **CREDIT SCORE** – This is a numerical score ranging from 300 to 850 that reflects your current credit history and worthiness.

It is from each of these reports that creditors and lenders derive the information to make decisions about whether to grant credit to you. Your personal credit rating has a huge impact on your ability to borrow money and personal finances. It is the system that lenders collectively use to judge your credit reputation based on your past personal finance history. Lenders base their decisions on these scores for virtually all borrowing, from those with no credit history to those with extensive credit backgrounds. Some of the key factors that negatively influence your individual score include things like losing your job, missing a major bill payment, foreclosure, medical conditions, excessive borrowing, higher ratios of consumer credit to net worth, and bankruptcy. It can also be a result of identity theft, a growing problem worldwide today. Past due medical debts alone can shave up to one hundred points off your credit score and may even go undetected for years.

The top of the credit score tier is 800–850, although no perfect credit score has ever been recorded. The average score is in the 700–750 range, while lower scores fall below 600. The median score in the United States today is 723, and the largest group of consumers, 28 percent, was in the 750–799 range. Scores under the 600 level are considered to be marginal or high credit risk and are subject to the highest rates and fees or are even denied loans altogether. Lower credit scores highlight individuals who have a statistically greater and probable risk of defaulting on their loans it has been determined from FICO studies.

Other useful tips include the following:

- ❖ *Use your credit cards but use 10 percent or less of your credit limit.*
- ❖ *Remember that a late payment can easily knock up to one hundred points off your score.*
- ❖ *Check your credit report for errors that are not yours.*
- ❖ *Don't apply for a new credit card for six weeks before making a large loan application.*
- ❖ *Avoid running up a big balance on any single credit card during a short period.*
- ❖ *Use your cards lightly but regularly and pay them off in full every month for the best scoring.*

Strategies to Offset Inferior Credit Scores

There are many things that you can do to create a better credit score. The only real way to repair bad credit over time is through the use of good credit practices, ones that show lenders ability on your part to manage and pay back debt responsibly. Before you even begin the process, it is important to understand that this repair will take months and even years to accomplish and not mere days or weeks. With patience and diligence, however, you can repair your credit and personal finance reputation.

Some rules for doing it are the following:

1. *Understand how to read and, if necessary, correct any errors on your credit report.*
2. *Know what credit scores measure and how they monitor your history.*
3. *Realize the right and wrong ways to use credit cards.*
4. *Educate yourself how and when to apply for new credit.*
5. *Consider taking a class or course in personal financial literacy.*

The work that you do to improve your credit score can pay off handsomely over the long term. There are specific steps that you can take to better your scoring number and prevent it from moving in the wrong direction. To accomplish this requires your active involvement in the process, a discipline to do it, and the commitment to take the necessary action.

Among some of the methods used to improve your overall score are below:

A. ***Take the Initiative and Shop Harder for Credit*** – There are a lot of lenders out there today and many specialty and diverse ones that are willing to overlook occasional flaws in your credit history. The trick is to isolate and locate them. In the end, it's worth it to find one that will give you a better deal. This is especially true with vehicle loans that, because of their volume, can be subject to more competition among lenders. For example, finding a specialty lender that can shave two to four points off the interest rate can be worth $750 to over $1,500 or more over the forty-eight-month terms of a $21,000 vehicle loan. This is even truer when it comes to a home mortgage. Finding a lender that can save several interest rate points on a thirty-year mortgage can result in a savings to you of over $100,000 on a $400,000 loan. Another way is to obtain a mortgage that is backed up by the FHA (Federal Housing Administration), which also results in less of a down payment and other up-front fees.

B. ***Research to Find Cheaper Insurance*** – Many insurers today base a major portion of their calculations for premiums on personal credit scores. Their position is that statistics have (once again) revealed that those with a lower credit score tend to file more insurance loss claims. Regardless of the reason, the result is the same: *higher insurance premiums for lower score consumers. Solution?* Shop around for insurance and do some comparison shipping here too. Those that are hungry for new business will give you a better rate. Another option is to work through an independent insurance agent who will check rates for you with eight to ten of the insurance carriers.

C.   ***Work Hard to Improve Your Credit Score*** – There are some steps that you can take to improve your credit score and to prevent it from moving in the wrong direction. Fixing errors can be accomplished by getting a copy of your annual credit report. If you find errors, you have the right to dispute them and/or have them corrected. Another solution is to pay down your existing credit balances. This alone is one of the best and most effective techniques because less debt owed results in a reduction of your credit utilization, the ratio of debt to available credit lines, and a key factor in improving your overall score.

D.   ***Get Your Debt Proportionate and Get Your Payments Up to Date*** – If you are behind on any payments, make every effort to get current and bring them up to date as soon as possible. Communicate with lenders and disclose your plan to get current and then do it as agreed. Live up to your commitment and even request them to re-age your account, which means that you still owe the principal and interest, but the account will be brought current for the record. Around 30 percent of your score is based on the amount of money you owe. Less debt equates to the ability to responsibly handle more available credit. This is especially true of consumer debt (credit cards, revolving charges, and store credit cards). The higher your outstanding debt is to your credit limits, the lower your credit score. Make every effort to keep your credit card balances low and within acceptable limits, and you will witness your score slowly increase. In addition, you should keep you mortgage payment, including taxes and home insurance, below 28 percent of your gross (not net) monthly income. Nonmortgage debt, including vehicle loans, credit cards, and personal loans, should not exceed 20 percent of your gross personal income. By continuing to pay them on time, you will also be able to slowly ratchet up your credit score. Talk with your insurer if your rates have increased and find out why. You can also ask them to rescore you annually so that you will be able to benefit from any improvements. Finally, don't wait to ask for help. If you're struggling with your debts, the sooner you get things back in order, the better for you and your credit score.

E. ***Fix Any Obvious Mistakes on Your Report*** – Inaccurate information can really cause damage to your credit report, so it is vitally important to regular get a copy of it even every six months as you are working to rebuild it. If you find errors, notify the credit bureau *in writing, asking them to check out the specific mistake and to notify you in writing when it has been done.* It is also important that you keep copies of these letters for reference and follow-up.

F. ***Request a "Goodwill Correction" from Your Lender*** – By removing even one bad mark from your account, it will improve your credit score. This is especially true if it is only an isolated smudge on an otherwise relatively clean record. Depending on your overall record, many lenders will agree to this.

G. ***Don't Close Out Old Accounts*** – *By not* closing out old credit accounts, even if you don't owe anything on them, it will have the effect of negatively increasing your credit utilization ratio. This will have the net result in lowering your total score. Besides, a long credit history with a creditor is a major credit advantage.

Other Effective Ways to Improve Your Score

A score of at least seven hundred is needed to qualify for a good interest rate, terms, and fees. The standards today are significantly higher than just a few years ago when the benchmark was only six hundred. This is because of the financial meltdown of the financial services industry in 2008. You are allowed one free credit report per year. This is not your score that you have to pay for but merely the narrative report of your personal credit status. You should review this narrative at least once a year. This is also a method that you can use to determine identity theft and can also allow you to reverse any errors on the report or incorrect information from your account. These types of errors can have a negative impact on your score, and they occur more frequently than you might think because of the tremendous amount of information being input into millions of accounts by thousands of workers, and they occur for many reasons. Verify all the information on your FICO report. It will take time to do this, but it will be a worthy effort in the long run to do this regularly and consistently, especially as you are attempting to rebuild your credit. The credit reporting agencies have thirty days to correct erroneous information in your account and to notify you in writing.

Since your credit score changes constantly, there is no such thing as a permanent score. It literally goes up and down all the time each and every month with a range of twenty-five to fifty or even one hundred points, depending on how much active credit you use.

CHAPTER 8

Fine-Tuning Your Prosperity Plan

In this chapter, you will learn about the following points:

- *The New Rules of Twenty-First-Century Prosperity Building*
- *A Unique Prosperity-Building Perspective*
- *Fine-Tuning Your Personal Prosperity Number*
- *How Prosperity Is Determined*
- *How Prosperity Is Measured*
- *How Prosperity Is Achieved*
- *Proven Prosperity Builders*
- *How Long It Takes to Become Prosperous*
- *Understanding Prosperity Arithmetic*
- *Creating Your Personal Prosperity Paradigm Formula*
- *Developing an Accurate Prosperity-Building Algorithm*
- *Property and Prosperity*
- *The Personal Prosperity Success Codex*
- *Success Qualities*
- *A Prosperity Warning Light*
- *Adding Retirement to Your Prosperity Portfolio Building*
- *The Definition of a Good Investment Opportunity*
- *The Many Benefits of Personal Goal Setting*
- *Creating a Needed Target*
- *What Happens When You Miss the Goal?*
- *Ten Steps to Personal Prosperity*
- *Increasing Your Personal Prosperity IQ*
- *Tips for Developing Financial Self-Discipline*
- *Determining Wants, Needs, and Nice-to-Haves*
- *Avoiding Family Finance Fiascos*
- *Prepare to Make Sacrifices*
- *Where You Can Find More Prosperity Education*

The New Rules of Personal Prosperity
Building in the Twenty-First Century

<< *Key Principles Needed in Achieving the Results* >>

E ach of the following principles will significantly assist you in building a higher level of personal prosperity in today's challenging economic markets:

1. *Improving your prosperity learning, training, and education*
2. *Learning how to create more income streams and assets in your life*
3. *Creating more protection for your personal capital resources*
4. *Understanding how to develop an effective spending and budgetary plan*
5. *Utilizing your existing resources more wisely and more productively*
6. *Learning how to invest your money and financial assets to improve your future*
7. *Creating an effective retirement program to maintain your lifestyle*

A Unique Prosperity-Building Perspective

➤ Each of us has an opportunity to build our version of a unique prosperity formula in our lives. A prosperity perspective can be a change in the way that we look at our personal opportunities for successes and/or failures in our way of doing things.

➤ They may often not be nearly as dramatic as lightning bolts or eureka moments, but they can be witnessed in even the smallest things that we do in our lives and careers every day. Many times, the tiniest alteration or change in doing something can have a major impact on the results. It can become a different path that we choose in life and one that can become increasingly more challenging and difficult *because each of us is, unfortunately, a creature of a few bad habits and behaviors that we need to work on and improve to bring us to higher levels of achievement and accomplishment.* Often, the ability to recognize and improve those bad behaviors can result in significant positive results over time.

➤ *When you think of the numerous options and variables you have experienced in life from the time you were born through the many circumstances that you have lived through, you begin to realize how many positive changes there are to be able to improve your "odds in life" once you choose to recognize and accept each of them.* Even more compelling is the fact that each of us has control over many of them. When you study many of your successes and failures, it is frequently a repetition of a singular positive habit done time after time that can make a tremendous impact on the eventual outcome of our lives.

> ➤ In the grand scheme of life as we know it, it is something that each of us shares as we journey through our earthly existence. Our pursuit of prosperity is an incentive to make the right decisions and take the right risks and chances and our ultimate personal motivation to do it better and well. It comes down to desire and commitment, and these two factors can often become the difference between *want and have* in our lives.

Fine-Tuning Your Personal Prosperity Number

What is the ultimate numerical equivalent of your personal prosperity plan? Is it a statement of your net worth? Is it the total of all your assets? Or is it something much greater than any of this? The difference between wealth and prosperity is similar in nature to the differences between being physically fit and being healthy. Being physically fit implies great bodily strength; but being healthy connotes an exceptional balance of overall well-being, including other aspects, such as heart, mind, and other key organs in your body.

Personal prosperity works the same way. It is the overall state of your well-being and not necessarily a single aspect of it, such as only income or assets. What then is the very definition of personal prosperity? How do you go from being "well-to-do" to "prosperous"? What does the process involve? What does the result even look like? What is the very criteria of prosperity in your life? This narrative writing examines many of the issues relative to the differences between wealth and prosperity. What comprises prosperity? How is it achieved? What does it feel like? In the end, it is perhaps the difference between looking at money resources with only your head and pocketbook and viewing it from your heart too.

How Is Prosperity Determined?

When you glimpse at someone for the first time, how can you determine their level of prosperity? Is it their appearance? Their mannerisms? Their communication? Their aura? Or is it a combination of each of these factors? Prosperity, it seems, like beauty, is often in the eye of the beholder. It often is determined by what the viewer feels is actual prosperity regardless of whether it is really valid. Yet is it possible to be perceived as prosperous even if you really are not? Are there actually visible signs of prosperous people? Do they look differently, act differently, or communicate differently? Is prosperity just another term for being wealthy, rich, or well-to-do?

Webster's **definition of prosperous:** *To succeed, to thrive, to be enriched, to fare well, to do well, to be of good fortune, to rise in the world, to be fruitful, to blossom, to make a fortune, to advance, to accomplish, to flourish, as well as the commonly known and familiar terms as to be wealthy and to become rich. It implies a sense of higher values than simply money in a bank account.*

It turns out that prosperous people are uniquely different from most people, including even rich people. In the widely read book that was written in the late 1990s called *The Millionaire Next Door* and its sequel *The Millionaire Mind*, the authors researched a number of highly prosperous individuals throughout the United States and took a close look at the qualities of each of them that helped define who they were. As it turns out, they are much different from others in lots of meaningful ways.

First, for them, it is not all about the money. Most of them, as it turns out, live relatively quiet, simple lives and maintain modest, resourceful, and meaningful lifestyles despite the fact that they can easily afford to do otherwise. Another key fact is that virtually all of them are involved in some sort of philanthropy, volunteerism, or other process of giving back. For them, this study revealed, it is perhaps the mental challenge of ambitious wealth building rather than an active and obvious desire to want to display their wealth. Prosperous people, it seems, have a large streak of humbleness and humility within them that belies who they are. Large, ostentatious displays of wealth are unknown to them. Instead, they are content to drive only late-model vehicles, wear conservative clothes, and live in comfortable but not lavish homes. Their lifestyle could be considered comfortable but not flashy.

How Is Prosperity Measured?

What is the ultimate measurement of one's personal prosperity? Is it portfolio value? Is it total assets owned? Is it the type of personal financial accounts? Is it a mixture of various capital resources? Or is it merely net worth? Even if there is a specific measurement of personal prosperity, how is it actually calculated? What is the formula that is used? Practically speaking, prosperity is actually a measurement of each of these calculations that is sprinkled with a healthy dose of actuality, humility, common sense, and resourcefulness. In truth, its total has more to do with the healthy use of economic resources than by the outward display of the "sizzle" that many high-income earners use as their audacious personal displays of wealth. It is essentially a combination of personal economics, joy, happiness, and peace that creates the virtual definition of prosperity.

How Is Prosperity Achieved?

If prosperity is more of an emotional attitude versus the portfolio size, bank account, investments, or net worth, then how does one go about obtaining it? What is the overall formula for accomplishing prosperity? As it turns out, that too carries an assortment of various "flavors" since there is no one-size-fits-all in the prosperity process, and no two people achieve it in the same way. To suggest that prosperity in a highfalutin word for mere wealth is like saying that everyone who can sing will make it to *American Idol*. There is a great disparity between mere wealth and prosperity, while there are many ways and paths to get there. There are, however, several proven methods of prosperity building that are well recognized by many over the years as being capable of creating long-term and sustainable prosperity that could be considered. Each of them involves an element of risk-taking, however; and for that reason alone, many shy away from engaging in them or attaining prosperity.

Proven Prosperity Builders

1. **ENTREPRENEURIAL ENTERPRISE** – This is widely recognized as a major long-term strategy for building large wealth for thousands of years going back to antiquity. Regardless of the type of business, it is a proven builder of income and wealth. It does, however, involve a high level of risk and a proportionate amount of personal risk-taking to achieve it.

2. **REAL ESTATE INVESTING** – This too is a well-used technique for building increased personal assets and net worth. It is a long-term strategy, and its results are well substantiated by countless numbers of wealth earners over the years. It is one of the underlying techniques of all high financial achievers regardless of the category and type of property investments made.

3. **PORTFOLIO INVESTING** – This is a reasonably "hands off" method for increasing net worth if properly executed. The process involves knowing and understanding the various financial investment markets, including paper investments like stocks, bonds, mutual funds, money market funds, notes, and many others. It involves using your personal money in areas that offer both growth and value. The effects of compounding do much of the work over a number of years; and you, as the investor, profit over time.

WHAT'S THE TIMETABLE?

How Long Does It Take to Really See the Results?

Today people live in an atmosphere of instant gratification as a result of numerous conveniences available, including microwave cooking, same-day FedEx deliveries, and even medical weight-loss programs. Unfortunately, they want to apply these same timetables to their investment results, and it is simply not possible. Prosperity building does not provide a get-rich-quick strategy but rather a get-there-slowly one. You cannot push a button or are able to do it overnight. Instead, it is a lengthy process that is attainable and possible through a process of education, learning, and proper training to learn the strategies and techniques that will help them achieve true prosperity.

Those who have the patience to reach for prosperity are destined to improve their lives, their happiness, and their overall net worth via moderate and reasonable risk-taking. Those who want to get there quickly often fail to do so because of taking extreme levels of risks that can often be compared to high-stakes gambling. Others, who have achieved higher levels of wealth building, are not able to sustain it because of poor money management and lack of personal financial education. *In the end, personal prosperity is often more of an emotion that comes from the heart as well as the head and the pocketbook. It is ultimately created by a finely tuned education program.*

Understanding Prosperity Arithmetic

True prosperity building is not necessarily only about complex numbers, accounting, and figures on a spreadsheet or computer screen. It *is*, however, about the arithmetic involving in addition and multiplication as opposed to division and subtraction when it comes to increasing the factors that help achieve it. There are, indeed, many ways to build your prosperity; but it is a fact that increasing each of the proven factors that can help create it can significantly help you in accomplishing it. It is not always done through an accounting process as much as it is done via a-c-c-o-u-n-t-a-b-i-l-i-t-y. Your future prosperity will only come about as a result of the exponential increases of each of the proven prosperity factors that make up your personal and unique paradigm formula.

This is why the addition and multiplication factors are two of the proven processes that can serve as a catalyst in bringing you to where you want to be in your preparation and planning. Any economist will tell you that using only simple numbers will eventually achieve a modest level of "ho-hum" results some day and some way, yet you should understand that learning the process of doing it and adding and multiplying those same numbers will considerably speed up the timetable that is necessary to succeed.

The keys are 1) creating an effective personal formula (this is admittedly that more difficult part); 2) beginning the slow, steady process of choosing the right steps to take; 3) starting adding your successes together; and 4) achieving the multiplication and compounding process that will create the exponential long-term success growth that is needed to accomplish your results. By using this basic arithmetic quantifier, your long-term prosperity building can produce the afterburner effect that will boost your level of prosperity success through the use of this proactive personal approach.

Creating Your Own Personal Prosperity Paradigm Formula

The specific ingredients in your personal prosperity-building paradigm are the result of many factors in your life and are carefully developed and created over time. An example of one of these is the prosperity-building pyramid shown in the attached illustration on the next page. This sample is for a hypothetical forty-five-year-old married male earning $50,000 per year of earnings income and who has three teenage children.

This prosperity paradigm provides a discipline to set aside $200–$250 per month of net (take-home) wages or $2,400 to $3,000 per year that funds this portfolio. By increasing the amount by $50 or $75 per month each year, this individual could easily have $600,000 to as much as $850,000 or more in their prosperity portfolio by age sixty-two in addition to Social Security and IRA investments. This prosperity success is achieved because of several important factors:

- *The positive effects of compounding over the investment period*
- *The results of rebalancing the portfolio once a year*
- *Maintaining a good prevailing interest rate on all investments*
- *Realizing an average amount of investment risk tolerance*
- *Understanding the effects of the rule of 72*

The annual growth of this particular portfolio will continue to increase even if *no other money* is added to it in the future for each of the above reasons.

Although this is a basic illustration, your specific personal prosperity success paradigm could conceivably far exceed these results by (a) adjusting the level of risk upwards; (b) adding more money to it, such as bonuses, inheritances, windfalls, profits from property sales, refunds, and other income sources; and (c) reducing debt, resulting in more discretionary income being contributed.

What is the perfect paradigm formula? The answer to that ubiquitous question lies within several key factors, including the following:

> *Your lifetime goals and ambitions*
> *Your knowledge and understanding of prosperity building*
> *Your capabilities and abilities as a successful investor*
> *Your willingness and desire to stay committed to doing it consistently*
> *Your ability to stay proactive in the investing process*

Developing an Accurate Prosperity-Building Algorithm

Definition of an Algorithm

Any systematic method of solving a certain kind of mathematical problem;
a set of specific instructions with a limited number
of steps for solving a particular problem.

Learning to spot potentially successful prosperity achievers in advance can frequently become a combination of both art and science since no two prosperity achievers are exactly alike. It can also be a huge factor in determining the likelihood of accomplishing it by future prosperity seekers. However, to do it successfully, it requires a two-step process, including the following:

1.) Creating a unique prosperity algorithm based on many of the unique prosperity habit and behavioral qualifiers that set PAs (prosperity achievers) apart from the general population
2.) After creating the unique formula, continually fine-tuning it by using the data gathered to identify and assist other prosperity seekers in the methods used in accomplishing it

Many of these traits are included in the ProsperiScore® evaluation criteria, yet some of the other ones include such qualities as owning rather than renting or leasing your home and vehicles, investing in real estate property and small business enterprises, maintaining a savings rather than a spending attitude, living within your means instead of utilizing a paycheck-to-paycheck existence, effectively using insurance to protect your personal assets, ability to use debt wisely and constructively to create long-term yields and cash flow incomes, choosing good partnerships, utilizing a professional team of advisors for key decisions, and many others. These personal traits, when utilized, along with the ability to recognize, spot, and seize on meaningful and profitable opportunities, will quickly begin to add more credibility and power to your individual prosperity algorithm. Some characteristics are more neutral than others, such as job or career involvement, marital status, leisure-time hobbies, and personal pastimes and interests. A few of the negative factors that exist in postponing, diluting, or even eliminating prosperity opportunities include *compulsive or addictive habits and behaviors, illegal activities, extravagant lifestyles, and personal character issues.* In the end, some of the variables that sharpen the prosperity algorithm are the key elements of both **desire and commitment**. These specific factors alone can ultimately give your personal prosperity algorithm formula much greater predictive power. Those who possess these two traits, above all others, have been proven to be the intensive factor in achieving personal prosperity than virtually any other markers used.

Property and Prosperity

Of the three different types of income available to each investor—earned, passive, and portfolio—there is only *one category* that allows you to build your prosperity via borrowed money and be able to leverage the investment. This method falls within the category of passive investments known as real estate property, and it is one of the catalysts to significant prosperity building.

Those who would doubt this technique should ask themselves if they could borrow an equivalent amount of money ($50,000 to $150,000 or more) to purchase stocks, bonds, mutual funds, or other paper portfolio investments. In addition, even earned income from wages or payroll earnings cannot typically be leveraged without putting up a substantial asset (such as real estate). The answer is that only real estate property investments offer the solid investment strength that appreciates in value over the long term and is recognized by all banks and lenders as a solid, long-term investment.

Some of the ways that an investor can make money in real estate include (but are not limited to) the following:

a. *Regular appreciation*
b. *Principal pay down by a tenant*
c. *Equity that is created over time*
d. *Numerous federal and state tax deductions and incentives*
e. *A bricks-and-mortar, "see, touch, and feel" peace of mind*
f. *Ability to purchase asset protection through insurance*

It is for each of these reasons and more that many highly prosperous individuals over the years have chosen this prosperity builder over others. Even banks and other lenders recognize the power of real estate property investments, which can be used to continue to build individual prosperity success over the long term. It is, indeed, one of the *best overall prosperity investments* that investors can use to create long-term sustained financial success. It is true that the real estate markets *do move* up and down occasionally just as they did in the year 2008 when many property values fell from 10 to 35 percent in parts of the country. Many also forget that these same property values steadily rose for the past twenty-five to thirty years by 6 to 8 to 10 percent per year, making it one of the best prosperity builders available (and think of the huge discounted buying opportunities for investors when this does occur from time to time).

Coupled with other portfolio investing consisting of stocks, bonds, mutual funds, and other financial securities and you have effectively created a solid one to two punch in your overall prosperity-building paradigm. As many smart investors have come to realize, the gains that individual investors can realize from real estate property investing rival any other form of significant prosperity success building results in every category.

And the best news? You can go to the bank to borrow money to do it!

The Personal Prosperity Success Codex

The term "codex" is used as a descriptive term when exploring the fundamentals of the educational text and materials created by the author. "Codex" is an ancient term used to describe a bound information manuscript and was chosen for use because of many of the core learning lessons, which are age-old concepts that can still be applied today in personal prosperity building. Some of these strategies include three of the best and most significant income opportunities that underline major wealth creation over the years and are referred to in the codex as the top 3 of income production:

1. **EARNED INCOME** – This is the income that is received as a result of performing work from a job, career, or profession and also sometimes known as payroll earnings. The downside to this income, regardless of how large, is that when you quit performing the job, the income also ceases.

2. **PASSIVE INCOME** – This is the income that is generated as a result of an investment in a small business, real estate property investment, venture capital investment, or other similar type of nonactive investment. The benefit in this category of income is that it continues to earn income even if you are not at work performing.

3. **PORTFOLIO INCOME** – This is the income that is created as a result of stocks, bonds, mutual funds, and other paper investments in the financial markets. Again, this income continues even if you are not working actively at it every day.

Other than portfolio income, the other two commonly recognized methods in achieving financial prosperity (earned and passive incomes) have existed for ages and are not new or revolutionary concepts. The difference, however, is that in our educational training, we show participants how to apply these age-old concepts to twenty-first-century America. Income, however, is only one step of the overall process since most people have some income; yet fewer of them reach a state of significant prosperity creation. During a four-year period, from age fifty-six to age sixty, this author researched and studied many of the ancient prosperity-building techniques and strategies that helped him create the Personal Prosperity Success Codex that is used to teach and train at the PdP® Learning Center in Arizona. He studied many of the well-known prosperity builders of the past, including J. P. Morgan, Cornelius Vanderbilt, Andrew Carnegie, the Rothschild and Rockefeller families, and many others as well as many modern-day prosperity achievers, such as Ross Perot, Donald Trump, Robert Kiyosaki, Bill Gates, and Warren Buffet. He created a uniquely personal view of method and implementation that complements the legendary Napoleon Hill's early twentieth-century writings and philosophies that described many wealth-creating concepts.

The impact of money and personal finances in our lives is significant, yet the Personal Prosperity Success Codex does not only expound on what prosperity is or how it accomplishes it, but it also teaches and instructs participants how to create, manage, invest, and even spend their resources more efficiently and more effectively. It is a complete and comprehensive study that includes classes, courses, workshops, and seminars in personal finance, business entrepreneurism, success training, and real estate investing, along with numerous "how-to" methods in accomplishing it. In addition, instead of just another get-rich-quick motivational read, the Personal Prosperity Success Codex is a detailed, thought-provoking, well-designed, highly satisfying educational learning experience that focuses on many of the practical and commonsense answers to the prosperity conundrum today. It takes that time to address and define each of the critical issues that confronts individuals in these challenging times today. It is created through a one-of-a-kind series of questions and answers, quizzes, tests, and exams that are designed to take the foundational prosperity-seeking knowledge and learning to help make it personal for each participant. It is further accomplished through a multilevel system that consists of basic, intermediate, and advanced training. Finally, it is accomplished in a highly personal and even occasionally humorous style of instruction via the use of an effective and creative format, including such techniques as graphics, charts, graphs, images, "chalk talk," numerous anecdotal examples and illustrations and many comparative analogies, as well as flip charts and high-technology media that drive each of the learning points and pearls of wisdom home to participants to make it a personal experience for each one of them.

Necessary Success Qualities

In his book *Talent Is Never Enough*, author and motivational speaker John C. Maxwell makes many success affirmations that can apply to anyone in their life and career. Among the most important of them are the following:

If you cannot be teachable, having talent won't help you.

If you cannot be flexible, having a goal won't help you.

If you cannot be grateful, having abundance won't help you.

If you cannot be sustainable, having a plan and preparing won't help you.

If you can't be reachable, having success in your life and career won't help you.

LEARNING LESSON #1: Don't let your talent get in the way of your success.

LEARNING LESSON #2: The most important thing in life to remember is not to only attempt to capitalize on our gains. Anybody can do that. To be able to achieve more requires us to profit from our mistakes, failures, losses, flaws, and shortcomings.

Adding the Element of Retirement to Your Prosperity Portfolio Building

Successful retirees share many of the same common traits according to Drs. Fredrick Fraunfelder and James Gilbaugh, geriatric physicians, in their coauthored book *Retirement RX* (2008 by The Penguin Publishing Group), including each of the following:

1. *They planned for their retirement, both financial and nonfinancial aspects of post work, and regularly revised their plan at least once a year.*
2. *They were positive thinkers with positive attitudes and who were generally optimistic in their thoughts and ideas about age, health, income, and life positions.*
3. *They learned to accept changes and develop self-confidence in tackling new challenges.*
4. *They had a wide and varied support group with people of all age groups and further, including spouse, friends, and family and even social organizations, special interest groups, religious organizations, and family pets.*
5. *They have developed a number of physically and mentally challenging activities that help them reduce stress and unwind them mentally and perform these activities on a regular, consistent basis with spouse and close friends.*

6. *They maintain a healthy lifestyle, which is the main ingredient for longevity, and realize that it is often not the hand they are dealt but how they play their hand that is important.*

7. *They engage in a passionate activity that keeps them engaged and with a sense of personal fulfillment.*

8. *They have a sincere and devout belief in spirituality that offers them strength, solace, and hope when faced with disappointments, setbacks, and traumas.*

On the Issue of Taxes . . .

It is the part of a good shepherd to shear his flock, not to flay it.
—Tiberius, Roman Emperor

If it moves, tax it.
If it keeps moving, regulate it.
If it stops moving, subsidize it.
—Ronald Reagan's humorous definition of
government taxes

Nothing is certain in life but death and taxes.
—*Benjamin Franklin Maxim*

Factoid©

Didja know that from 1868 to 1913, exercise taxes in liquor and tobacco accounted for 90 percent of all internal revenue collections? Today the IRS (aka the tax gestapo) has more power in the lives and properties of Americans than any other agency of the federal government. Sadly, in a great many cases, the government does not have to prove that the individual is guilty; the individual has to instead prove that he or she is innocent.

What Is the Definition of a Good Investment Opportunity?

There are a lot of investment options to consider in your prosperity-building efforts. Some of them include stocks, bonds, mutual funds, gold, silver, real estate, annuities, entrepreneurial business, art, collections, and many others. However, all investment making is very much a matter of making the *right choice* and *selection* at the *right time*. It is a fact that most savvy, experienced, and successful prosperity achievers have utilized two specific investment categories in their long-term strategies as mentioned earlier in this book—entrepreneurial business and real estate investments. This is essentially the one to two punch of those who have mapped out a personal prosperity-building plan and have done so over their lifetimes. When you research the well-to-do and the highly prosperous individuals since the beginning of civilization, these two strategies stand out as the twin engines of nearly all their prosperity. They each create the type of cash flow and disposable incomes that provide major incomes to their investors and predictably do it time after time despite the occasional market fluctuations.

It really all comes down to this instead of some top secret investment one-of-a-kind formula.

The Many Benefits of Personal Goal Setting

A unique aspect of personal prosperity building is the process of goal setting, which is another word for setting priorities. This is the opportunity to document your dreams and ambitions so that you can build a personal template formula on how you will be able to achieve each one of your objectives in the future. It is an important time to use your imagination and creativity to harness each one of your aspirations so that they can become your realities in the future. Make sure to give each one of those elements of your planning plenty of time, or you might somehow forget the purpose of the plan itself. For some, it might become an ironic challenge since you may have to get ready to increase your acceptance of those things in life you really want. Sometimes it is difficult to do this since it requires stepping out of your comfort zone, and you may even feel unworthy to desire many of these items on your list.

One of the biggest challenges in creating personal goals is recognizing that you are both deserving and capable of achieving the results. When you start moving in the directions of your dreams, you begin to shed the self-created perception of your limitations. A good strategy if this occurs is to ask yourself this: what would your life be like if you could have anything you wanted? The "how" is what we will focus on later. Perhaps it is even time to go back to your childhood and start thinking bigger again. Children are the epitome of dreamer and make-believe, and maybe your dreams all began to shrink a little as your "life," and all its frustrations began to take over. It is now time to revisit those hopes and dreams. It is time to remember how to think larger again.

What exactly is it that you *really want* in life? To achieve each of your new goals in life, you must even be a little selfish for a while now. Each of your goals needs to be clear and specific in your mind. Most of all, they need to be written down and documented. Dare to create the affirmation of *exactly* what it is that you want in life. Remember too that this is a private experience (for now anyway), so you don't have to worry about how others will think or feel. It is nobody's business what your dream list looks like or even includes. Part of the process of reading your newly established goals involves the ability to give up those things that you really determine you don't want or need. Knowing what you do not want or need is somehow, magically, just as important as determining what it is that you *do want*.

This process involves taking a realistic look at many of the things in your life that you may feel are important but in the final analysis are not really that earth-shattering. Does your lifestyle get in the way of your prosperity goal somehow? Are you sure that the McMansion you are considering is worth the monthly mortgage payments? Do you have a handle on your personal debts to be able to achieve your monetary goals? If not, it is a sign that perhaps that should be one of your goals as well.

Creating a Needed Target

If you really desire something—anything—you first need to know what the target is.
That's especially true when it comes to developing the skills in your personal prosperity planning and development.
Your objectives are important in being able to achieve your level of prosperity success.

—L. S.

What Happens When You Miss the Target?

Let's face it. No one hits the target each and every time. Even the best and most successful achievers have their share of misses and near misses that bring new reality to their scorecard. So what do you do when this occurs? How do you keep this minimized and keep your "shots" near the bull's-eye more often than not? What can you do to increase the likelihood that your ultimate successes will far outweigh your defeats? It's as important to develop a personal strategy to be able to pick yourself up and dust yourself off as it is to have a long-term set of goals and ambitions. For this reason, I am listing a few effective ways to be able to do this when it happens.

Here are a few tips to remember when you have fallen short of your target goals:

1. **LEARN FROM YOUR MISTAKES** – As the familiar saying goes, "Big achievers know that it is important to learn from your mistakes." This is especially true today when the costs of failure are high economically as well as emotionally.

2. **DON'T CONTINUE MAKING THE SAME KIND OF ERRORS** – It's okay to make errors. That's where we all grow and learn, but you should avoid at all costs making the same kinds of errors frequently. This can have disastrous results to your long-term success.

3. **LEARN FROM THE MISTAKES OTHERS MAKE** – You don't have to experience the actual problem to learn from it. The mistakes that others make in your career, business, or profession can serve as useful learning lessons to you.

4. **KEEP THE MISTAKES SMALL** – Try to avoid waiting too long to admit a mistake. This will keep each of your errors small enough to be dealt with at a reasonable cost. The expensive lessons are the ones that hurt you the most.

5. **KNOW WHEN TO SEEK HELP** – One of the signs of success in life is to know when to seek out the advice of someone who has "been there and done that" to be able to minimize the damage.

6. **CREATE BACKUP PLANS** – "Even the best laid plans of mice and men often go astray" so make sure that if there is a lot on the line, you have a good backup plan to put into effect the minute that it's needed.

7. **KNOW WHEN IT'S TIME TO RE-ADJUST** – Even if you have carefully thought out your entire plan and spend hours doing all the "what-ifs" to prevent failure, you should recognize when it's time to huddle and readjust your strategy. This is the single biggest cause of failure among success achievers.

8. **KEEP FOCUSED** – Don't make the further mistake of allowing your temporary setback to destroy your macro focus. Be smart and learn to maintain your intensity and on the long term of the success.

9. **THINK: MACRO PICTURE** – It's easy to experience that a failure of some sort will singularly destroy your future. When seen in the grand scheme of things, it will probably only create a short-term hurdle, so you need to think about the macro picture more.

10. **FAILURE PRODUCES MORE KNOWLEDGE THAN SUCCESS** – It is a fact that you will learn more from your failures than from any of your successes. Think about it. When you have had a setback, most of us will take the time and examine the reasons why it happened and prepare a better plan for future projects. That's called experience and one of the rewards of failure.

You might as well face it now. There will be failures in your job, career, business, and professional life. There just isn't any way to get around it. It will happen many times in your life, so you need to concentrate more on what to do when it happens than on trying to prevent it from occurring. The strategy that you are comfortable in using and that produces the most effective results for you is the one that you should apply in your rebounding to minimize the damages and keep you pointed in the right direction. Mistakes can be minimized but not avoided entirely.

Ten Steps to Personal Prosperity Success

In her book *The Four Spiritual Laws of Prosperity*, author Edwene Gains describes her ten-step formula that has become wonderfully successful for her and others. Those ten steps are briefly described as the following:

STEP 1: Write down each of your desires in a spiral notebook. Carry this notebook with you in your pocket, briefcase, or purse; and as you think of new ideas and dreams, write each of them down and document them in your notebook. This is an effective way to begin creating your life priority items.

STEP 2: From the above list, choose your most significant and important goals and desire and prioritize them. Be specific here. If you cannot be specific, it may be an indicator that our dream might have to go to the bottom of the list or go on the backburner for a while. Make sure that these are *your personal goals* and not the goals of someone else (spouse, significant other, parent, friend) that has been imposed on you.

STEP 3: What are the action steps that you will need to take to achieve each of your goals and dreams? This exercise will become the difficult part, ascertaining what exactly must be done to get to where you want to be, but do it anyway because the results will surprise you.

STEP 4: Create your own personal timetable for each one of your newly created goals. This will be the date you wish to accomplish each one of them. If you get near that date and have not yet achieved it, it is time to develop a more realistic expectation of it.

STEP 5: Refer to your list of goals and objectives frequently—several times a day. Focusing on these will help you affirm that they are important to you and your future life and will benefit you by drawing power to it.

STEP 6: Use your creative imagination and see yourself in your mind's eye, subconsciously accomplishing each one of them. The more you do this, the easier it will be for you to attain each one of them. The power of the subconscious mind is significant, and many books have been written by successful people who have learned to do exactly that to be able to achieve their personal and career goals.

STEP 7: Take the attitude that you believe that it is possible to achieve each of them. Accept that the successful completion of each of them will be the result of a lot of hard work, but it will occur. Taking this proactive position approach will become a major part of your accomplishment of each of your objectives.

STEP 8: Keep this private. There will be lots of time to disclose your dreams and ambitions to others, but for now, keep the list between you and your Creator. This will avoid the inevitable criticism and doubt by others. Only your most trusted friend and loyal supporter can know about your plan (if you, indeed, are lucky enough to have one).

STEP 9: Cross off each of your goals as they are accomplished and achieved and become part of your reality and continue to add new ones regularly to replace the ones you cross off. This should ideally become an ongoing proccss and not a single event.

STEP 10: Develop an appreciation for everything that you have and how you were able to finally achieve it. it is simple for many to develop *convenient amnesia* the moment that they have successfully accomplished a goal and forget the work, sacrifice, and effort that went into achieving it. Maintaining a healthy appreciation for the time, effort, and energy that you (and others) have put forth will send a strong message of sincere appreciation as you continue to do it in the future.

By following each of these steps, you will be on track in being able to develop, document, seek, and create an effective plan to get you from here to there. It is not easy, however, and having an *accountability partner* can help you in the process. This can be a trusted friend, spouse, or family member whom you confide in and "report to" on a regular basis that can encourage and motivate you to achieve your dreams. You are well on your way now with a sound and effective strategy map showing you how to do it.

> *Now take a bow, catch your breath, and set your notebook and pen down for a moment. You can now start feeling a little prosperous!*

Increasing Your Personal Prosperity IQ
<< *Learning How to Be Smarter with Your Personal Resources* >>

The Top 6 "How to" Methods in Accomplishing Personal Prosperity:

1. *Learning How to Create More Income and Earning Streams*
2. *Learning How to Better Budget Your Money and Spending*
3. *Learning How to Improve Your Borrowing of Money and Better Use of Credit*

4. ***Learning How to Protect Your Capital and Personal Assets***
5. ***Learning How to Better Invest Your Money and Make It Grow***
6. ***Learning How to Better Utilize Your Personal Resources***

Tips for Developing Financial Self-Discipline

As with many things in life, it's easier to be able to *walk the walk* when you develop a sense of self-discipline when it comes to personal finances. Listed below are twelve key techniques in learning to develop a successful strategy in being able to do it:

1. Remember that patience is required. Debt won't be eliminated overnight. Changing what we originally learned in the past is key to improvement.
2. Don't try to impress those who are broke or worse off than you.
3. Avoid *instant gratification* personal finance mistakes.
4. Talk regularly with your spouse and kids about personal finances, set up a budget or spending plan and show them how to do it also, and *don't deviate from your budget* once you set it up.
5. *Earn, save, and invest wisely* instead of *earn, spend, save* to improve your personal finance situation.
6. Don't buy *big once in a while* or even a *little always* to be able to improve your personal finances. Instead, choose each one of your purchases carefully and *realize that price is what you pay, but value is what you get.*
7. Realize that food is the number 3 expense in your budget so learn to plan your weekly menu wisely when shopping for food and take advantage of coupons whenever possible.
8. Leasing is the same as renting and is seldom a good thing for you financially. It is essentially a symptom of not being able to afford something.
9. *If you don't have the cash, you probably don't really need it yet!*
10. Vacation after vacation after vacation doesn't work or put any money in your investment portfolio.
11. Transportation is the number 2 personal expense in your budget. Late-model used vehicles are substantially cheaper in the long run than new cars, and you can *really tell the difference in your budget.* Depreciation accounts for nearly one-half of the expense of a new vehicle today.
12. A large tax return means that the government got to use your money for a year instead of you.

Determining Wants, Needs, and Nice-to-Haves

Many of us have fallen victim to the temptation of buying something that sounds like a good idea at the time but in the final analysis creates a personal financial hardship. This is especially true if it is something that you cannot really afford and had to charge it via a credit card of department store card. This is unfortunately one of the biggest problems facing consumers today.

As Americans, we live in the greatest capitalistic nation in the free world and are not used to hearing the phrase "I can't afford it." It brings to mind depression-era situations and events where people survived with the barest of necessities. How does one address the issue and effectively draw the line between *wants versus needs and nice-to-haves*? What are the parameters that need to be considered when making large purchases and frequent smaller purchases that can add up to large purchases?

Here are some useful tips to use in making significant purchase decisions. By asking yourself these questions *in advance,* it might be possible to talk yourself out of that *must-have* purchase and stall it off until you have the resources to pay for the item in full *(or you may even decide that you can really live without it):*

1. *What is the fundamental reason that you are really considering the purchase? If necessary, could you document and write down the reason in fifty words or less? Would it make sense to a rational person?*

2. *Can you afford to pay cash for the purchase? If not and you have to charge it on a credit card, can you afford to double or triple your monthly payments on the card for a few months to pay if off in a short period?*

3. *Is the purchase being considered an investment in your life, or instead, is it an expense that you can really live without?*

4. *Will the item be out of style in a year or less? Is it a fad purchase?*

5. *Do you have to talk yourself into buying the item? If so, this is a huge indicator as to the nature of the proposed purchase.*

6. *Is the item something that you will be tired of by the time you have finished making the payments on it? Or will it be out of vogue in six months or less?*

7. *Will the item appreciate in value or simply depreciate after a year or so?*

8. *Will your incentive to purchase the item or service become less or more if you wait forty-eight hours before purchasing it?*

9. *Does your spouse, family, relatives, friends, and others support your buying decision, or will they not favor purchasing it? This is another key indicator.*

10. *What will the effect be if the purchase is not made? How will it affect your lifestyle? What category is the item considered to be—a want, a need, or a nice-to-have?*

By being able to follow each of the above guidelines, it may serve to look at your major buying decisions more objectively and, at the very minimum, allow you to consider not purchasing it until you have enough cash to pay for the purchase upfront. *Remember, in the end, it's all about making your money go as far as it can, isn't it?*

AVOIDING *Family Finance Fiascos*

Without even realizing it, many families jeopardize their personal financial futures by loaning or outright giving money to adult children for questionable (albeit questionable) purposes. On top of this, the majority of them do it without even insisting that it be paid back on any type of regular payment schedule, asking them to sign any formal loan agreement documents, or even for them to insist on providing collateral, which then creates a number of future relationship issues in the parent-child relationship and at family events, including holidays. When your son or daughter comes to you for a loan request, you should first ask yourself if one of the reasons that they are coming to you is perhaps because they have already been turned down by a conventional lender. This, in fact, should be one of the stipulations of a loan consideration. They should first go to their bank, credit union, or other lender and apply for the money before even coming to you. If they cannot secure a loan from them, you should carefully consider loaning them money (unless, of course, you can afford to do this without negatively affecting your own personal finances). *This should also send a warning sign to you that they are unable because of credit, income reasons, or other reasons to be considered a good credit risk.*

On the other hand, if you can indeed afford to make a cash gift for a reasonable amount of money ($5,000 or $10,000), you should make a copy of the check for your own personal records (since you are allowed to make an annual gift of up to $10,000 or more to family members without tax liability), and you will then need to have a written record of the transaction. Writing a brief narrative letter to them, including the date of the gift, is also suggested. This can be an opportunity to describe the circumstances of the monetary gift so that several years down the road, all the facts are documented so that there is ample description of why it was done, how it was done, and when it was done as well as formally signing the letter. In my work with people over the years, this has been a powerful source of good advice for both giver and receiver. It also helps you keep track of who was gifted and when in the event that there are several children that must be treated equally when it comes to family money. You may also want to include a notation in the letter that the amount of the gift will be deducted from any future inheritances if this is your desire and agreement.

I am not suggesting whatsoever that this practice not be done. What I am saying is that it must be done with both of your eyes open as well as your heart and pocketbook since once this money is gifted or loaned, it may take a number of years to get it back in small increments or perhaps not at all. Frequently, the problems with parents in this situation is that the transaction is done in a loosey-goosey format and that there is no real documentation as to when the payments can or will be made; and often, it is handed over with a "pay us when you can" repayment policy statement. Unfortunately, these five words have ruined many parent-child relationships over the years. If in doubt as to whether loaning money to your children is a good idea or not, ask yourself if you are not required to provide more personal financial scrutiny than this *when you seek a loan from a bank or other lender.* If the answer is *yes*, then perhaps you should look at this money transaction as more of an arm's length transaction than a purely emotional one. In addition, if the money is a loan, you as the lender can include in the formal agreement such items as modest interest rates, default penalties, collateral assignments, and other typical lending requirements, which make this a doable possibility but protect you from a personal finance nightmare that can result in years of anxiety and struggle with your offspring. Using this method, the borrower, your son or daughter, realizes that you want to make this a formal bank-type loan and will be more encouraged to pay you back. It does not mean that you necessarily have to enforce all the covenants of the loan. If only part of the loan is paid back and in good faith and on time, you may, at some time in the future, forgive the balance as a token of your good intentions. Some parents also escrow the interest paid on the loan and set up an account to finance their grandchildren's college education with it since this is interest that would have been paid to a conventional lender anyway.

Making loans to adult children can be a positive experience as well. It can help them build their personal credit, get started on the right foot in life, overcome personal credit or loss of job issues, and other purposes. Only when it is done professionally, however, will it result in a transaction that will benefit both of you. In my household, we also held a "loan committee" meeting consisting of my wife and I, and we went over the details of every aspect of the loan repayment. Only after we were satisfied by looking at my son's income, finances, and ability to pay back the money did we even consider loaning him/ them any money. They had to fill out a loan request, specify how they would pay it back, agree to the loan covenants, and understood that this was an arm's length transaction that we were prepared to undergo but that there would be ramifications if they missed payments or reneged on the loan at any time in the future and that we would insist on every aspect of the covenants being adhered to (ironically, many times, after going through this process, they would eventually decide to go to a conventional lender and get a loan, which then took us out of the loop, and this had the effect of avoiding many future problems and issues with family finances).

The Drawbacks to the Bank of Mom and Dad

Loans to children aka the infamous bank of mom and dad, while good intentioned, often have disastrous long-term results as detailed below:

- *It is too easy for them to ask and stifles incentives for them to gain the necessary borrowing power themselves.*
- *It is usually done with no formal documentation, which can cause resentment later to the lender when they realize how much personal finance opportunity they are losing.*
- *They are often not collateralized, which makes them a bad investment for the lender.*
- *It creates family hardships when payments are not made on time or are minimized. No one likes to have to call a family member each month to remind them of a financial obligation.*
- *It is seldom treated as the event that it really is—a financial loan that needs to be paid back.*
- *It often creates friction between mom and dad when they realize that they could use the money for something else like retirement.*
- *It promotes dependence on children to their parents.*
- *It can cause resentment between siblings when one child is favored over another.*
- *It often creates long-term hard feelings when the loans are perceived to be taken for granted by the borrower as a condition of their birthright.*

So How Can All This Be Prevented?

Learn To Say "No."

REPEAT: *Learn To Say "No."*

Or emphasize to them the need to maintain their financial responsibility so that they can be approved for financing lending. If they cannot borrow money from a financial institution, it is a sign that they just might be financially irresponsible in some way, and they need to work hard on improving their financial discipline.

PREPARE TO *Make Sacrifices*

All of us regularly spend money on many things that we do not really need to live. It is imperative in building a business enterprise to use and apply that money that will make a huge difference in your venture-building efforts and will ensure and protect your ability to be able to get it off the ground. I look at this issue very seriously because it will be impossible for you as a business builder to both enjoy a lavish lifestyle as well as get your venture off the ground. Balancing your personal needs and that of your business is an issue that is important to the success of your organization. The problem is how to effectively do it. Part of the answer, the easy part, is to reduce both your personal and business spending until you have the level of sales and profit to be able to earn a larger wage. As you become more confident in your efforts and abilities to take on more customers, your opportunities for personal income growth become better and more proportionate. But you should not pretend that there is going to always be harmony between our personal economic lives and that of our business since there will always be ups and downs in the marketplace and unexpected costs in each area.

So what should you do? Sometimes you should choose to protect the business and those that depend on it, such as customers, employees, and vendors, even if that denies economic opportunities to yourself. You should, of course, try to find alternatives in each scenario because the goal is neither to live as a church mouse nor as a Hollywood celebrity but instead as one who recognizes that it will take time to build your personal income and that the first few years, you must concentrate on your business income. The cost-benefit analysis certainly favors this approach. The method to assigning a value to your enterprise building certainly trumps any short-term personal spending. Even if you ignore this rationale, the reality is that the offset provides that in the first few critical years, you probably won't even have the time to do any lavish personal spending anyway.

New entrepreneurs tend to trip up on the issue of whether to discount the future profits too. Suppose that you believe that in ten or twenty years, you feel that you can discount the present-day profit by 5 percent per annum. Such a discount cannot be justified on the basis of the real rate of return on capital. It implies that the future matters much more or much less than the present, yet unless you are willing to personally sacrifice some of your personal spending, the reality is that there may not be any future for your business since significant personal spending also involves more time off from the business building, which is something that you can ill-afford to do either. Given equal weight to each of the arguments provides you with strong reasons to be concerned about your discipline and commitment about your venture as well as the more immediate concern of reducing personal spending. You should be willing to sacrifice for your business future but not at the risk of reducing or minimizing joy and happiness in your life, which can be created without a significant level of spending. Many successful entrepreneurs would agree that the ability and the means to succeed in their business-building efforts can replace the tendency to spend money on materialism. Some would argue that there is no reason to develop your own business if you are not able to experience any of the financial gains from doing so. It must be clear that it is not an all-or-nothing situation and that over time, you will know and understand when it is possible to build your personal finances and not at the expense of the enterprise.

At the End of the Day, If It Breaks, You Must Fix It

Another compelling reason to live within your economic means for the first critical few years is that excessive debt (borrowing) is often the death sentence of many new businesses. By self-funding and personally paying for any of the out-of-the-ordinary expenses in the beginning stages, you are ensuring that your commitment will sustain your venture and not have to have loans to offset each of them. Indeed, all the ethical arguments point to the owner taking the lead when it comes to bearing the responsibility that can befall a business. It can be stated that this is the literal definition of financial responsibility and, if handled well, will serve to irrigate and cultivate the enterprise and make it available for incremental harvesting. It is a fact that such proportionate distribution of income and profits is a strategy that virtually all successful business owners have utilized in the past. No one would argue that you should sacrifice to the extent of not putting food on the table for their families; but when you think of the alternatives, including the options of larger home, vacations, vehicles, and other possibilities that exist, you should opt for practicality over luxuries in the first ten years. This is especially true when it comes to setting a leadership standard with your subordinates. It is possible to take your fair share of the profits and abundance that are a result of your hard work, ingenuity, risk-taking, and long hours; yet you should not reject the idea that you also have an ethical obligation to future generations. It seems that selfishness and avarice have no place in the long-term attainment of your personal and business goals, and my opinion is that you should do what you can to encourage your own success by maintaining the sacrifices necessary for your business enterprise to achieve its own success and not become one of the financial reasons that it could fail by not living within your means.

Where You Can Find More Prosperity Education

How do you find the necessary prosperity and educational fundamentals to do better in life, to make your life more prosperous? Where do you go to find a place that teaches this? When is the best time to begin the process? How long does it take to learn it? Who are the people who are the best instructors to teach these lessons? The ultimate course of action each person takes is unique to their individual goals and objectives in their life, and there are many options available. Some of the choices include the following:

1. *Self-help books and materials*
2. *Investment seminars*
3. *Working with a financial planner or advisor*
4. *Attending community college or adult education courses*
5. *Banking and lender symposiums*
6. *Education received from financial newspapers, magazines, and newsletters*
7. *Prosperity trainers, mentors, and coaches*

However, even though some of these alternatives are not costly, they are time-consuming and often difficult to comprehend. Worse, many of them that are less expensive also involve buying a product or service or even use a trial-and-error investment method that, as a result, they might never fully realize how investing actually works and why certain investments outperform others. Indeed, perhaps the *best alternative* form of prosperity investment planning comes about as a result of working with an experienced and successful financial trainer or mentor, who has already achieved a high level of individual prosperity and net worth in life and might be willing to meet with you over a period, schooling you in achieving personal investment knowledge. Unfortunately, these types of individuals are rare and even harder to contact. There is literally no listing in the phone book or Internet for them. They often judiciously guard their own success-building formula, and even if they are willing to share it with others, they frequently don't have the necessary time or inclination to even do it.

So where do you go to find the type of educators to help you create a successful individual prosperity plan? Who can you contact to sign up for this training to learn the methods to develop your personal program? Where is this education located? Who teaches it? How do I find it? These are the very reasons that the author of this book wrote the book and founded The Prosperity Success Institute™ in Gold Canyon, Arizona (further information about the learning center is located in Appendix A or at the **www.prosperitysuccessinstitute.com**).

CHAPTER 9

Personal Prosperity Principle Beliefs

__In this chapter, you will learn about the following points__:

- *Prosperity Building in a Nutshell*
- *Building Your Prosperity Foundation*
- *Key Prosperity Principles Illustrated*
- *Ten Established Personal Prosperity Principles*
- *Details of Each of These Principles*
- *Six Steps in Achieving a Higher Level of Prosperity*

Ancient Economic Advice

You are supposed to keep a surplus during good times and deficits only in bad times.
—Advice that Joseph gave to the pharaoh
over three thousand years ago

(And who was probably the last politician who took that advice with the possible exception of today's LDS members)

Prosperity Building in a Nutshell

The true concept of building an effective, long-term, and significant personal prosperity plan can become a daunting experience for many individuals. In truth, there are hundreds of options, techniques, strategies, and formulas that can be used in this process. In addition, there are a great many mistakes that can be made as well.

Here is a translation of the concept reduced to its most abbreviated form in ninety words or less. This is a concentrated version of how it works:

"When you earn more than you consume, you create a surplus that is known as discretionary or disposable income. This is really simple arithmetic. This particular income creates and then becomes your investment capital. You can use this along with any other income(s) to purchase investments, such as real estate and paper assets, or perhaps even to start a business enterprise. This investment capital will then grow and compound many times over the years, along with the money that you are setting aside from earnings. At some point in the future, your investment money starts to earn money on its own."

This is how long-term, significant prosperity is created. It is a rather simple formula, and the "secret sauce" is in creating the right formula based on your own individual and unique situation. *This is exactly what I am illustrating to you in this book.*

Building Your Prosperity Foundation

"Creating Your Long-Term Personal Financial Freedom Paradigm"

The following are some of the key steps in building a firm foundational prosperity base that will serve to get you off to a good prosperity start. The depth and size of virtually any foundation will determine the strength and height of the structure that it can withstand. Any building that is constructed on a weak or insufficient foundation will soon come tumbling down or might even implode. It takes patience and perseverance to accomplish true prosperity. By following each of the following strategies in priority order, you will be able to survive even the worst personal financial and life difficulties, including "earthquakes," "avalanches," and "tsunamis."

- *Proper choice of job/career/vocational work*
- *Proper selection of a life partner*
- *Develop a Personal Prosperity-Building Success Paradigm®*
- *Create and fund a tax-deferred IRA*
- *Decision to buy or lease vehicles*
- *Decision to rent an apartment or buy a home*
- *Purchase of necessary insurance protection*
- *Decision to consistently set aside 10 percent of annual earnings**
- *Fund a rainy day account equivalent to 10 percent of annual earnings*
- *Commitment to not abuse credit cards and live within your income*
- *Development of a lifelong tax strategy*
- *Establish a will and estate planning documents*

*By doing this alone, you will be able to live off your investments in twenty-five to thirty years and ensure that you will *never* run out of money and that your earnings will stay ahead of both inflation and deflation.

Key Prosperity-Building Principles Illustrated

It frequently makes sense to condense and summarize key concepts and principles and condense them into their most concentrated form to be able to define, relate, and understand each of them better and more thoroughly. It also serves as a guide to refer to from time to time and helpful to be able to stay on track with your own personal strategies. This chapter details ten of the most useful prosperity principles that reveal the very core principles that serve as the major foundation blocks in significant prosperity building. When layered together, they form a cohesive fundamental base in which to create you unique individual plan.

These principles were created after many years of intensive study and interviews with hundreds of individuals from all walks of life who (a) were financially struggling because of not following any of them, (b) were slowly building personal prosperity by following some of them, and (c) were experiencing significant results after carefully and religiously following each of them. This prosperity code is a proven formula that can work for virtually anyone who makes a sincere effort to follow it. Its design is intended to illustrate to the individual that it is possible to build a long-term "wealth" plan despite either a bad economy (often, it has been proven that this even works to the investor's favor) or their current financial condition. It is a system of prosperity achieving that has been successfully occurring for hundreds of years around the world. Yet it is not taught anywhere today, including the formal public school system in the United States.

Ironically, it employs many of the key concepts that many immigrant families, including Italian, Irish, German, Russian, Vietnamese, Indian, Chinese, Hispanic, and others, quickly grasp when they come to America. They immediately see the opportunities for fame and fortune in this country and can easily identify with each of these ten principles. Furthermore, they have the necessary discipline, commitment, and desire to follow them and achieve results. Grasping the concept, however, is only one step in the process. To be successful on a long-term basis, you have to implement each of the principles in your overall personal prosperity planning and preparation. Take the time to carefully go over each of the principles and see how they affect you now and how they will affect you in your preparation and planning in the future. Later in the chapter, we will go over the principles in more detail and give descriptive explanations and details why each of them is important in your prosperity building.

Established Personal Prosperity Principles

The following is a list of ten personal prosperity principles that are the fundamental foundation, teaching, and training of the Circle of Competence® Prosperity Concept:

i. *THAT IN ORDER* to be more prosperous on a long-term basis, you should create and maintain a savings and investing attitude in your life instead of a spending and consumerist one.

ii. *THAT THE VERY PROCESS* of designing and engineering your personal financial future is an ongoing and lifelong effort that needs to be regularly and continually updated and maintained through a combination of reading, studying and education.

iii. *THAT PROSPERITY BUILDING* is as much about learning to live within your means as it is in growing your total income, assets, and net worth.

iv. *THAT THE KNOWLEDGE* and understanding of the power of compounding in personal finance needs to be understood and implemented to help and assist you in investing as well as how it negatively affects you in your money borrowing.

v.   *THAT HAVING THE RIGHT* financial advisory team in place is an essential part of prosperity building; but it is also important to remember whose investment money is involved and why you, as the beneficial recipient of the effects in the future, need to be involved in the entire planning and preparation process.

vi. *THAT THE STRATEGY* of creating your retirement fund should start with your very first job when even a small amount of money set aside each month will be able to produce a sizeable nest egg in your senior years if it is properly and regularly invested via the powerful effects of compounding.

vii. *THAT INSURANCE PROTECTION* needs to be carefully understood, used, and applied to protect your personal assets and that too much insurance can be just as damaging to your discretionary income and overall finances as too little insurance can destroy the prosperity that you have created.

viii. *THAT EACH OF THE* following can make a significant difference between a good lifestyle and a great lifestyle: creating a small business enterprise, purchasing real estate investment property, and portfolio investing and that each of them is directly proportionate to your level of risk-taking, experience, and knowledge.

ix. *THAT ULIMATE FINANCIAL* prosperity often results in working within a job or career that suits your personality, talents, and skills and thereby creates the necessary passion, motivation, desire, and determination to be able to achieve a better life.

x.   *THAT THE UNDERSTANDING* of personal finance education principles should be taught in the home by parents and other knowledgeable persons as well as in the school system instead of using haphazard trial-and-error and "make do" processes of personal money mistakes and bad financial choices to gain the necessary experience and know-how to understand how to do it.

Details of Each of the Ten Personal Prosperity Principles

A detailed and carefully explained summary of each of the ten prosperity-building principles is translated in each of the following:

1. **IT IS MAINTAINING A SAVINGS AND INVESTING ATTITUDE WHILE AVOIDING A SPENDING AND CONSUMERIST ONE.**

This item is listed first because it epitomizes the core belief that prosperity cannot be achieved in life to any significant degree without adopting this single, all-important prosperity principle conviction. It is the attitude that there should *always* be a percentage of net (take-home) earnings that needs to be set aside regardless of income. It is the further view that without this foundational block principle, any prosperity plan is destined for failure.

2. **IT IS AN ONGOING, LIFELONG EFFORT.**

The very process of prosperity building is a long-term and actively pursued plan that is fashioned from the creator's unique set of skills, talents, goals, objectives, and preparation and must be continually adjusted, revised, edited, and improved throughout life for it to be effective. It is further achieved by the continuous alteration and refinements through knowledge and education.

3. **IT IS LEARNING TO LIVE WITHIN YOUR MEANS AND RESOURCES.**

Instead of artificially supplementing your income through the use of credit cards, equity loans, and consumer credit, it is created through the use of a carefully constructed budget or spending plan that can tell in advance what your money will be used for so that you can make the necessary adjustments to stay within your income.

4. **IT IS ACHIEVED THROUGH UNDERSTANDING THE POWER OF COMPOUNDING.**

One of the underlying secrets to significant prosperity building is the knowledge and application of the principles of compounding and how it works *for you* (as in investing) and how it works *against you* (in consumer indebtedness). The magic and powerful effects of this important financial tool must be completely understood and practiced in your personal prosperity building to gain exponential growth in investments and to minimize personal debt.

5. **IT IS HAVING THE RIGHT ADVISORS IN PLACE.**

It is absolutely critical to have each of the financial engineering team members in place, including advisors, planners, teachers, trainers, accountants, insurance agents, attorneys, stockbrokers, real estate agents, and others; yet you must also remember that you too must be proactive in the building and investing process because it is *your money* and resources that are being used in the process.

6. **IT IS FROM STARTING A RETIREMENT FUND EARLY IN LIFE.**

Creating a disciple and commitment to set aside a percentage of earnings starting with your first job is very important in long-term success with prosperity building. Even though good results can be obtained later, starting earlier in life often provides dramatic results because of the powerful effects of compounding all categories of investments.

7. **IT IS THROUGH THE PRUDENT USE OF INSURANCE PROTECTION.**

Prosperity builders know and recognize the advantages of personal asset and liability protection that is available through the use of insurance protection, including life, health, accident, vehicle, and home and umbrella liability. They do not try to exposure themselves to 100 percent of any of these potential losses and instead choose to use insurance to protect themselves. They avoid insurance "gimmicks" and stick to the tried-and-true coverage with recognized insurance carriers that have proven results.

8. **IT IS THROUGH THE USE OF PROVEN PERSONAL INVESTMENTS.**

Savvy prosperity builders realize that there are three major and proven income-production methods: (a) small business enterprises (the "Mount Everest" of personal income production), (b) real estate investment property (a proven long-term prosperity strategy), and (c) portfolio investing (stocks, bonds, mutual funds, and other securities). They understand how each of these techniques works in relationship to their personal prosperity building and creates an individual success strategy in addition to earnings that are a result of a job/career or even in place of it later in life.

9. **IT IS FROM A RESULT OF SELECTING A SUITABLE JOB AND/ OR CAREER VOCATION.**

Prosperity achievers all recognize their unique, individual skills and talents and choose a job/career that takes advantage of them and that gives the passion and motivation for them to excel at their work. Many of them are entrepreneurs and leaders in their fields and industries and know how to seize on carefully chosen career opportunities as they appear. Furthermore, they refuse to get involved in opportunities that are highly speculative or too risky or that they know nothing about.

10. **IT IS THE UNDERSTANDING THAT FINANCIAL EDUCATION MUST BE LEARNED EARLY IN LIFE TO HIGHLY SUCCEED.**

Virtually all prosperity seekers are active in the role of teaching financial literacy in their families and with others who are close to them. They realize that it is an ongoing process and recognize that it is necessary to teach them "how to fish" as opposed to merely "providing the fish" to them. They also promote this financial learning process and may even formally teach it at some level of public education.

Six Steps in Achieving Higher Levels of Prosperity

✓ *Learning How to Create More Income and Earning Streams*
✓ *Learning How to Better Budget Your Money and Spending*
✓ *Learning How to Improve Your Borrowing of Money and Better Use of Credit*
✓ *Learning How to Protect Your Capital and Personal Assets*
✓ *Learning How to Better Invest Your Money and Make It Grow*
✓ *Learning How to Better Utilize Your Personal Resources*

Each of These Strategies Is Outlined Next

PART 1
Learning How to Create More Income and Earning Streams
<< Examining Many of the Opportunities to Create More Income >>

The critical first step in creating an improved personal financial IQ or PIQUE© (Prosperity Intelligence Quotient) is through the generation of earnings from your job, career, vocation, or profession. There are, indeed, many various methods to achieve this; and the best ones involve working within a field that is well suited to your talents and skills as well as it is compatible with your personality and motivations. Many people often make the decision to seek employment based only on income needs and forget that balancing income with personal passion for the work involved will usually result in the optimum formula for long-term financial income success. In addition, one of the prosperity-building considerations in building greater income is in realizing that there are several category choices of earnings that are available to everyone:

1. **WAGE EARNINGS** – This is the income that is created as a result of your personal efforts. It is commonly referred to as a job and can include everything from A to Z. The downside to a job, however, is that when you leave it at the end of the day, your income stops too. With a job, the work that you perform is rewarded with earnings; and they can be low, moderate, or high based on your talent, skills, experience, and opportunity.

2. **PASSIVE EARNINGS** – This is the earnings that are derived as a result of (a) a small business enterprise; (b) real estate property (ies) investments; (c) an idea, innovation, or concept that is properly marketed; or (d) similar types of earnings. The key is to remember that once again, this income is created 24/7/365 and whether you are on the job, and it can produce significant earnings over the long term. This is why it's referred to as *passive earnings*.

3. **PORTFOLIO EARNINGS** – This is income that is created as direct result of financial security investments, such as stocks, bonds, mutual funds, treasury notes, CDs, annuities, ETF funds, or other paper investments in the stock markets. Essentially, these are earnings that make money after being invested; and even though it is subject to occasional volatile financial market conditions, it can often produce highly predictable incomes over time in addition to other categories of income.

It should be noted that none of the other stages of personal financial IQ building can be taken or even considered until you have accomplished this first step in identifying the various income opportunities that are available to you. Only after you thoroughly know and understand its effect on you and how they are used can you build on this essential foundational block in your personal prosperity plan.

Once you have a thorough understanding and comprehension of the various types of income and earnings, you are ready to take the next step in your personal financial IQ—learning how to budget your earnings to get the biggest bang for your bucks.

PART 2
Learning How to Budget Your Money and Spending
<< *Learning How to Be Able to Do More with Less* >>

On the one hand, it's a good idea to have a significant income (or incomes) regardless of the category or type; but on the other hand, income alone is not nearly enough to increase your personal prosperity building or personal financial IQ. You must also be able to use your income wisely and resourcefully to make the maximum use of it. Many high-income earners are also big spenders and, as a result, have little discretionary (money that is left over after paying all your bills) income that could be used for savings and investing as discussed in step number 1.

Learning to use and apply a budget or spending plan is an extremely important strategy technique in improving your personal financial IQ. It involves a process of creating *predictable spending*, which simply means that you can forecast your personal spending and expenses a month or more *in advance*. Using this method, you can avoid coming up short at the end of every month. A good budget contains a level of flexibility so that if you overspend during a given month, you can then cut back the following month to balance out the average monthly expenses. It is a highly useful technique that all successful prosperity builders use.

An effective spending plan also includes a recognition of the *big four* personal expenses that, when combined, can involve between 75 and 85 percent of your entire net income. In order, these four highest personal expenses are as follows:

1. **SHELTER** – This is the cost of a home mortgage, rent, and related expenses.
2. **TRANSPORTATION** – This is the cost of vehicle(s) loan payments as well as the related expenses, such   as fuel, repairs, licensing, maintenance, insurance, and other costs.

3. **FOOD** – This is the cost of groceries, food, dining and restaurant meals, and take-out meals and a necessary expense.

4. **TAXES** – This is the cost of government services and is often not considered to be one of the larger expenses because *they appear in smaller bits and pieces,* yet when combined, they represent a formidable total expense. These costs include income taxes, FICA, real estate taxes, sales taxes, luxury taxes, capital gains taxes, fuel taxes, and others too numerous to mention.

The process of identifying a suitable budget or spending plan template formula as well as the implementation of it in your personal lifestyle is a major step in further developing your personal financial IQ. It provides further levels of assistance when you apply the following other techniques:

- *Good negotiating, bartering, haggling, and purchasing skills*
- *Knowing how to ask for discounts and items on sale to get a better price*
- *Utilizing warehouse-style retailers for everyday staple items*
- *Understanding the value of appreciating items versus depreciating ones*
- *Using coupons and other price-reducing techniques*
- *Purchasing late-model vehicles rather than new ones*
- *Practicing resourcefulness and value in every aspect of your personal life*

If you are cash tight yet anxious to take advantage of many of the bargains and discounts available today, creating a war chest of cash will make your opportunities more achievable. The more cash you have, the better deals you can get. Sellers are more willing to take a lower price from buyers who have cash, realizing that they are probably better fixed financially. As a result, creating a cash savings program is important and worth it.

Some pointers for those who wish to create a cash savings program include the following:

1. *Examine Your Views and Attitudes About Spending.* What are the issues that prevent people from sticking to a money diet? Usually, they involve emotional barriers and not a lack of professional financial guidance. Many come to professional advisors seeking a miracle but quickly learn it comes down to their personal discipline and commitment to do it. People who attempt a crash savings program first need to deal with the reasons for their bad money habits and behaviors, such as impulse spending, credit card abuse, or a sense of material entitlement.

2. *Create an Inventory of Your Current Financial Situation.* Often, a major obstacle to saving money is uncontrolled day-to-day spending. Before you can even decide how to allocate your spending funds, you need to

review where your money resources have gone for a period of several weeks or months. This can be done with a simple paper and pen or through the use of a personal finance tool, such as Quicken. This review can often bring a host of surprises. Many are shocked to learn exactly how much they are spending on restaurant meals, coffee stops, carryout food, and entertainment. Creating a spending inventory can be time-consuming because you may have to sift through credit card, debit card, and checking account statements. For those who don't routinely track their spending, this process could take the better part of an entire weekend, so an easier method is to simply purchase an inexpensive journal at an office supply store and write down all, and I do mean A-L-L, of your daily purchases for a thirty-day period regardless of how you pay for them. The summary results will reveal where you are spending your money and how much of it you are frivolously wasting. *In* the end, it's essential to determine where cuts are possible before you can slash spending.

3. ***Create a Budget That Allows a Degree of Flexibility.*** Given the increasingly higher cost of living, it's more and more difficult to trim expenses enough to allow for a serious savings program. Savers need to closely examine their largest outlays, including regular supermarket spending, which is a variable cost among the *big four (shelter, transportation, food, and taxes)*. It is well recognized that eating out is   costly, but grocery store food can also add up quickly. Purchasing fewer processed foods, doing more home cooking, monitoring food waste closely, and even taking bag lunches to work are all savvy and effective ways to cut food costs. Transportation costs (the number 2 cost in the big four) can also put a big dent in most household budgets; so savers should challenge their long-held assumptions about vehicle ownership, including attitudes about new versus late-model used car, asking yourself if every adult in your household needs a vehicle, if public transportation or carpooling a realistic alternative to/from work, and other options, such as shopping only once a week instead of doing it daily, using the Internet for gas shopping, and seeking estimates for car repairs, which could all potentially lead to hefty savings.

Since many people live paycheck to paycheck, they find it hard to summon the necessary discipline and commitment to extract a percentage of their net income each payday for savings. For these people, automatic deductions might be the answer instead of methodical setting aside actual cash. Those who have direct debits taken from their pay rarely miss the money goals and objects, and meanwhile, their savings accounts add up rather quickly. In the words of the famous kitchen appliance promoter, Ron Popiel, "You can just set it and forget it"; and that's a big plus for anyone trying to save money during these challenging times.

Once you recognize, know, and understand how to bet the best use of your money resources, it's time to go on to the third step in your financial IQ training: knowing how and when to better borrow money when needed.

PART 3
Learning How to Better Borrow Money When Needed
<< Everyone Needs to Seek a Loan from Time to Time >>

Let's define exactly what the term "borrowed money" really means. First of all, it's not only the *biggies in life* like your mortgage and vehicle payments. Those loans represent the obvious and traditional source of borrowed money for many people. But did you know that there were other forms of borrowing that many people use that are not quite as obvious and, if improperly used, can serve to peck away at your prosperity-building efforts? One of those that quickly come to mind is the abuse of credit cards and consumer loans. When you stop to consider the basic concept of the credit card, it is easy to see that this is money that is *advanced to you* from a lending source, such as a bank, to pay for a particular purchase because you do not have the cash in hand or in your checking or debit account to buy it. As a result, you are essentially borrowing the money from a lender (and paying a high rate of interest and fees) to pay off the accumulating debt each month. Call it what you will, this is borrowed money, and you pay for it royally. This is the very essence of ineffectively borrowing money, yet many people fail to comprehend this concept and instead use their credit cards to supplement their incomes and lifestyle. The average household today in America has five different credit cards and owe between $15,000 and $25,000 in cumulative credit card debt that results in payments that are somewhere between the cost of a vehicle payment and a mortgage payment every month. This is not good use of your hard-earned income and is simply borrowed money. The second frequently used form of costly and ineffective borrowing is the use of home equity lines of credit or HELOCs. These consumer loans became very popular in the 1990s when banks and mortgage companies made consumers increasingly aware of the rising amount of equity that many were creating in their homes as a result of highly appreciating real estate prices. This abusive form of consumer loans creates a stated amount of money that a homeowner can borrow for any purpose whatsoever that is backed up by the equity in their residential homes. We all know what happened to these loans when the market crashed in 2008 when many borrowers used this equity to pay off large balances on their credit cards only to begin doing it all over again.

PART 4
Learning How to Protect Your Money and Your Personal Assets
<< *It's hard enough to build it, but it's even harder to protect it* >>

Once you have begun to see results from your prosperity-building efforts and financial IQ, the next step is learning how to protect your money, assets, and the very lives of you and your loved ones. This is an essential strategy to prevent you from losing all of it in the event of a catastrophe. This can be done in a variety of ways from recognition to protection, to prevention. These are the top methods to minimize the numerous opportunities that exist today that could potentially separate you from your hard work, efforts, and personal financial resources and wreak devastation to your prosperity building. Some of the best methods of accomplishing this involve the following techniques:

1. **RECOGNITION** – There are a host of opportunities that exist today for financial schemers, scammers, con men and women, hackers, and charlatans of every conceivable dimension that will try to take advantage of the unsuspecting and the too trusting. Intuition counts a lot here. If you feel that you are being pressured or are being given the *hard-sell approach,* walk away or simply hang up the phone when confronted by these types of nefarious individuals. Other protective approach techniques include asking for written quotations, Better Business Bureau's inquiries, Angie's List summaries, and other ratings, referrals, recommendations and asking to see their contracts for review by a third party *before* you sign it. Due diligence is an important strategy in protecting your financial resources, and a few simple techniques can assist you greatly from being taken advantage of or ripped off.

2. **PROTECTION** – The next layer of security in personal finances and prosperity building with your money, assets, capital resources, investments, and even your life and income generation is through the judicious and wise use of insurance. There are many, many forms of it available today, and you need to become familiar of those that offer good value and the ones that are *retail priced* and make better investments for the insurer than the insured.

Some of the categories of coverage are as follows:

- *Property insurance*
- *Vehicle insurance*
- *Life insurance*
- *Liability insurance*

- *Comprehensive insurance*
- *Health insurance*
- *And many others too numerous to mention*

The use of insurance can best be described as one of those items that you pay for and hope that you will never need. But having it on hand gives you a great deal of peace of mind, and it is a significant and important step in your personal financial IQ training. Having too much of it and the wrong types is just as bad as not having enough of it. Like many things in life, it pays to shop around for this protection; and even when you have coverage, make sure to periodically (once a year when you get your bill for coverage) get other quotes.

3. **PREVENTION** – This is the ultimate safeguard when it comes to insurance and involves a literal state-of-mind perception that carefully monitors such things as the opportunities for identity theft, one of the most common crimes involving large sums of money that can be lost today. Here, simple precautions, such as careful use of passwords, access codes, PIN numbers, Social Security number, credit cards numbers, and other banking and financial account numbers, all need regular and diligent monitoring. In addition, the use of a crisscross paper shredder at home for sensitive financial documents received in the mail or over the Internet also serves to prevent this type of theft of your money and assets. Even if you have insurance to cover many of these losses, there is much in the way of time, effort, and energy that a few steps involving prevention can eliminate.

Understanding the Concept of Insurance Protection
< Protecting Your Hard-Earned Personal Assets >

Many people underinsure themselves from many of the personal and material aspects of life. They feel that it is a waste of money to spend it on something that they will probably never even use. They fail to understand that basic economic value of certainty and instead choose to play the odds with much of the results of their hard-earned income and assets. This is especially true when it comes to the concept of health-care coverage insurance. Insurance involves transferring the risk from you to an institution that specializes in that risk-taking. It is a sound prosperity strategy, especially when it comes to our own lives via life insurance. It is our human life that is arguably our largest and best asset that must be protected at all times through the use of insurance. The amount of insurance maintained should be directly proportionate to the level of assets owned since prosperity building is not a do-it-yourself experience. Having the proper amount of protection gives you the opportunity to focus on the really important things in life and provides the ability to create an amount of certainty that is unavailable any other way. The more certainty that we can establish, the more risks, challenges, and opportunities we can control and personally pursue in our lives. Among the ways that you can develop the understanding include following each of the below steps.

PART 5
Learning How to Invest Your Money and Make It Grow
<< Discover the Powerful Effects of the Ninth Wonder of the World >>

Once you have accomplished steps 1 through 4, you can now focus intently on the next step of the personal financial IQ process—learning how to invest your resources and money. The two unique and compelling concepts that are a fundamental part of this process are the following:

1. *Regular compounding of your investments*
2. *Exponential growth of your investments*

Each of these two factors plays an increasingly huge role in learning how to invest your money.

Compounding is the process of making good yields in your investments through a time-honored process that allows investors *to make money on top of the money that they have already made.* It is a technique that all successful investors know and understand. This is either from money that is invested, such as paper financial investments, or from money that is leveraged (borrowed) from such investments as real estate and small business enterprises. *This is a principle that literally cuts both ways.* It has been said before that those who do not understand the way that compounding can benefit them in investing are destined to have to pay it to others through their personal borrowing and obligations.

Exponential growth is the result of substantial increases in your investment portfolio through a personal prosperity-building formula that is developed over a period. It is directly related to several factors, including *the category of investment, risk-tolerance level, age, the timetable you are working around, and personal long-term goals and objectives.* The successful results are achieved by combining each of these principles into a personal prosperity strategy (PPS) that is both unique to your particular situation and also completely and thoroughly understood by you.

The particular investments that you choose are based on many factors, and each of them should be carefully considered before selecting them. Some of the common criteria used in selecting investments include the following:

✓ *Knowledge of the potential investment being considered*
✓ *Understanding the techniques needed to achieve the results*
✓ *Recognizing the risk versus rewards involved in gains or losses*
✓ *Creating defined personal goals and objectives*
✓ *Utilizing a customized formula that you develop that outlines your approach to the investment*
✓ *Using a competent and trusted investment guide or advisor*
✓ *Old-fashioned experience and savvy in doing it*

All substantial prosperity-building achievements include the knowledge and understanding of each of the key concepts and principles of investing. This is not a subject that can be learned in a few hours at an afternoon investment seminar. Rather, it is a series of defined actions that when combined can produce a unique personal investment strategy that can lead to substantial long-term prosperity results. *It is an absolute requirement of the financial IQ learning series to accomplish the highest levels of prosperity-building accomplishments and success.*

PART 6
Learning How to Better Utilize Your Personal Resources
<< *Engage in a Virtual Reality Check of Your Use of Money* >>

This last and final step is not necessarily only about the most efficient use of your money and assets as it is about the ultimate and best use of it once you have finally achieved your prosperity goals and ambitions. When many people are asked what they plan to do with their recently acquired prosperity, visions of exotic vacations, expensive homes, luxury vehicles, and expensive jewelry purchase often come to mind. Each of these, however, is merely the external expressions of legitimate prosperity creation. It's all right to enjoy the fruits of you efforts and labors, but there are other better and more sustainable uses of it also. Those that should be considered are the internal, emotional, and heartfelt applications of it in various other areas. Some of this involves creating lasting memories with family members and close friends, using some of it for good causes and charitable giving, building a prosperity legacy in your community, and even applying a portion of it, along with your personal skills and expertise to help others achieve prosperity in their personal lives too.

Often, prosperity can be defined better as an attitude, view, or concept rather than the size of a bank account, portfolio, or net worth statement. There are, indeed, always more ways to spend money and buy things than there are to be able to build them. You should also remember that in the prosperity years of your life, a certain portion of your *initial seed money* should be applied and used to help foster the long-term growth and motivation of others who need your help and encouragement in negotiating their hurdles and obstacles.

Another effective method to do this is to not always simply give your resources away but to give of yourself as well. This is demonstrated in the expression, "Teaching others how to fish instead of just giving them fish." Those who have achieved a respectable level of personal prosperity in their lives have the ultimate responsibility of sharing and teaching others what they have learned and experienced so that other lives can be positively affected as well. It is the virtual pebble in the water that creates larger and bigger rings as it continues to grow.

After all, when it really comes down to it, it's not only about the money. This method is a way of maintaining a *scorecard* but not the only or best way to win at the game of prosperity life. The best and most successful prosperity achievers have all developed a sound strategy of giving a portion of their monetary acquired resources and talents away in a manner that will benefit many others in the future.

Make no mistake about that whatsoever!

CHAPTER 10

Creating Change Through Personal Improvements

Change Is Inevitable

The process of change is ever before each of us. Nothing in our lives can escape change. There is nothing in this entire world that will remain forever as it is forever. Even the largest glaciers and the highest mountains located around the world are slowly changing and have done so for millions of years. Change is everywhere around us. The true reality of change, however, is good. It becomes the open door to all accomplishments, achievements, advancements, and success; and there is no progress that can be made without experiencing it. Looking at it another way, nothing can improve in your life without some sort of change taking place. It is the literal process of taking you from "here to there" that makes it so compelling and important. Until a change occurs, we are left with our existing habits and behaviors while lacking the impetus and motivation to do anything differently. It has been said that one of the most accurate definitions of insanity is to keep doing the same thing over and over, expecting a different result. Although this may be an extreme view, it is nonetheless the attitude that many people experience when it comes to change. They expect improvements but are unwilling to make the effort to see the change that needs to take place.

Another word that is helpful in understanding change is "evolution," which means progress or purposeful change. This is the type of change that results in positive personal growth and achievement. It is the modification experience by needed change in your life that takes you further down the road to accomplishing your goals. The reality of the law of change is written deep down within each of us. It is the process of transition that is used to improve ourselves and is the reason that change is so compelling within each of our lives. It is inevitable that we will somehow experience change in our lives and in our aspirations. Change is a constant, enduring law; and without it, everything would remain forever as it is. There would never be any growth or progress, and we would become static.

The real question when pondering change is this: will your change be ultimately for the better or for the worse?

> **"Creating needed change in your life involves**
> *S-T-R-E-T-C-H-I-N-G Y-O-U-R-S-E-L-F*
> *to fulfill your ambitions."*

Change Is Bound to Happen to Each of Us

Change can be either good or bad, yet often, it is inevitable. If you learn to embrace change instead of fearing or avoiding it, you could find that it will improve your life, career, and prosperity building. ***Change is scary!*** It is different from the security of the "here and now." It is the unknown and requires adjustment and adaptation. It is no wonder why many prosperity seekers resist change and its effects on long-term outcomes. Change can be both scary and positive at the same time. Collectively, they can often be very good for us and our prosperity building. Change might make your situations better, or without them, your situation could become worse. Change may provide the opportunity you need for your plan to take off like a rocket ship to Mars! Do you resist change or embrace it? Do you try to make seamless changes that make effective improvements or fail to make changes and become just another financial casualty? Change is the quintessential ingredient to personal prosperity progress regardless of the size, type, category, or degree. *Ask yourself which is better:* making the needed changes to your preparation and planning or experiencing yet another "uh-oh" or, even worse, a ubiquitous "crash and burn."

> **CHANGE:**
> *When carefully studied and researched,*
> *change has both physical and*
> *psychological attributes.*

Making Needed Personal Changes
< Do You Need a Dramatic or Subtle Improvement? >

Some people are of the mistaken impression that all major improvements are a result of large changes in their life. This is usually not true. A small and significant change improvement is often all it takes to notice results. Change is frequently a product of either one or a series of two or three modest alterations to behavior that can substantially alter the outcome. Often, a simple tweak or adjustment, depending on the issue, is enough to create the necessary results. The line, it seems, between *now* and *not me yet* is a lot narrower than it appears. Knowing just where the needed changes need to be created can literally make all the difference in the world as you are going through the process of change. Redoubling your efforts is not always a requirement.

The trick is finding that needed small change or changes that will significantly alter and improve your long-term achievement. Sometimes the smallest details can have an overwhelming impact on your immediate personal life. In the end, it is not such a radical or unbelievable idea at all. It is a rather single and straightforward strategy that has been found to work successfully for many people. This process seems to work best when you learn to identify precisely the right *tweak* that is needed to effect change and improve your behavior and situation. It can be done through the influence of special kinds of people, people of extraordinary personal communications and with the personal motivation to sincerely want to help another overcome their challenges rather than merely applying a Band-Aid adhesive bandage to it.

Some of the unique factors in achieving this are the following:

- *Overcoming defeatism*
- *Realizing the things you are capable of changing*
- *Understanding needed changes*
- *Identifying the right types of influences in your environment*
- *Isolating the specific capabilities of needed change*

Each of these can have a dramatic effect on how we behave, who we are, and our level of prosperity achievement in life. It is indeed possible to do a lot with a little bit of carefully developed and choreographed teaching, training, and education. With the slightest nudge in the right direction, you can experience needed change in your life without completely reinventing yourself.

Making Needed Changes in Your Views and Attitudes About Money
< Do You Need a Dramatic or Subtle Improvement? >

Some people are of the mistaken impression that all major improvements are a result of large changes in their life. This is usually not true. A small and significant change improvement is often all it takes to notice results. Change is frequently a product of either one or a series of two or three modest alterations to behavior that can substantially alter the outcome. Often a simple tweak or adjustment, depending on the issue, is enough to create the necessary results. The line, it seems between *now* and *not me yet is* a lot narrower than it appears. Knowing just where the needed changes need to be created can literally make all the difference in the world as you are going through the process of change. Redoubling your efforts is not always a requirement.

The trick is finding that needed small change or changes that will significant alter and improve your long-term achievement. Sometimes the smallest details can have an overwhelming impact on your immediate personal life. In the end, it is not such a radical or unbelievable idea at all. It is a rather single and straightforward strategy that has been found to work successfully for many people. This process seems to work best when you learn to identify precisely the right *tweak* that is needed to effect change and improve your behavior and situation. It can be done through the influence of special kinds of people, people of extraordinary personal communications and with the personal motivation to sincerely want to help another overcome their challenges rather than merely applying a Band-Aid adhesive bandage to it.

Some of the unique factors in achieving this are:

- *Overcoming defeatism*
- *Realizing the things you are capable of changing*
- *Understanding needed changes*
- *Identifying the right types of influences in your environment*
- *Isolating the specific capabilities of needed change*

Each of these can have a dramatic effect on how we behave, who we are, and our level of prosperity achievement in life. It is indeed possible to do a lot with a little bit of carefully developed and choreographed teaching, training, and education. With the slightest nudge in the right direction, you can experience needed change in your life without completely reinventing yourself.

The Clock Is Ticking on Excuses
< You *Can* Transform Your Life Step by Step >

You can carve out the time to make the needed changes, habits, and behaviors in your life and career; but when it comes to making the changes, we have heard all the excuses, and the one we hear most frequently is "I just don't have the time." People who say they don't have the time or, more specifically, do not want to take the time to get better and improve are just making excuses for their present condition. What I teach people is that one good reason for improving overrides a dozen excuses. Often, the motivation for giving up excuses is that in the end, you are the one who ultimately benefits from the transformation. Some may have fears, such as risk-taking, learning the right strategies and techniques, or failing; or even if they can afford it, the ones who are most successful at changing their lives state that they simply do not want to be the victim of their own excuse anymore. Instead, they make the decision to take immediate action even if it involves taking small steps at first.

When you give up your excuses, you can begin to take responsibility for your life. Nearly every transformation that I have witnessed over the years was preceded by a dramatic increase in self-discipline and personal responsibility. You have to accept the fact that you need to "pilot" your own life. Instead of using lack of time as an excuse, you need to look at your life in an entirely new way. For example, the excuse that you just cannot change can be replaced with "How can I change?" The excuse that you cannot afford getting the right kind of help can be replaced with "How can I afford the right kind of help?" Instead of the excuse that you do not have the time to do it, think: "How can I find the time to change?" The following is an outline for turning around different areas of your life and career:

1. **WRITE DOWN THREE OF YOUR GOALS**
    You can begin by coming up with three goals in areas that you would like to have more control over, such as the following:
    *   More control of my financial destiny
    *   More personal independence
    *   Greater happiness and enjoyment in my life and career

2. **IDENTIFY ACTION PLANS FOR EACH OF THEM**
    You can then decide on an action that you can take in each one of those areas like the following:
    *   **Destiny** – You are going to focus on this aspect of your success so that you can achieve better, more long-term results.
    *   **Independence** – Spending time planning and preparing for success in advance and choosing a coach who can help you create firm boundaries and measure and monitor your achievements.
    *   **Happiness and Enjoyment** – Choosing to alter your habits and behaviors can result in more joy in your life by choosing new strategies that will view setbacks and adversities as opportunities to learn, grow, and improve.

3. **GET SPECIFIC**
    You will be able to achieve greater success in your life and career if you have more detailed plans for acting on your goals. For instance, when it comes to building a bigger accomplishment, you might pledge to yourself, your support team, and your coach to do those things on a regular and consistent basis, such as the following:
    *   *Following the guidance and instruction while applying it to your life career*
    *   *Refusing to fall back into a temporary relapse*
    *   *Continuing to improve through new techniques and strategies*
    *   *Using the new methods to build on existing successes*
    *   *Learning when to ask for help when you get off-track*

4. **ACCEPT RESPONSIBILITY**
    You will begin to change and improve when you realize that there are some things that you will never have any control over, such as market conditions, negative influences, and actions of others, such as random events that affect your success building. You need to accept this and decide in advance that it is up to you to control your self-discipline and

mind-set in those situations. Do not let them affect you by focusing on your objective and not always on the hurdles between you and your goals.

Thought of the Day

Ninety-nine percent of the failures come from people who have the habit of making excuses.
—Washington Carver, American Botanist (1864–1943)

Identifying Needed Changes in Your Life

"If it shrieks pain, you must have hit it directly on the nose!"

Creating Change Through Positive Personal Improvements
<< Seven Stages in Accomplishing Sustained Self-Improvement >>

In virtually all my previous self-improvement work with people of all ages, backgrounds, incomes, and genders, I have come to a startling conclusion:

People simply do not like to be reminded what they have done wrong in the past.

GUESS WHAT. None of us do, including me, yet it is essential in achieving the desired results.

The reason behind this emotion is many and various, which should be openly discussed. Let me be the first to advise you that even though the presenter has achieved a certain level of success and financial prosperity in his life, it has not been without a major or significant effort in his own self-improvement. Because of this, I feel I have a unique perspective of self-improvement that I can relate to each of you; and as a result, I will use strategies and techniques that each of you can greatly benefit from, relate to, and implement. As we move further along the educational training, I will relate some of my personal anecdotes, past experiences, and some humorous stories that will help you better relate to the personal development improvements that we all seek in our lives. I promise not to dwell on any of your failings.

First, let me again remind each of you that there are some fundamental stages involved in making positive developmental changes in our lives that need to be addressed. What I am referring to is a "prescription for prosperity" that is actually a list of various stages that each of you has either gone through in the past, are going through now, or anticipate going through in the future that can help identify the meaningful process of self-improvement development. Even though we might not like to be reminded of our past mistakes, shortcomings, errors, and faults, it is, indeed, part of the self-improvement process and is one of the crucial steps involved in the training process.

The Seven Stages of Improvement

STAGE 1. <u>RECOGNITION OF NEEDED CHANGE</u> – Self-improvements are not something that occurs on their own. They are the result of our personally recognizing that there is a problem that needs to be made to better our lives in the future.

STAGE 2. <u>DESIRE TO IMPROVE</u> – This is the fundamental benchmark of self-improvement development. Without this stage, improvement will probably never happen. It is proven that someone with the necessary desire to improve and change is a prospect that has a *very good* chance to achieve a successful outcome.

STAGE 3. <u>MOTIVATION TO IMPROVE</u> – We all have personal motivators in our lives. Some of them may include more income, better use of our existing earnings, improved relationships, more prosperity, or other reasons that often are defined as motivational functions. Without proper motivation, improvements stall.

STAGE 4. <u>CREATING A SENSE OF PURPOSE</u> – There is always a purpose, obvious or not so obvious, that explains why human beings do things. It is the cause of our actions and represents the reasons why we undergo them.

STAGE 5. <u>COMMITMENT TO IMPROVE</u> – Even the most needed improvements will not take place without a personal commitment to change and improve our past behaviors. This is the human element that makes each of you stay with the program to achieve the desired results.

STAGE 6. <u>DISCIPLINE TO DO IT</u> – Each of the other stages is meaningless without the necessary self-discipline and willpower to follow the process. Arguably, this is one of the more important stages because it involves the gut-level approach to achieve that desired changes and results.

STAGE 7. <u>IMPLEMENTING THE CHANGES</u> – The final and most critical aspect of the teaching, training, and learning is ultimately the implementation of the knowledge. Without application, the process is meaningless. It literally defines the entire experience.

Is It Time for a Needed Change in Your Life?

Most of us would agree that we do not like change in our life, especially if it involves altering our habits, beliefs, behaviors, views, and attitudes. It is always much easier to resist them and continue our existing patterns even if we know changes are needed. But what happens when our views and methods don't seem to work? Isn't the ultimate litmus test the ability to get things accomplished the way we want and be able to meet our life goals and ambitions through a process that really *does* work? In the end, the challenge is clear. If we are somehow lulled into thinking how good we are yet the results of our thoughts, actions, accomplishments, and results fall considerably short of where we want to be because we have made error, pursued the wrong strategies, and not accomplished our objectives, perhaps it is time for a new perspective or change in our thinking. When that happens, ready or not, it is time for a change.

REMEMBER: *No one can change you from the* **outside.** *It* **always** *has to occur from the* **inside.** *Are you ready for a change?*

Dealing with the Fear of the Unknown Territory

Just imagine the courage and bravery of the legendary Meriwether Lewis and William Clark who underwent the arduous and lengthy early 1800s expedition, which involved threading their way to the American West Coast, eventually arriving at the Pacific Ocean. As we know now, their journey was made much easier as a result of the efforts of the female Shoshone Indian guide, Sacagawea, who served as their pathfinder and interpreter throughout their journey. Have you ever looked at our personal finances and prosperity-building plan as a trip into an unknown territory, perhaps a foreign language or even some form of high-tech proverbial rocket science? The unknown is always full of haunting and surprising "what-ifs." To be able to chart unknown territory requires a map, a compass, and a trusted guide to take you through it safely. Often, it further involves temporarily giving up some of the things that provide your existing level of security comfort or pleasure that might leave you in the scary territory of unknown outcomes and conclusions because you have never visited them before.

The fear of the unknown can even cripple your capacity to follow the right path over the weeks and months ahead. During the process, the results may appear to be so far off, so distant, and removed that it is easy to become discouraged and frustrated. You may even choose to procrastinate in obtaining the results as a consequence of this longer-term payoff. This is especially true when you don't always know or understand the process of getting there or how it works. Much of this can be controlled or even eliminated when you have the right set of instructions (a textbook, guidebook, and materials), a compass or GPS system (your personal paradigm prosperity formula), and a well-experienced guide (instructor, mentor, coach) to help and assist you in this important life process. It must, however, be remembered that many of the really good things in life are never easy or quickly achieved. They each take willingness, focus, discipline, and perseverance. Eventually, if you have studied and researched it well enough, if you have carefully detailed your goals and ambitions, and if you have diligently followed your personal prosperity formula, you can achieve your objective with only a minimal amount of errors, mistakes, blunders, and omissions.

Long-term prosperity building includes journeying into unknown territory for many people. It is ironic that most people spend their entire life working and earning income, even setting aside a portion of their hard-earned wages and creating a suitable lifestyle, yet they spend proportionately *very little* of their time, effort, or energy actually planning their financial life, including income and expenses, and their future personal prosperity success. Even though the specific formula varies from person to person and no two formulas are ever identical, the long-term results are frequently worth it in the end. The process is neither unreasonable nor impossible. It is a highly personal achievement that is accomplished by having the right essentials in place, along with the willingness to enter the unknown financial territory.

Bettering Our Own Self-Assessments

Research shows that very few of us are very good at critical self-assessments. Because most of us generally don't have a good idea of how we think and why we act in certain ways, we simply don't do as well at some activities in life as we could. Anything that can help us understand ourselves better will also serve to improve our long-term performance over time. In the end, doesn't it make good sense to pursue a career field that takes advantage of your natural abilities and strengths as opposed to putting yourself into a mold that is ill-suited for your talents and abilities? There have been a countless number of books written by highly intelligent people concerning this subject, but essentially, what it comes down to are three (3) distinct factors in making this determination. Each of them is important and key in our long-term career success:

1. **HOW YOU WERE RAISED** – Your upbringing, it seems, has a whole lot to do with your ability to make critical self-assessments and factors in issues of self-esteem and confidence, depending on whether you were encouraged as a youngster to pursue your passionate pursuit or instead told to follow a more secure path.

2. **YOUR VARIOUS LIFE EXPERIENCES** – It seems like the School of Hard Knocks is another critical factor in this process, and many

of your previous trials and tribulations have a huge impact on your abilities to assess ourselves.

3. **YOUR GENETIC MAKEUP** – It should not be surprising to learn that genetics play a highly important role in our ability to look at ourselves in the looking glass and determine where we might be able to improve for maximum benefit.

However, this process that many call introspection comes at a price. Once you have identified a specific behavior in your life or career that you have determined needs to be improved, it becomes your responsibility to do something about it. Taking a class; studying a self-improvement book; seeking the counsel of a trusted friend, mentor, or coach; and creating an effective strategy to overcome the challenge are all extremely useful methods to accomplish your self-improvement goals. Those who desire higher and higher levels of self-betterment know that isolating a certain behavior is only the first step. After identifying the change, you must take action and do something about it.

> ## Creating Positive Habits That Can Help You Create Needed Change
>
> *It has been said that it can take up to 28 days to make something a habit;*
> *Yet, ironically, only three days to undo it.*
>
> —Anonymous

Behavioral Changes
<< Are You Resistant to Making Changes? >>

Every day millions of people around the world engage in behaviors that they know and realize are bad for them—smoking cigarettes, drug abuse, gambling excessively, riding a motorcycle without a helmet, and exceeding the speed limit with their vehicles. Why? Because they want to! People derive pleasure, a thrill, or just a break from the daily doldrums. Getting people to change their behavior and habits, even via a friendly, rational argument, is not easily done. The seat belt was introduced in the early 1960s by Robert McNamara, who eventually became the Secretary of Defense during the Vietnam War. Sadly, the seat belt was not regularly used until the government made it mandatory, which was not done until hundreds of thousands of people were killed in traffic-related deaths every year.* And yet there are still people who refuse to wear a seat belt because they are told they have to.

A central, frustrating reality of human behavior is that personal conduct change is hard. It takes effort, discipline, and desire and commitment to clearly see both the cause and effect of actions that cause our self-inflicted actions that bring us harm. Surprisingly, many people already know what causes their lack of prosperity building. They may even be aware of the solutions to their problems but are unwilling to create the necessary changes that will positively affect their lives. Sadly, no one can be forced to improve. This is an unfortunate part of the human condition. Some people have to hit rock bottom for them to recognize that drastic changes are necessary.

In the end, you must remember that it is never too late to commit to change. It is a whole lot easier to make the "adjustment" types of changes a little at a time as you go along in life as opposed to the more radical changes that are necessary as a result of not wanting to alter your behavior until it is too late to be able to see much positive results from any of the changes that you have to now undergo. Changes force us to admit that our previous habits and behaviors just might not have worked as well as we previously thought. This may explain why so many people are so resistant to making changes until it is painfully obvious that change needs to be made. One of the best and most effective techniques in maintaining necessary change is to use an accountability partner who can help you "keep score" of your ability to maintain until a new and better habit is formed. This accountability partner can be a spouse, family member, neighbor, coworker, or trusted friend who knows you and understands your desire to change and can act as your barometer to access and monitor your actions and the desired results. By using an accountability partner, you will know and understand the progress being made and be able to separate the self-imposed positive results from the reality of you actions. As stated earlier, change is part of the human behavior and what separates the prosperity builders from the mere prosperity seekers.

*Taken from the book entitled *SuperFreakonomics* by Steven D. Levitt and Stephan J. Dubner (2009)

It is not the strongest of the species that survive, or the most intelligent, but the one most responsive to change.
—Charles Darwin

Embracing Instead of Resisting Change

The ability to accept, adjust, and even embrace change is an ongoing, ever-evolving life skill and is the very basis for significant and long-term prosperity building. A person who adapts well to change regardless of the type of change can learn to create a so-called built-in "endurance machine" that adapts well to needed change. The capacity to rise above life's financial and other challenges and difficulties is the type of resilience that is necessary in building personal prosperity in your life. It is a fact that resilient people often can rise to the occasion and accept the changes to improve themselves, their surroundings, and their families.

Embracing change is a technique that can be learned by being able to teach ourselves to better deal with frequent challenges; and it creates a sense of self-confidence, better decision-making abilities, and a further sense of personal financial independence. This is one of the reasons that having a carefully scripted personal prosperity plan makes so much sense. It is a method to be able to document your long-term preparation and planning that can often referenced by yourself and others. It literally becomes your "blueprint map," showing where you are currently and what direction you want to go, including the exact route you will use to get you safely to your prosperity goal. This also involves the key ingredient—*change*. Recognize that it is not unusual to experience anxiety when you go through the change process. Some of the proven ways in dealing with this anxiety experience include the following:

1. **WRITE DOWN YOUR THOUGHT COVERING THE ISSUES INVOLVED.** Documenting your feelings and emotions regarding proposed changes that will affect you long term is a powerful method to adjust to contemplated changes. Journaling is another method to overcome any apprehensions or fears.

2. **EASE INTO CHANGE OVER A PERIOD.** None of the recommended steps in building personal prosperity have to be done overnight. Allow yourself the necessary time to get used to the idea and take slow steps in achieving the necessary proposed changes for your ultimate benefit. Numerous changes can have a tendency to overwhelm you so avoid making too many changes at one time.

3. **SEEK ACTIVE SUPPORT FROM OTHERS.** You are not alone in the change-making process. You have a spouse or life partner, family, trusted friends, professional support, and even others who can support you during this evolutionary process.

4. **IT'S NEVER TOO LATE TO UNDERGO CHANGE.** Regardless of your economic position, career/job/profession, age, or personal situation, remember that it is never too late to embrace change that

will improve your prosperity planning and results. Instead of running away from change, you can learn to meaningfully embrace change for its needed advantages.

5. **DEVELOP A KEEN SENSE OF INSIGHT.** Change involves moving away from being self-centered and selfishly using your pending prosperity for only personal gain. Think of ways that you can use positive change to help and improve other people's lives.

6. **SEEK NECESSARY HELP WHEN YOU NEED IT.** Occasionally, we all get off track. Smart people know when this happens and get the necessary help to be able to get back on track. Frequently, prosperous people travel in the same circles. This allows for support and networking closely with each other for mutual benefit.

7. **LEARN TO PUT EVERYTHING IN PERSPECTIVE.** Take a good look at your life now, your past, and where you want to be in the future. Remember the concept of the glass being half empty or half full and apply this to your prosperity-building plan. If necessary and useful, develop an inventory of advantages that the changes will have on you and the lives of those closest to you.

8. **<u>REFER TO YOUR PROSPERITY PLAN OFTEN.</u>** Having a clear idea of who you are, how you want your life to develop, and how you see yourself in the future provides the necessary motivational strategy as you are experiencing the change. Capitalize on your personal talents and skills, your uniqueness.

In the end, making the changes will create a sense of total freedom that you never before experienced in your life. It is not a simple or fast-moving event or without its share of challenges and efforts. Making the necessary changes in altering previous habits and behaviors will serve to create a new sense of purpose in your life that will result in positive prosperity building.

How to Make a Big Change in Your Financial Life

We all seek to improve certain aspects of our lives, and yet we could probably use a little help in the process.

Here are a few good tips on how to make a big, life-altering change in your life:

Go on Record with a new project, behavior, or habit. Publicly declare to spouse, family, friends, neighbors, and coworkers that you are ready to take on this new chapter in your life.

Create a Support Team and you will be far more successful than going it alone.

Make an Affirmation, such as "From this day forward, I will . . ." Download your goal and post it in your office, kitchen, bathroom mirror, locker, and car.

Tackle the Small Stuff by paying bills, returning e-mails, cleaning clutter, etc. Handling small tasks improves your self-esteem, and when you feel more effective, you are closer to your goal.

Get Through the First Thirty Days. Once you have reached this first milestone, you have set a precedent, and you are more apt to success on a long-term basis.

Above All, Do Not Give Up! Life is full of ups and downs. None of us should get too familiar with the high points since there seems to be always a corresponding low period. The secret to improving your life is through personal change.

Redirecting Your Efforts

When your dreams are shattered, how do you react? Often, your actions reveal your true character and even your faith in the future. Instead of giving in to self-pity and self-indulgency, you should be willing to redirect your efforts and your long-term prosperity plan to create a new path for yourself. This is one of the benefits of positive change that you will experience when you are faced with an economic challenge in any stage of your life. Change can result in redirecting your efforts in a completely different direction and perhaps even with an entirely different motive. Often, it is not a complete makeover that is needed or necessary. It is a realignment or recalibration that is needed. By closely examining the problem and its origins, it is conceivable to isolate the cause and effect, which can redirect your efforts in a completely different direction to help you achieve your prosperity ambitions. You don't always have to "wipe the slate clean" and create a literal "do-over." You might just simply have to "erase" a few things and redefine some of them. Having a good mentor, financial coach, trusted friend, or accountability partner can assist you in this entire process. These individuals are hard to find and, when obtained, should be cherished like gold. Each of them, depending on your personal situation, can help you get back on track and back to speed; yet you must be willing to have the gumption to make the needed changes and adjustments.

There are no step-by-step guidelines that will guarantee your prosperity success, but there are some general guidelines that can help you. Acknowledging the necessary change is one of those guidelines. In the end, much of life is about tradeoffs and compromises.

Change Boosters

It is hard to make a significant change in your life. You are bound to experience discouragement in your efforts to change. That is why you need some surefired change boosters. Some good tips are the following:

PARTNERS IN CHANGE. Some people may feel threatened by what you are attempting to do. Others will not believe that you will be successful in making your changes. Don't let their attitudes drag you down. Learn to spend more time with optimistic people and those who are also working on changes. Another good strategy is to seek those who have successfully completed a major change in their lives and ask them how they were able to succeed at change. These people will have the effect of inspiring each other!

REASONS TO CHANGE. Ideally, change happened from within, an internal desire, but you can look externally or outwardly for extra motivation. It is said that often, people will do more for others than we do for ourselves. Instead of accomplishing change for your own good, think about knowing what your change can do for others, including your spouse, family, and others.

VISIBLE CHANGE. Give yourself a vivid and brilliant reminder of the change you are choosing to make, something that you will view daily on your person, on your bathroom mirror, on your vehicle's dashboard, or on your computer at home or at work. This may take the form of a motivational quote, a note, or a letter from someone who cares about you or an image or photo. One glance at it will remind you of the purpose of your journey.

As we get older, it becomes increasingly obvious to each of us that change is never easy. It is hard work and demands a lot of effort and "intestinal fortitude." However, it can be achieved if you develop a successful strategy, and these tips can help you in the process.

Improved Prosperity-Building Changes

It is often the experience of many prosperity trainers that would-be prosperity seekers simply do not know how to change their existing personal financial habits and behaviors. They may not even know where to start. Making key fundamental changes can be a frightening experience for people who have to consistently set aside what they already know, even the status quo, for something that they may not yet completely understand or comprehend. However, at some point, to improve, we soon realize that we must try something difficult and that hopefully, it will produce better results.

The truth is that each of us has the ability to make the time and the changes for what is really important to us, especially if it involves progress toward prosperity and happiness. Indeed, financial freedom trumps many other life challenges. It is, however, up to you to find the best approach and personal formula that nurtures your individual prosperity building. To a large extent, our current perception of what to do with our prosperity building is largely shaped by banks, stockbrokers, insurance companies, and mutual fund companies, where advice is based far more on what is good for them and not necessarily what is good for us. This misinformation is the cause of frequent prosperity blunders. The secret in overcoming bad prosperity advice is with *prosperity education*, plain and simple. If you undertake prosperity education, you will soon discover that you are in the top 5 percent of everyone in terms of personal financial freedom. Ultimately, it is up to you to make your prosperity happen. After all, you are the one who will benefit from it in the end.

Making Really Important Personal Changes in Your Life

Many of us give up in our efforts to improve ourselves way too soon. Often, we do not allow the necessary time and space needed to make significant changes in our lives and merely assume that we cannot really change. Amazing transformations are possible. Here are some useful strategies to consider when making personal changes in your life:

- **HAVE FAITH THAT CHANGE WILL OCCUR.** Even if you seem trapped in the worst possible situation, don't lose hope. Change will happen. It is a fact that change is a basic and fundamental part of life.
- **FIND A SUPPORTER.** Someone who believes in you and sees your potential is your best support fan. Always remember that you are not alone in your desire for change. Having another person who sees your capabilities can produce encouragement and help to make up the difference between where you are presently and where you want to be.
- **ALLOW TIME FOR CHANGE TO HAPPEN.** Frequently, we underestimate the time that it will take for needed change to come about. If it has not come about in a few weeks, we give up and give in; we quit. You must have patience. It may take a few months or maybe even a year or two to undergo the transformation that you desire.
- **BE FLEXIBLE IN YOUR CHANGES TIMETABLE.** Do not give up on the changes you desire. Even though deadlines are important, it may be necessary to adjust them to compensate for a personal situation or event in your life. Carry your changes with you at all times in your heart and mind.

Changes in behavior are never easy, but if you have enough *desire* and *are committed* to achieving the positive results, change can and often does come about. Do not give up and do not ever quit. This is always the easiest thing to do but never produces any positive results.

Steps to Take in Creating Needed Change in Your Financial Life

To be able to grow and improve in your life and career, it's important to face some of the basic truths about ourselves. In the book *Talent Is Not Enough*, noted author and motivational speaker John C. Maxwell offers a formula to help us get through this difficult process:

- **_Identify the Issue_** – *Usually, it is something that we really don't want to hear about.*
- **_Recognize the Temptation_** – *Instead of confronting it, we may choose to want to ignore, rationalize, or even spin it.*
- **_Confront the Challenge_** – *Realize that change is not easy to undergo and that you will be tested daily.*
- **_Make a Decision_** – *To improve, it's necessary to face the truth, take personal responsibility and accountability, and make the needed personal changes.*
- **_Create a Positive Response_** – *Others may be slow to respond until they see your behavior change.*
- **_Validate Your Improvement_** – *Respect comes from others when they see your words and your actions coincide.*
- **_Realize That It Happens S-l-o-w-l-y_** – *Genuine growth and improvement is slow and doesn't happen quickly. It takes time as well as effort to make needed changes.*

CREATING THE TYPE OF CHANGE YOU CAN BELIEVE IN
<< *Key Things to Remember About Change 2.0* >>

Making any kind of changes in your life, big or small, can be fraught with identity crisis, financial stresses, and impatience to return to previous behaviors and habits. Taking such a leap of faith is never without risks. Change is often a good thing, and it's part of everyone's life. It is always easier and quicker when you can interact with others who have been through similar experiences and can relate to what you are attempting to do. Taking risks to follow your passions can often pay off. Don't worry about what others say and remember that you can succeed if you believe in your heart that you can do it.

Consider the following factors that were taking from the recent book *The First 30 Days: Your Guide to Making Change Easier* (2009) by Arianne de Bonvoisin, founder of first30days.com.:

- *Change is often a very good thing.*
- *Change happens to each of us and is an important aspect of life.*
- *Change creates an opportunity for you to grow in a new area.*
- *Change can mean that something good is about to happen.*
- *Change can bring new people, new opportunities, new developments, and new perspectives to your life.*
- *Change can help you strengthen yourself, boost your self-confidence, and improve your knowledge so that you can tackle anything in the future.*
- *Change is not a form of self-punishment.*
- *Change can allow you to understand or learn something new about yourself.*
- *Change can remind you to let go of a former habit or behavior that may have been holding your back.*

Understand That Many Personal Problems Are Often All About Finances

Money is how society values its goods and services. This is the method that we pay for those things in life that we value and that mean the most to us. We live in a much more complicated world today than what previous generations did twenty-five or thirty years ago. This is especially true when it comes to our personal finances and use of our money. In previous years, longevity after retirement was a far less period than what it is now largely because of health-care improvements. Currently, many of us can expect to live *after retirement* as long as we lived *during* our working years. This alone has completely changed how we look at our long-term financial preparation, planning, and especially when it is time to begin starting to save for retirement.

As a direct result of this, it is important today to create a long-term plan for this period in your post-working life and also for the income that you need to fund it and your lifestyle in future years. In addition, there are many other competing factors and events that will also become increasingly apparent as you reach that period in your life, such as the following:

- ✓ *Issues with aging parents*
- ✓ *Education and college funding for children*
- ✓ *Personal health-care issues and expenses*
- ✓ *Dependent children who may be living at home*
- ✓ *Monthly living expenses that arguably might not go down as much as you may think*

This all boils down to a strong possibility that many people might even have some financial problems that they do not even know about yet, much less have planned for over the years, such as the following:

❖   **Lack of effective long-term financial planning**
❖   **Overcoming bad financial advice and strategies**
❖   **Offsetting ill-suited investments**
❖   **Overcoming improper estimates of needed income production**
❖   **Creating increasingly higher levels of financial education**
❖   **Rebounding from bad economic period**

However, it should also be quickly mentioned that it is not *all* doom and gloom when it comes to repairing and improving your overall personal finances and planning. Often, it is possible to repair damages and to even put together a viable prosperity plan that will achieve good results and even better results over a period. Remember that *you* are the one who is *most affected* by your financial situation, so it makes good sense for *you* to do something to uncover some of the existing problems and issues that affect you. Unlocking the key to your financial personality is one of the steps that is necessary to begin your road to saving and investing. This is a compelling exercise that is included in this book in chapter 2. Another step is to correct any misinformation and misunderstanding that you may currently possess regarding personal finances and prosperity building. Even a modest bit of financial literacy training will serve to help you learn to change your habits and behaviors. This can result in better overall use of each of your money resources. Still, other steps include overcoming previously held beliefs and principles that might be deeply rooted in early childhood through witnessing how your parents handled their money in positive and negative ways.

Learning to Deal with Self-Inflicted Wounds (SIWs)

There are certain other common problems that are seen today in many people who have desire to build a higher level of personal prosperity that may include self-inflicted wounds that are a result of a bad financial decision in the past. These are created with individuals when one or more of the following occur:

1.   <u>THOSE WHO DO NOT EASILY UNDERSTAND THE MATH</u>

Most personal financial mathematics is relatively simple and involves the four basic functions of arithmetic: addition, subtraction, multiplication, and division. It is, however, made increasingly more difficult as you begin using other financial concepts, such as compounding, ratios, yields, gross and net earnings, portfolio gains, and others. The secret? Taking lots of notes, writing down personal questions (and the corresponding correct answers), using a preprogrammed software program or programs, and/or working with a patient prosperity teacher, advisor, or planner to know and understand how to effectively and efficiently do it are critical to successful achievement. In the end, learn to apply the concepts to your personal finance situation.

2. THOSE WHO HAVE EXTREME RISK VIEWS

These extreme views come in two forms: extreme low risk, which often results in minimal rates of return and usually borders on being too conservative and polar extreme, and high-risk investing, which can be compared to gambling and speculation. Each of these extremes will greatly affect your prosperity results. The optimum is in creating the *balance* that is ultimately needed.

3. THOSE WHO ARE COMPULSIVE SPENDERS AND HAVE EXCESSIVE DEBT

This is, sadly, one of the most frequent problems of many people today. It is caused by the abuse of credit cards and consumer loans to fund and supplement personal incomes and is a symptom of lifestyle that is essentially living beyond its means. In some cases, this often becomes a compulsive and addictive behavior.

4. THOSE WHO HAVE A POVERTY ATTITUDE

This view is more fully explained in chapter 4 and results in an imposed set of beliefs and values that are often are produced by bad economic decisions and poor choices made in the past and a feeling that your personal financial life will never improve or get any better. Furthermore, it is an attitude that your earnings are below your capabilities and are evidenced by frequent struggles with money.

5. THOSE WHO SQUANDER THEIR WINDFALLS

Each of us receives windfalls in life, not always the humongous winnings as a result of lottery, sweepstakes, or casino money consisting of hundreds of thousands or millions of dollars but rather the more modest dribs and drabs, such as year-end bonuses, profits from home sales, divorce settlements, sale of assets, inheritances, unexpected rebates, refunds, lawsuit settlements, insurance claims, and others. Instead of using the majority of this "newfound" money for long-term prosperity building, many use it for consumerism and short-term indulgences and wonder why their investments don't grow faster.

6. THOSE WHO HAVE AN UNWILLINGNESS TO CHANGE OR IMPROVE

This is the hardest personal finance situation and one that is all too common. This is realized by the individual who simply is unwilling to change or improve their money management behaviors and habits. It is this group of people that will undoubtedly struggle most with personal prosperity building because they fail to realize that small adjustments and adaptations in their money management and investing style can often result in large gains down the road.

<< Important Self-Analysis >>

It is important now, after studying each of these common financial problems, to do a little self-analysis. Often, we can recognize our shortcomings if we experience them face-to-face. Are there any of these problems that you feel that you have? If so, what do you feel is the solution to it/them? The answer to these questions is usually pretty straightforward and can greatly assist you in your continued prosperity building. As it has been explained before, it all starts with discipline and commitment.

The Need to Recognize Needed Changes in Your Financial Life
<< The Powerful Effects of Altering Your Present Condition >>

"An obstinate person does not hold opinions, but instead they hold them."

As we grow older, it becomes harder and harder to teach the proverbial dog any new tricks. After all, we often have taken a lifetime to build on our wisdom and experiences, yet we need to ask ourselves if those views, opinions, habits, and behaviors help or hurt you now. Have your routines become so ingrained that you cannot seem to break away from them to change, improve, and refine them to grow in the right direction? Human nature in the mid to latter stages of life is a compilation of many elements of patterns and behaviors that create a literal mosaic of who we are and what we want the world to think we are—successful or unsuccessful, prominent or just getting by, prosperous or less than prosperous, wise or uninformed, savvy or naive, or other qualities. For this reason alone, it is sometimes difficult to consider making a change in your life to improve it even if needed. Our stubborn personas may say one thing about us, but the reality might say another.

The beginning of this process is identifying the existence of a need to make a necessary change in your life. You can start by asking yourself if this is a major or minor change (the techniques are vastly different for each of them). You should also ask yourself the following when it affects your long-term retirement and financial planning: Are your finances in good order? Do you have enough income to meet your expenses? Do your investments meet your expectation for a comfortable retirement? Is your debt proportionate to your income? Do you have leftover or discretionary income to be able to enjoy your hobbies, leisure, and pastimes?

If the answer to any of these questions is "no," perhaps you need to consider making some needed changes in your financial life—sort of like starting a new exercise regimen—that will produce the needed results over time. It should also be mentioned that obviously, each of us wants the highest and best results possible; yet the formula and individual efforts will be uniquely different for each of us since no two of them are ever alike, just like your mother's favorite meat loaf recipe.

Useful Tips to Help Create Needed Changes

Like many other undertakings, it is helpful to have a solid strategy in undergoing needed change in your life. The alternative is a haphazard wandering that will not produce the needed results and can leave you with even more frustration than before. Having an effective set of techniques to use in creating these changes will significantly assist your efforts.

Some of the suggestions that need to be considered when making any needed changes in your life include the following:

- **Determine the Priorities** – An old Italian expression says, "He who chases two rabbits, will lose both." Instead of attempting to make major changes in many areas at one time, take the time to prioritize each of them and begin to work on one of them at a time. Once you have succeeded in overcoming one of your challenges, go on to the next one. Like all worthwhile activities in life, make sure to write down each of them and refer to your life often.
- **Exactly What Are the Real Issues?** – Issues and negative situations in life seldom occur by themselves. What is it that caused the problem? How did it start? Are there habits and behaviors that need to be altered and changed to prevent them from taking place in the future?
- **Take Inventory of Your "Sins"** – An honest assessment of your "addictions" and "compulsions" is a sure way to get to the bottom of the needed changes that you are considering. Often, these are at the very heart of the problem and must be gently peeled back one at a time to reveal the heart of the challenges.
- **What Are Your Goals and Objectives?** – What direction do you want to go and what system will you use to measure your success or

improvements? Keeping a chart or other records is one viable method to determine the velocity of your success in accomplishing the needed changes in your life.

- **What Are the Options and Alternatives?** – What happens when you fall short of your aspirations? What does your backup plan look like? How will you pull yourself up when you get off track? Creating alternatives and options is an effective strategy in making the needed changes.

- **Take a Close Look at Education and Training** – There are countless number of self-help books, materials, CDs, and DVDs available to help you in many areas affecting the improvements that you are attempting. Take time to carefully consider each of them and how they could assist you in progressively making the alterations that will result in the desired changes that you seek.

- **What Is Your Timetable?** – What is the length of time that you have established to accomplish your change goals? Many times, it is helpful to have a written idea of how much time you have given yourself to achieve a new behavior. Even if you arrive at the due date and need to adjust, it is useful to have a firm date in mind to make it a part of your overall goal.

- **Create a Support Group** – Support groups, such as your spouse, family, trusted friend, or accountability partner, can be sources for motivation and inspiration, which can be frequently used to remain on target. Sometimes just talking about the needed changes can bring about the renewed desire to continue improving. This allows you to be able to voice your frustrations and concerns, which allows you an ability to work together with others rather than alone. It is important to seek help when you feel discouraged. You should look for someone with experience in this critical area of your life and happiness.

It is important to remember that change is where improvements begin to take place. If all your past efforts are not working as well as you hoped they would, you may need to examine the need to make some personal changes to your previous prosperity strategies. It is all about planning and preparation. Some people are better at change than others. But it doesn't mean that you should not begin a process of making changes when they are needed to improve your life and your prosperity.

Somehow Avoiding Groundhog Day

For many people, change can often involve something similar to what happened in the movie *Caddy Shack*, where Bill Murray's character got up each and every morning and proceeded to go through the exact same routine over and over, and his life never ever changed. Unfortunately, this is the reality that many experience in their daily lives. In the real world, this virtual *Whack-A-mole* experience fails to produce the kind of results that can improve our lives. By continuing to address your life in this way, it can also end up resulting in a virtual replaying of events that can cause frustration, anxiety, and confusion and little, if any, improvement or needed change. The key to a more desirable result is *change*, and that process doesn't occur without effort and commitment. The first step, recognizing change, is often the one that people have the most trouble dealing with; yet with a little thought and strategy, it doesn't have to be something that is feared. Like all things that are good for us, however, there is no *gain* without a little *pain*. Although it may be only short-lived, the discomfort that we experience is often worth the effort.

Here Are Some of the Ways to Effect Needed Changes in Your Life:

1. **RECOGNIZE THE NEEDED CHANGES** – This is often the most difficult one for people to undergo. It is easy to postpone or sidestep needed changes in our lives, yet by doing this, we also run the risk of delaying the results. To secure success in the area of improvement, it is necessary to admit that there is a problem that exists.

2. **DOCUMENT THE ISSUE(S)** – Once you have decided that something must change, it's necessary to write down your perception of the problem in as much detail as possible so that you are aware of all the aspects of it. By documenting the problem, you formalize it and take responsibility for its solution.

3. **UNDERSTAND WHAT CAUSED IT** – Often, this will take some needed research and soul-searching since the issue might have started long ago, but it's very important to understand its root cause to prevent it from occurring in the future.

4. **REALIZE THE EFFECTS** – What are the short- and long-term effects of the problem in your life? Exactly how is it impacting your life, relationships, finances, and future? How will improving it positively affect you?

5. **WHAT ARE THE COMPONENTS?** – Often, a major problem has many components. Each of them frequently compounds the issue. What are they, and how do they interface with your particular situation?

6. **WHAT ARE THE POSSIBLE ALTERNATIVES?** – There is usually more than one solution to any problem. After giving it a lot of thought, what are some of the alternatives? List and prioritize them on a sheet of paper.

7. **WHAT IS THE BEST SOLUTION?** – This is not to be confused with the *easiest solution*. Many people error in thinking that the best

alternative is the fastest or the easiest one. Identify the best alternative for you.

8. **CREATE AN ACTION PLAN** – What are the specific steps that you must take to put your solution into place? What are the moves that you must make to see results?

9. **DISCIPLINE YOURSELF** – This is where most changes fail to take place. You must commit to a regimen of self-discipline to see and witness the results. This can involve creating a measurement or reporting system to monitor your success.

10. **CLOSELY MONITOR THE RESULTS** – The gains are probably not going to be huge at first; but over a few weeks or months, depending on the issue, you will start to see the needed results. Establishing a reward system to maintain your motivation to stay on track is also a viable option for many people.

Creating needed changes and improvements in life is never easy. After all, it may have taken years and years to create the situation that you may be dealing with, so it will not occur instantly. By following each of the above steps, however, you will be able to establish a game plan to ensure that your change will ever become permanent. Another option is to find an *accountability partner* who can help you maintain your focus, help you monitor your results, and share in your successes.

Learning Lesson:

It is far easier to change yourself than to wait for the rest of the world and its systems to change.

Change >> Transform >> Improve >> Succeed

CHAPTER 11

Spending Versus Investing Lifestyles

In this chapter, you will learn about the following points:

- _Defining Your World_
- _Unlocking Your Financial ID_
- _There Is an Ultimate Cost in Spending "How" and "When" You Want_
- _Determining Wants, Needs, and Nice-to-Haves_
- _The Delayed Consequence Effects_
- _Consumerism Definitions_
- _DEBT: A Four-Letter Word Meaning Too Much Spending_
- _Five Fundamentals of Prosperity Success_
- _Positive and Negative Emotions_
- _Improving Your Financial Habits_
- _The Reality of Fear of Prosperity Failure_
- _Replacing a Spending Habit with a Savings One_
- _Are Your Dollars Bruised and Stretched?_
- _The Secret Sauce to Your Personal Financial Success_
- _Larry's Prosperity Proverbs_
- _Finding Your Way_
- _Wise Money Use_
- _The Principle Finance Rule: Learn to Save Money_
- _How Much Should You Save?_

Defining Your World

<< *Choosing Your Personal Prosperity Lifestyle Destination* >>

When given a choice, who among us would not choose a prosperous lifestyle over any other one for all the obvious reasons? The next logical question then is what are you capable and willing to do to achieve it? The answers to each of these questions will serve to define your life and your world in the future. What really constitutes personal prosperity? Is it the size of your bank account or net worth, or is it the possibility of something that is even much greater than any of these? Is it the result of an attitude or of a carefully chosen wealth-building process, or is it instead the result of it? Is it a cautiously scripted personal formula for producing income or something else totally different? Is it achieved by earnings, investments, or securities, or is it a sort of secret financial recipe? Is it something that can be accomplished by anyone, or is it reserved for only a chosen few?

These many other questions, issues, and investigations are the subjects contained in this book in an effort to define, examine, and translate the true meaning of prosperity in twenty-first-century America; and furthermore, how it is still possible to achieve prosperity under the right circumstances and the correct amount of effort. This book serves to quiz and test you, the reader. It examines and challenges you while assisting you to formulate and design your own personal definition and interpretation of your prosperity building that is often characterized by individual goals and objectives. Prosperity building is a challenging, even daunting, experience in developing an individual and personal formula; yet it is also a journey that is full of personal examination, identity, creation, and exploration. For many, this may be the first time your personal prosperity building has been researched. For some, it provides a more in-depth observation and analysis of your life's ambitions and objectives. For others, this is a peek at the recipe formula that will help bring sustained and achievable financial and emotional success known as personal prosperity.

In the end, it is a journey that is both challenging and exciting; it digs deep into the very core of collective and individual initiatives and incentives. This is a thorough examination of the method, the means and the preparation steps that need to be taken to gain financial improvement and ultimate happiness in these troubled times. Finally, it is the essential blueprint map that has been used by much of the "old moneyed" individuals throughout history to create and accomplish their own prosperity and one that still works exceedingly well today.

Welcome to the ubiquitous, timeless world of personal prosperity building.

Unlocking Your Financial "ID"

The quintessential Dr. Sigmund Freud, the father of modern psychology, championed the term "unsatisfied ID," which was his concept of a selfish inner child that he said exists in each one of us. It is that inner child who wants desperately to be taken care of and to have all its wants immediately gratified. Is it possible to take this theory a step further and suggest that it is one of the factors that create impulsiveness and emotional personal spending habits and behaviors in many people? Is it reasonable to say that compulsive "spendaholics" are trying to satisfy an innate inner demand to placate the inner child in them?

Whatever the reason, it is a fact that personal spending must be controlled in an effective prosperity-building plan whether the reasons are psychological. Only when we are aware of its negative consequences can we offset the disastrous effects of impulsive and compulsive spending to your prosperity planning. Although Freud's theory is interesting, the effects of spending can wreak havoc to any personal prosperity plan. Without a disciplined approach to your spending habits and behaviors, you will constantly be struggling to find enough discretionary income (defined as the money that is left over after paying all your financial obligations) to be able to set aside for other investing and for your nest egg. Psychology or not, satisfying the inner self when it comes to compulsive spending is a *major* prosperity issue because if left unchecked, it will always result in creating more personal debt, which is the number 1 cause of all prosperity failure. There are many ways to control spending, but just like any other looming personal problem in life, you have to first recognize the problem before acting on it. One proven and effective technique is to ask yourself the following question before purchasing anything of value:

> *"If I had to write a check or pay cash for this item,*
> *would I still want to purchase it?"*

The answer to this question can be used as a highly effective technique that can serve to *qualify* many potential purchases and help you recognize if the purchase is a "want," a "need," or a "nice-to-have." *Try it. It really does work very well!*

There Is an Ultimate Cost in Spending "How" and "When" You Want

Most of us enjoy spending money on those things in life that bring us the most pleasure, such as vehicles, boat, RVs, clothes, furniture, appliances, jewelry, homes, and vacations. There is, indeed, something to be said for working hard, living within your means, and setting aside a portion of your net income for savings, investing, and long-term nest egg. In fact, those who follow a disciplined approach to money management and personal finances often have fewer problems developing a higher level of prosperity building as they become increasingly older than those who don't follow this practice. But what about the other percentage of people who spend their income resources on whatever and whenever they want and never seem to get around to developing any kind of short- or long-term prosperity plan? What ultimately happens to those individuals? The answer to these questions may lie in the "eureka moment" in life when they wake up one day in the future and realize that their spendthrift lifestyle has not created much or even any discretionary or leftover income to be able to grow their "prosperity tree" over the years. Worse, this defining moment often occurs when there is little timetable left to be able to react to the positive and proportional effects associated with compounding of any investment.

Instead of assuming the role of the proverbial "ant," these people have chosen to live the "grasshopper" lifestyle and fiddle away their prosperity until they suddenly realize that they may not have accumulated enough money resources and other investments to be able to live a comfortable lifestyle in their post-working life. It is never too late to start saving and investing in your life. Even those who are in their late fifties can develop a program that will result in building some degree of prosperity (albeit much less than the "ants" in life who have been saving for many years). When you look at the mathematics and numbers, it is so much easier to start an effective prosperity program at an early age, even at your very first job, by setting aside $100 or so each month than it is to try playing "catch up" much later in life because of the missed opportunities as a result of compounding.

The reality is that many never learn this at an early age, and when the "eureka moment" suddenly occurs, they are quickly trust into a panic mode and attempt to offset their lack of planning and preparation with a series of highly speculative investments that border more on gambling and good luck rather than well thought-out, educated investments, and it usually results in further personal economic disappointments. There is ultimately a cost for the grasshopper approach to prosperity building, so it is a far better strategy to develop a modest "pay as you go" program that gets you where you want to be throughout your life without affecting your lifestyle too much.

Determining Wants, Needs, and Nice-To-Haves

Many of us have fallen victim to the temptation of buying something that sounds like a good idea at the time but, in the final analysis, creates a personal financial hardship. This is especially true if it is something that you cannot really afford and had to charge it via a credit card of department store card. This is unfortunately one of the biggest problems facing consumers today. As Americans, we live in the greatest capitalistic nation in the free world and are not used to hearing the phrase "I can't afford it." It brings to mind depression-era situations and events where people survived with the barest of necessities. How does one address the issue and effectively draw the line between *wants versus needs and nice-to-haves?* What are the parameters that need to be considered when making large purchases and frequent smaller purchases that can add up to large purchases?

Here are some useful tips to use in making significant purchase decisions. By asking yourself these questions *in advance,* it might be possible to talk yourself out of that *must have* purchase and stall it off until you have the resources to pay for the item in full *(or you may even decide that you can really live without it):*

a.   *What is the fundamental reason that you are really considering the purchase? If necessary, could you document and write down the reason in fifty words or less? Would it make sense to a rational person?*

b.   *Can you afford to pay cash for the purchase? If not and you have to charge it on a credit card, can you afford to double or triple your monthly payments on the card for a few months to pay if off in a short period?*

c.   *Is the purchase being considered an investment in your life, or instead, is it an expense that you can really live without?*

d.   *Will the item be out of style in a year or less? Is it a fad purchase?*

e.   *Do you have to talk yourself into buying the item? If so, this is a huge indicator as to the nature of the proposed purchase.*

f.   *Is the item something that you will be tired of by the time you have finished making the payments on it? Or will it be out of vogue in six months or less?*

g.   *Will the item appreciate in value or simply depreciate after a year or so?*

h.   *Will your incentive to purchase the item or service become less or more if you wait forty-eight hours before purchasing it?*

i.   *Do your spouse, family, relatives, friends, and others support your buying decision, or will they not favor purchasing it? This is another key indicator.*

j.   *What will the effect be if the purchase is not made? How will it affect your lifestyle? What category is the item considered to be—a want, a need, or a nice-to-have?*

By being able to follow each of the above guidelines, it may serve to look at your major buying decisions more objectively and, at the very minimum, allow you to consider not purchasing it until you have enough cash to pay for the purchase upfront. *Remember, in the end, it's all about making your money go as far as it can, isn't it?*

The Delayed Consequence Effects

When the rewards and punishments come quickly after a behavior in a young person's life, the rationales between cause and effect are unmistakable. When you become an adult, however, your life becomes increasingly more complex; and the consequences of your prosperity planning are not always as immediate or even visible. When your future becomes jeopardized because of erratic spending, it can seem that it is of little importance until you sit down and look at the results of your lifelong spending behaviors.

The far-range effects of failure to plan and prepare become more visible and more apparent the closer you get to the "big R"—retirement; and without the responsibility and discipline to get it going at an early age, you might have less to look forward to than many others. Delayed action is better than inaction, but it must be remembered that a few simple steps can make all the difference. Some of the techniques include the following:

- ➢ *Start your savings and investing early in life.*
- ➢ *Set aside at least 10 percent of your net pay to use for your plan.*
- ➢ *Live within a defined spending budgetary plan.*
- ➢ *Read and study to equip yourself better financially.*
- ➢ *Educate yourself to boost your personal finance IQ.*
- ➢ *Remember that it is never too late to do it.*
- ➢ *Don't quit! Ever! It can be done. Everyone can succeed!*

Consumerism Definitions

1. **SHOPARTUMIST** – An individual who looks for opportunities to spend money lavishly on virtually anything at any time without regard as to whether they can afford it.
2. **FASHIONISTA** – An individual who is fashion conscious and must always be in touch with the latest designs, clothes, furnishings, jewelry, technology, vehicles, or even homes.

Does either of these sound familiar to you or anyone you know?

Earning Versus Spending

Almost any man or woman knows how to earn money; but not one in a million knows how to spend it.
—Henry David Thoreau, Writer and Philosopher

Morale:

Debt exists because you spend more than you earn. Debts are a
symptom of a spending habit.

DEBT: A Four-Letter Word Meaning *Too Much Spending*

Of all the prosperity-building hurdles and pitfalls, none of them will wreak
more havoc on your personal economic success than this particular issue. No
matter what your income or asset level knowing how to effective deal with debt
can be a convincing prosperity lesson for each of us. However, did you know that
debt can work in your favor and that good things can actually happen when you
incur debt? It is because essentially there is such a thing as good debt and bad
debt and prosperity builders need to know and understand the effective use of
each of them in order to achieve their goals and ambitions. Ignorance of these
fundamentals differences can often result in a major negative financial impact
over a lifetime. *In this writing, I am going to briefly explain both bad debt and good debt
and give the reader some compelling reasons how to distinguish between each of them so
that you know and understand how each of them are created.* I will also demonstrate
to you what the effects are to your prosperity plan long-term-wise. A thorough
knowledge of the differences between these types of debt can, alone, alter and
improve your prosperity-building efforts over your life.

*First, let's start with bad debt since that seems to be the cause for so many personal
finance failures and economic calamities.* Bad debt can be broadly defined as a term
referring to consumer debt. This is the personal debt that is created through
the use of credit cards, department store cards, and other types of buying and
spending methods. It often includes wasteful or even frivolous shopping and
spending for items and merchandise that depreciates quickly in value or have
no long-lasting effect (other than perhaps memories). Some examples of this
type of debt are expensive clothes, furniture, vacations, trips, high-cost autos,
vehicles, expensive gifts, boats, costly jewelry, regular attendance at major
sporting events, and other similar types of expenses. Often the use of credit
cards for these types of expenses is a signal that the purchaser cannot really
afford to be buying this type of merchandise and therefore it must be paid via
borrowing money a/k/a credit cards.

It should also be mentioned that paying too many taxes is also a sign of bad
debt since it is an indicator that you have not taken the precautions of building
a viable tax-minimization strategy to offset the tax liability you are responsible
for. Granted, taxes do pay for many municipal and governmental services at the
local community, state, and national level but you are legally responsible for
only paying your *fair share* of them and overpaying taxes is not a cause of good
debt. Bad debt has a tendency to snowball creating the need for HELOC (home

equity lines of credit) loans, remortgages, personal loans, and other types of borrowing. When studied, those that make a habit of regular borrowing of these categories of expenses are the ones most affected when there is an economic slowdown. The result is what we have witnessed as a result of the economic downturn over the past few years in America. Those with significant consumer debt are the ones most affected by this situation.

The critical difference between the issues of affordability of each of these items is whether or not you can pay cash for each of them or pay them off when you receive the bill in the mail at the end of the month on your credit card statement. However affordability in and of itself is not necessarily a key indicator that they are good investments in your income. This is especially true when you consider that, by comparison you could be investing this *disposable income* in some sort of investments that will pay regular dividends and will appreciate over a longer period of time. *What is the best description of good debt and how does it impact each of us.* Good debt can be best explained as debt that is assumed by an individual that will produce income and/or will produce an asset that *appreciates over time.* This is the type of debt that does not go down in value, but instead, goes up in value. Obviously, there are fewer of these types of items available as compared to bad debt but in order to build long-term prosperity in your life, you must know and recognize what they are.

Specifically, they include your home and other real estate investments such as rental homes, condos, duplexes, foreclosed property, and tax lien certificates to mention only a few; an assortment of several types of small business investments; tools and equipment if they are used to produce an income stream for you; and other paper investments such as those that are found in the stock or bond markets. *Virtually anything that can be considered as a good source of income-producing can be considered good debt.* Even insurance coverage, since it has the effect of protecting your personal and business assets, can even be categorized as good debt. Education for you, your spouse, or children, is also acceptable good debt as the end-result positively affects the effort in building a greater amount of wages and income for you over your lifetime.

Five Fundamental Requirements of Sustainable Prosperity Success

By following each of the following fundamentals, you will create a solid prosperity-building foundation that will serve to benefit you from an early age all the way through your second career and retirement years.

These are the keys to developing the type of financial strategies that will work for you throughout your lifetime. If you ignore even one of them, it will result in greatly affecting your personal prosperity success:

1.   *Discipline yourself to consistently save or invest at least 10 percent of your monthly net (take-home)   earnings.*

2.   *Create adequate income to support your lifestyle and learn to live within your means.*

3.   *Begin funding your retirement through various investments at an early age in life.*

4.   *Purchase a home that is proportionate to your earnings and add other real estate property investments over time.*

5.   *Keep your credit cards and consumer loans at an absolute minimum.*

Seven Positive Emotions

- Desire
- Faith
- Love
- Sex
- Enthusiasm
- Romance
- Hope

Seven Negative Emotions

- Fear
- Jealousy
- Hatred
- Revenge
- Greed
- Superstition
- Anger

Improving Your Financial Habits

A habit is a "mental path" that your actions have traveled over for some time. Each passing makes the path a little deeper, a little wider, and a little stronger. As humans, we all have them, the very good and the not so very good. Good habits are the result of repetition along a certain well-worn path. Consider a piece of paper that is folded a certain way that will fold along the same lines the next time it is folded. A pair of well-worn gloves will form into creases according to the hands of the person who uses them. New machinery is optimized only after it has been "broken in," proving this law is in operation everywhere. Old habits are hard to break and are best removed when new ones are created to replace them. Each of our daily lives is a result of a series of habits, good and bad. Much of our effectiveness can be significantly improved when we take a hard look at our various daily habits and see how they can be changed to improve our changes and opportunities for success.

Ask yourself if you have any of the following habits, and if so, what can be done to improve or eliminate them:

- *Wasting too much time*
- *Watching too much TV*
- *Sleeping too much*
- *Eating too much*
- *Exercising too little*
- *"Playing" too much*
- *Involvement in too much trivia*
- *Talking instead of listening*

If your answer to any of the above is "yes," then consider one or more of the following "replacement" habits:

- *Reading or studying more*
- *Exercising more*
- *Writing more letters*
- *Creating personal goals*
- *Engaging more in worthwhile activities*
- *Use self-help materials*

The process of just adding <u>one good habit</u> can significantly increase your daily productivity and level of success while making the world of difference in the overall outcome. The habit, an act repeatedly performed in the same manner, has a tendency to become permanent; and eventually, one performs the act automatically and unconsciously.

Think About It!

Typical Problems Resulting from a Lack of Financial Literacy

➢ **Low income**
➢ **Lack of budgeting of income and expenses**
➢ **Absence of a tax strategy**
➢ **High living expenses from impulsive spending**
➢ **Excessive debts through materialism**
➢ **Poor financial advice**
➢ **Flirting with bankruptcy**

➤ **Possibility of foreclosure**
➤ **Sadness, hopelessness, despair, anxiety**

And worse yet, these same people don't even think that they have a problem. They simply hope that something will change in their lives and fail to realize that *they are the ones who have to change!*

Blame It on the Lack of Money

Have you ever noticed how hard it is to change old emotional habits and how easy it is to blame all your emotional problems on money or the lack of it?

For Example:

"I would have become a _____, but there wasn't any money in it." Or "I would have done _____, but I couldn't afford to do it."

Morale:

Either money will be allowed to dictate the terms of your life or you will. Either you will blame your failures on the lack of money or you will accept your failures and use money to get back on track again.

The Reality of the Fear of Prosperity Failure

One of the biggest secrets in building your personal and prosperity success is to learn how to look failure in the eye and not blink an eyelash. The reality in this process is that the fear of failure can often become a self-fulfilling prophecy and cause you to err on the side of too much caution or self-doubt and back away when you should charge ahead full speed. The more you dwell on your deficiencies, the more pronounced they will become. Even though it is difficult at times to act confidently when it seems that all your creativity and ideas are being turned down, your top investments have tanked, or you or someone in your family develops a health problem or issue, you have to somehow, someway shrug it all off and learn to take it in stride. Things will get better. It's literally always darkest before the dawn, and perhaps it's just the prosperity gods testing you again to see if you can survive all of it. Besides, the anticipation of success can become a self-fulfilling factor too. Success can be elusive, it seems, but practicing the key principles that you've learned to get through the ups and downs in life will help you get through these difficult periods. It isn't a record income or single investment returns, but as you struggle to maintain your head above water in those first critical years, it's good to remember that many others also have walked this path before, and they have undoubtedly experienced the same trials and tribulations as you are experiencing now. You must remember that you are building a carefully constructed and unique formula in your prosperity building, and at some point in the journey, you will begin to see a return on your physical, mental, and capital investment to offset all the anxieties, risks, and hardships. This is when it's time to reflect on the many times that you were discouraged, disheartened, and even considered giving up; but as time goes along, it really does start to become less of a struggle and more of a fight to keep your prosperity moving in the right direction. It seems that building it is difficult, yet keeping it away from predators and those who would take advantage of your hard work is just as challenging.

Now aren't you glad you didn't give up the first time that things didn't go your way and you thought of failing more than succeeding?

Replacing a Spending Habit with a Prosperous, Saving One

Overcoming the "debt monster" can be accomplished one step at a time by replacing a **spending habit** with a **saving habit**, which will serve to redirect your overall efforts toward financial prosperity and independence. The long-term results of this transition will significantly add to your success and accomplishments in the area of personal finance and wealth building.

We Are All the Victims of Our Habits

The process of saving on a regular basis a portion of your net income each week or month is a significant step in accomplishing this process even if your initial savings is only a few dollars to start. Very soon, this new habit will begin to take on a life of its own, and you will actually begin to find great joy in watching your savings account grow each month. In addition, this new habit will be the beginning of your new wealth-building strategy since if you seek to control spending and create savings simultaneously, it will result in the ability to save more money each week/month.

The Overall Effects of Inflation Over Fifty Years
<< Making It Personal >>

Factoid®

In 2008, it costs $7,398.45 to buy what you could

have purchased in 1960 for $1,000.

This Is, Indeed, the Hidden Cost of Inflation for Each and Every One of Us!

The Real Questions Is This: *What Are You Doing to Offset Its Effect on Your Prosperity-Building Efforts?!*

Effective Inflation-Fighting Techniques

Inflation is a continuing factor in any prosperity-building plan. By definition, it is an increasing cost at a decreasing value. Simply put, it is a declining level of our currency based on many factors out of our control, and it has a tremendous effect on every part of personal finances at every stage of life. As a direct result of this, you need to have an effective method for combating its effect on your personal prosperity-building plan. Some of the best techniques are the following:

- *Make every effort to maximize and maintain your cash flow and income.*
- *Learn more advanced techniques to offset such things as taxes through charitable giving and gifting.*
- *Use a system of trusts and family foundations to isolate assets that have favorable expense treatment and are more favorable to heirs and family members.*
- *Avoid passivity even in retirement. Stay engaged in your life and personal finances.*
- *Adjust your asset allocation to create liquidity to be able to seize opportunities as they appear (example: the real estate foreclosure market).*
- *Maintain a check list of contingency plans to prevent lost opportunities.*

Are Your Dollars Bruised and Somehow Stretched Out of Shape?

It's an obvious reality that it is becoming more and more costly every year to just be able to make ends meet and get by paying off our mortgage, buying food, making vehicle payments, paying those pesky taxes (these are typically referred to by me as the *big four*), raising our children, and trying to have a little fun along the way. It's also an unfortunate fact today that our money has really taken a beating for many reasons, especially in the last ten years, as a result of inflation and deflation and the effects of the various markets, including the stock market and the real estate market. This especially hurts *boomers* as they continue to approach retirement and seek knowing if they have set aside enough already and if what they have set aside will sustain them over the next twenty or thirty years. What are the techniques and strategies that you have in place to offset the effects of inflation and higher costs of living (you do have some of them in place, don't you, and I am not referring to only Social Security and Medicare benefits)?

As you get closer and closer to the time when you are less dependent on earning a regular working wage and more dependent on the results of your savings and investing, it becomes increasingly important to access each of the facets of your retirement plan and see where it can be tweaked and improved to provide the ultimate personal benefits for you in the years to come. If you have been one of those unfortunates who have not done much to set aside funds for the final period of your life, there is still hope. Realization of the potential problem is the first step in solving it. Some of the options available to you are the following:

- *Review your 401 (k) and other investments. Are they growing or shrinking? Should you be thinking about switching the poor performers and receive a tax benefit for doing this?*
- *Are there some investments that you have not yet been involved with? There are lots and lots of investment choices, and your risk tolerance and long-term plans are two of the elements of making other choices.*
- *Is your stockbroker and portfolio manager more of a salesperson than a performer? If so, maybe it's time to look for another one and transfer your investments. Fortunately, there are many choices available to you.*
- *Have you looked into the possibility of starting a small business? For many people, this can be the passionate pursuit as well as additional income stream that propel them through their retirement years.*
- *Are you getting hit hard with taxes? There are many, many options for minimizing personal taxes, yet it's important to know not only what they are but also how to implement them. This can be achieved by finding a good tax or financial advisor and good ones like other good professionals are challenging to find.*
- *Should you think about downsizing your home and using some of the equity dollars to invest in your retirement portfolio?*
- *What is your debt ratio? How much do you owe on credit cards? Is now a good time to look at paying down some of your disposable personal debt and entering retirement* **with a more minimal amount and reining in some of your spending?**

These are just a few methods and options that can be considered in this upcoming important phase of your life. The choices that you make now will certainly impact the next few years and your ability to enjoy a comfortable lifestyle or experience more bruising and stretching of your hard-earned dollars.

The SECRET SAUCE to Your Personal Financial Success!

The results of your efforts will be a state of personal financial freedom that will create an even greater degree of self-confidence for you. Once this habit has been firmly in place for a period (six months to a year), it will come as no great surprise that your financial problems begin to disappear, and you will enter into a period of financial success that you may have never visited before. In short, the accumulation of personal financial resources will not be difficult once you have mastered the savings habit even though personal success is not achieved or measured by net worth alone. *It does take money to live.* It is a cold, harsh fact that money has an important place in the materialistic society in which we live, and it cannot be overemphasized that life is much better when one has the necessary resources to finance their lifestyle whatever that might be. It doesn't matter the level of intellectual strength either when that strength is without money. **Simply stated, the person who does not have sufficient financial resources is at the mercy of those who do possess financial resources; and this is, unfortunately, without exception regardless of any skills, talents, or know-how.** This is the origination of the term "starving artist," one who has lots of talents but no way to earn a living from it.

Often, right or wrong, it is the standard of which many people are judged in the twenty-first-century democratic world. Those with significant financial resources are lionized by the general public as contrasted to those who are living paycheck to paycheck or are impoverished or even appear to be so. Can this be the reason that many choose the **perception of wealth** by adorning themselves with the "bling" of materialism instead of creating true wealth by the accumulation of real assets?

Larry's Personal Prosperity Proverbs

A Guide to the Thirty-Four Absolutes That Are Necessary in Building Your Personal Prosperity

The following is a list of the thirty-four dyed-in-the-wool prosperity precepts that will enable you to become more effect at the game of prosperity building in your life. Each of them has been carefully chosen by me as a result of witnessing an increasing level of prosperity in my own life and that of others. By following each of these time-honored proverbs, you will begin to see your prosperity increase over time. If necessary, photo copy this page and put it in a place where you can refer to it often and frequently. It is the Bible of prosperity success for each of us. As you go through the list, mentally check the ones that you are already good at doing and circle the ones that you could stand to improve in your life. No one is perfect, but knowing what the eventual effects will be if you follow them will help motivate you in your success-building efforts.

1. *You must become effective at making good decisions.*
2. *You must learn to know how to plan and organize yourself and daily schedule.*
3. *You must have documented and specific goals, along with an effective strategy to enable you to achieve them.*
4. *You must learn how to recognize good opportunities and be able to seize on them for long-term growth and success.*
5. *You must routinely build on your knowledge of prosperity building by regularly maintaining your prosperity education.*
6. *You must understand that hard work in your chosen job/career field is more important than being first in your class.*
7. *You must learn to understand and recognize value in what you buy and in what you do.*
8. *You must realize that the biggest investment you will ever make in your life is the one that you make in yourself.*
9. *You must know how to be able to effectively bargain and negotiate for what you want and what you are willing to pay for it.*
10. *You must know when to seek guidance and advice and who you can trust.*
11. *You must learn how to make the necessary improvements and changes that will positively affect your life and future job/career success.*
12. *You must constantly hone your prosperity tools and not learn to rely on others.*
13. *You must avoid materialism, bling, and false appearance of true prosperity.*
14. *You must learn to embrace and somehow overcome your fears.*
15. *You must be able to separate disinformation from sound reality, practicality, and common sense.*
16. *You must begin creating a sound nest egg for retirement early in life.*
17. *You must understand that it's far easier to buy something than to try and sell something.*
18. *You must realize that significant prosperity success is not a solo flight.*
19. *You must never quit. If you don't succeed at first, you must learn to try, try, and try again.*
20. *You must maintain a manageable personal debt and create a monthly budget or spending plan with your income that avoids consumerism and overspending.*
21. *You must understand that building a high level of prosperity takes time and that it's more than just about money.*
22. *You must understand what passive income is, such as real estate investments and financial securities, and the many advantages of them in building your long-term prosperity success.*
23. *You must understand that twin engines of prosperity success are real estate investments and a small business enterprise.*

24. *You must thoroughly learn how to make your money and earnings work for you instead of frivolous spending.*

25. *You must build a professional advisory A-Team and know which experts you can trust.*

26. *You must comprehend the difference between poverty thinking and prosperity thinking.*

27. *You must develop and maintain a good credit and a high FICO score by paying all your obligations on time and not utilizing all your available credit.*

28. *You must understand the difference between a spending and an investing lifestyle.*

29. *You must thoroughly comprehend how to make your money, income, and resources work for you.*

30. *You must possess the right motivation to want to do better and realize that it isn't all about money and assets.*

31. *You must learn how to create your unique, customized personal prosperity formula that will create your long-term achievements.*

32. *You must learn that prosperity building is an ever-changing educational environment and be willing to add to your knowledge on a regular basis.*

33. *You must understand that inheritances, lotteries, and gambling are not prosperity plans.*

34. *You must realize that procrastination is the venerable death wish of prosperity building.*

Finding Your Way in Prosperity

Some of your may have a decent sense of direction, but there may be certain times when you get lost and for specific reasons. If you glance at two points on a map, you may get a general idea of the direction that you want to go; and if you make the mistake of plunging into the journey without the necessary planning and preparation, you should not be surprised if you end up becoming lost. Sometimes your method to get back on track works, but at other times, it fails. It frequently fails when you are driving "in the dark" and a darkness that you had not thought to even plan for. The most aggregating type of lost, however, occurs when you know that your destination is in sight, over there, just beyond the mountains; but you cannot seem to figure out the way to get there. You may even be able to see the mark that you are aiming for, but the right road seems to elude you. Why do we get lost? It's often because we assume that we have our destination firmly under control at all times and forget that there are many things that happen to us in our lives or in our work that can mysteriously force us off the beaten track and into the jungle and serve to create barriers in being able to find our way again. Ultimately, we find ourselves in the dark.

We become proud. We ignore the guidance that may even be at our fingertips waiting to be utilized.

The good news is that it's a wonderful feeling to find your way again after being lost. Sometimes it's just a matter of tweaking your technique, your style, your implementation, or your goals. Other times, it requires more of a major investment in time, effort, and energy to get back where you need to be. In either case, when you consider the consequences, isn't it worth it to get the type of help you need to find your way out of the jungle?

Wise Money Use

Having reserve funds is absolutely essential to the successful operation of any household or business. Period. Seizing good opportunities that are available for those with cash is one distinct advantage, and having an emergency fund to counter an unexpected fiasco is another. It is a fact that the money that slips through one's fingers in a given month can eventually bring financial independence if one creates a savings habit. It is startling to see what the effects of the compounding value of a meager savings account (one that can eventually be used later as an investment vehicle with higher returns) can realize if only one has the self-discipline to begin the process. The prerequisite is the **willingness** to stop useless spending and start the savings habit.

It is simply not true that people can become prosperous by saving a certain percentage of their income each month. The accompanying charts prove that this process does, in fact, work for anyone who is willing to do it on a regular and consistent basis. This fact is something that should be taught in every school system in America, and no high school student should be allowed to graduate without taking a course in financial literacy and the powerful effects of saving and investing money, this author feels. It is positively amazing the amount of money that can be saved without any of the usual habits of gambling, drinking, drugs, and excessive entertainment (which are all sure to destroy one's character too) and **especially significant** when one considers the effects of compounded money when you are on the **receiving end** versus when you are on the **giving end**. *We are not teaching morality here; we are teaching personal finance.*

THE PRINCIPLE FINANCIAL #1 RULE: *Learn to Save Money!*

It is a proven fact that if a person creates and follows a habit of saving a portion of the money they earn or receive by inheritance or windfalls, they will eventually place them in a position of financial independence. **If, on the other hand, they fail to do that, they are sure to never be financially independent regardless of their income.**

The reverse of this is equally true—watching your spending. The more one earns and spends, the further one gets from financial independence since spending money as fast as one makes it is not a formula for financial success either. Unfortunately for many, money gained easily is often spent easily. By performing both functions of saving and controlling spending, one is well on their way to financial independence. As we all know, there is nothing as humiliating and causes more suffering an agony as poverty in old age when your personal and professional services are no longer marketable, and you must rely on governmental assistance and relatives for existence. To admit that one lacks the courage to cut monthly expenses to save money is the same as admitting that one lacks the desire to be a success in any other aspect of one's life.

How Much Should You Save?

The eternal question that arises is always how much savings is enough? Generally speaking, *saving 10 to 15 percent of your net weekly/monthly net income* on a regular, consistent basis is enough to create a viable nest egg for savings, investing for retirement. Obviously, anything more than this is of greater benefit to you, and anything less than this becomes proportionately less beneficial since it will require much more time to build. The important point to remember is to start the savings habit *now*! Unfortunately, many parents do not teach their children good financial savings habits, and they effectively teach them the wrong habits by overindulgence and materialism. Going from a consumer attitude of spending to a savings attitude of accumulating may be difficult but, in the end, is the essential step in building a significantly higher level of personal prosperity and lifestyle.

CHAPTER 12

Learning The Art Of Real Prosperity Giving to Others

> ## Noble Ironies
>
> *It is ironic that only the well-to-do and the very poor—*
> *Those with everything and those with nothing—*
> *Both have the time, the motivation, and the inclination,*
> *To dedicate their lives to pursuits of the highest order.*
>
> —L. S.

Your Prosperity Inheritance

E arlier in this book, the word "prosperity" was defined as the fulcrum or "tipping point" where one begins to understand and adapt to a better balance between giving and receiving in life. It is, literally, the process of realizing and learning that true prosperity in life has an ultimate price: the capability of time, resources, income, and freedom to be able to create many life-changing situations and events both with and for other people. The history of American prosperity is replete with numerous examples of prosperous individuals, such as J. P. Morgan, Andrew Carnegie, J. Paul Getty, Henry Ford, W. K. Kellogg, John D. Rockefeller, and Cornelius Vanderbilt, while more recently, Ross Perot, Bill Gates, Warren Buffet, and many others who reached the pinnacle of financial achievement and started a detailed path of philanthropic giving to others. Each of them created a unique and personal method of giving that helped define them more than the wealth they had accumulated.

Prosperity giving can take on many forms, including volunteerism, charitable contributions, mentoring, youth leadership programs, fund-raising for passionate pursuits, and even large-scale capital and venture philanthropy. They are all based on individual levels of personal prosperity, willingness, motivation, and time availability. Indeed, for many people in this situation, it has become virtually a second-career calling that has the effect of creating a sense of purpose in their senior years. It frequently then becomes their passionate pursuit. The beauty of it is that it can be done on the giver's own time and terms, making it a distinctive pursuit. The personal choices for prosperity sharing are as unique as the formulas used to build their personal life fortunes. It can also be a carefully designed composite of many various selections. Today's prosperity builders are truly creative and imaginative in their choices of giving options. Many of them even choose to work directly with the involved charities and use their lifelong entrepreneurial or professional strengths and skills to add personal value to their causes. Often, it is challenging to understand many of the compelling reasons to give. After all, isn't the result of your prosperity building the reason that you worked, saved, invested, and created it in the first place? Many ask themselves the question of why they should even consider giving it away to others who they may or may not know when they have sacrificed their entire lives to be able to afford a comfortable lifestyle.

The answer to this question is virtually the same response that people give when they are asked why they give to their church or to a fund-raiser at work because of a personal tragedy, to the police and fire departments' annual charity drive, or to one of the most successful character-building organizations of all time, the Boy Scouts of America. Simply put, it is the act of *giving*, and each of us *receives* something from that giving. It is the heartfelt appreciation from those in need that really makes the effort worthwhile for those who can afford or maybe even not be able to afford to give. Looking back at antiquity, even the Egyptian pharaohs eventually learned that they couldn't take their worldly treasures with them to the next life as evidenced by the vast amounts of gold and jewels left with them in their tombs. Despite all the pomp and circumstance that was a part of their life or death and by virtue of even building one of the wonders of the ancient world, the pyramids, the ruler's treasure eventually either was discovered next to their mummified remains or was looted by tomb robbers. Despite their power and influence, even they could not take it with them to the next life.

Giving Plan Lessons to Be Learned

The learning lesson here is that perhaps you should consider developing a detailed "giving plan" as a part of your overall prosperity building. Keep in mind that no one says that you have to give all or even a substantial part of it (even though it will always be graciously accepted by others). But maybe you could even consider giving a percentage of it as your personal act of giving in your estate planning. Creating a carefully constructed estate plan is fundamental to both being able to use your existing and future prosperity and being able to witness your prosperity plan at work and even planning what to do with it at death. Studies have shown that it is arguably never a good idea to leave *all of it* to your family or children since they each need to learn how to build their own prosperity too, just as Bill Gates and Warren Buffet have done with their own families.

By carefully selecting several charitable causes and even possibly becoming involved in them in your post-working years, you can help to qualify each of them for your personal acts of giving. Some of the formal, legal strategies that can be used to achieve this include the following:

- ✓ *Family Limited Partnership (FLP)*
- ✓ *Charitable Remainder UniTrust (CRT)*
- ✓ *Revocable and irrevocable trusts*

✓ *Living trusts*
✓ *Family and community foundations*
✓ *Wills and other estate planning documents*
✓ *Other forms of protection and distribution*

Obviously, the extent that you use formal entities depends largely on the size of your personal estate or prosperity; but by taking time *throughout your life* to work with a professional advisor to plan your prosperity inheritance, it allows your preparation to become a reality even if your demise is unexpected. An annual meeting with a prosperity planner or financial advisor can permit the essential planning for the ultimate act of giving. Once again, planning is essential toward the ultimate results.

The planning stage is also a great way to engage family members, including spouse and children or others, in being able to discuss life, career goals, and objectives while freely communicating personal interests and strategies that can be used to achieve them. It also is an effective way to be used in funding many of these goals later in life. Estate planning is a valuable tool in virtually anyone's prosperity-building plan. It is highly recommended and can be used quite effectively in accomplishing your personal prosperity goals. Without proper planning, a lifetime of hard work, sacrifice, and asset building becomes at risk. For that reason, it is necessary to commit your dreams and long-term aspirations into formal, written documents so that each of them can be carried out and fulfilled. It is the final step in the prosperity process that should not be overlooked.

The Essential "Tipping Point" of Prosperity Achievement

In this book, we introduced you to a phrase that we previously used and termed the "tipping point" in one's personal prosperity plan. It is defined as the critical point where one develops a healthy and meaningful balance between both "giving" and "receiving" in their prosperity building and in their individual lives. It is where it is finally recognized that a prosperous life is not only all about "getting" but also involves "giving." It is when we reach this period that we have finally achieved ultimate and true prosperity regardless of income, assets, or net worth. It is at this point that you can use your personal resources and prosperity to make positive personal changes and improvements in other people's lives. Most of us are familiar with the eighteenth-century British character, Ebenezer Scrooge, in the Charles Dickens annual Christmas novel *A Christmas Carol*. Ebenezer Scrooge was transformed from a life of self-indulgence, personal greed, manipulation, and abuse of his employees and others into a generous, warm, caring, and giving individual. It was through the act of being finally able to look at himself and his greedy acts and deeds by experiencing a series of dreams that revealed to him who he *really was*, a petty, selfish skinflint who took advantage of everyone he came in contact. Dickens metaphorically used the Scrooge character in the book to emphasize the added value of true prosperous giving: *true happiness in life.* Perhaps this is also the reason that this Christmas classic has endured for so many years. It somehow defines the constructive use of prosperity.

Although there have been countless books written on the ubiquitous subject of personal happiness in life, Dickens did one of the best jobs in defining it for us in this classic story that chronicles a selfish rich man's "eureka moment" when the life of a penny-pinching lonely old man forever changed into a responsible giver of his wealth and material resources to help others as opposed to being only a receiver of life's goodness and financial rewards. We have each experienced "Scrooges" in our lives. They can best be described as those who are hell-bent on reaching the top of the economic or bureaucratic power scale. They are those who will climb over anyone for any reason to improve themselves and their status while carelessly injuring many other in the process. Sadly, when or if they reach a level of wealth creation where they could be satisfied to even enjoy their efforts, they often have developed such a case of "gold fever" that they are unable to enjoy their money and other personal resources.

Often, these individuals have few other passions other than income production and even fewer friends and family members to share them with. High incomes, they *do have*; prosperity and happiness, *they do not have.* So how does one reach this "eureka moment" in prosperity building? It is by realizing that prosperity is not so much an "I" attitude as much as it is a "we" attitude. We realize that we can improve people's lives through our prosperity achievements. It is the process of learning how to discover happiness by finding the proper balance between giving and receiving that personal prosperity is achieved.

Focusing More on the "Root" and Less on the "Fruit"
<< Finding the Causes of Prosperity and Not the Effects >>

You were born to prosper. It is the nature of mankind. It does, however, come with certain inherent fundamental responsibilities. Most people immediately think of prosperity as wealth creation; and most assuredly, a portion of a fully functional personal prosperity plan does include monetary growth, although true and ultimate personal prosperity involves far more than merely money and material possessions. Prosperity, joy, happiness, and contentment are synonymous. Prosperity is the absence of selfishness, greed, and hubris that ultimately defines personal prosperity. If we are not happy, then chances are we are not prospering. It is the single best indicator of our level of abundance in our life. Prosperity is the aim of everybody to be able to do better, to achieve more, and to create a more comfortable lifestyle for ourselves and for our loved ones.

The process of getting from here to there, however, has a lot to do with the fundamental core principles that are a part of the "root" as opposed to the "fruit" in the prosperity-building experience. The best prosperity plans are those that have strong, deep, and well-nourished roots as a result of learning and education, which also include necessary sound personal financial habits and behaviors.

On one hand, many tree experts can confirm that a healthy, growing tree is just as substantial *below* the surface of the ground as it is *above* the ground. On the other hand, shallow roots will not maintain a tree's long-term growth for very long. The same is true with a well-constructed and fully functional personal prosperity plan. It also needs the reinforcement of many of the developmental steps that are used in the long-term growth process, such as watering, fertilizing, and protecting the seedling as it grows into a sapling, a tree, and finally, perhaps someday, even a giant sequoia.

Extreme Prosperity Accomplishments

Now you have followed most of the teaching and training presented in the building of your individual prosperity plan paradigm. You have carefully implemented many of the important techniques and strategies that you have learned as a result of your reading and may very well be at the edge of something called *extreme prosperity*. This is a unique situation where your earnings and investment incomes may very well exceed ten to fifteen times your living expenses or annual needs. You are now faced with the reality that you have more money than you could ever possibly expect to spend in your entire lifetime. Is this an oxymoron or, indeed, an enviable situation?

If you find yourself in this situation as a result of your diligent prosperity building, here are five possible solutions:

1. *You can begin by spending: either increasing your standard of living or simply spending more money. This is contrary, however, to the personal formula that got you to a high level of prosperity to begin with.*

2. *You can learn to develop some new "bad habits" or "unlearn" some of the good ones. Again, this seems to go against your previous disciplined financial behavior.*

3. *You can gift it away to your family member or through charities or charitable causes. This is a highly recommended strategy and often done through an organized system of a personal or family trust or foundation for tax purposes.*

4.   *You can start investing your prosperity in "memories" with your spouse, life partner, family, relatives, friends, and others. This is also a highly recommended strategy for at least some of your acquired prosperity.*

5.   *You can allow the government to take up to half or more of it when you die through inheritance taxes. This is never a good technique. We all know how the government will abuse your hard-earned income just as they abuse taxpayer's money.*

Whatever strategy you chose, this is a good problem to have. But don't wait until just prior to your imminent death to start thinking of a way to begin dispersing your wealth. This last chapter in your prosperity building is often the most engaging and enjoyable of all so take time to contemplate how you will spend it and enjoy the final chapter of your prosperity journey!

REMORAS

Consider the remora – It is a small and insignificant fish that inherently attaches itself to a shark. The shark stealthfully hunts, kills, and eats its prey; and the remora, in turn, feeds off the shark. It provides no benefit whatsoever to the shark. It only takes from the shark for itself. Ask yourself the following question: **Are you a remora?**

Prosperity Is So Much More Than Just About Money

The Rev. Kenneth Copeland makes many comments in his 1985 book *Prosperity: The Choice Is Yours* and makes a well-known statement that bears repeating:

> *Money is NOT the root of all evil. The LOVE OF MONEY is the root of all evil.*
> —1 Timothy 6:10

Copeland also says in his book that we must "realize that prosperity covers far more than mere finances. There is spiritual prosperity, mental prosperity, physical prosperity, as well as financial prosperity." Below is a detail of each of these prosperities:

- **SPIRITUAL PROSPERITIES** – A rich sense of divinity and appreciation for heavenly blessings defines this sense of prosperity.

- **MORAL PROSPERITY** – You must be able to control your mind's thoughts, your emotions, and your will to achieve this prosperity; yet knowledge alone does not equate to it.
- **PHYSICAL PROSPERITY** – Your health and sense of physical well-being is exemplified in physical prosperity. Literally, the first wealth in a prosperous life is health.
- **FINANCIAL PROSPERITY** – The possession of wealth and power is perhaps the most sought but least needed. Money is a poor substitute for true prosperity in life.

REMEMBER Money Is a Tool, Not a God

It is good to create prosperity in your life. That is what this entire book has been about. Rightly or wrongly, it is one of the ways that we measure personal success in life. It is a means to an end and that can result in personal comfort and a secure lifestyle and, if properly applied, can end up in a substantial investment in personal happiness. Yet it must be remembered that money is not an end in itself. Money is either a religion, a value system, or a suitable result. Use prosperity your prosperity for many, many good things in life. Do something meaningful with your prosperity. Invest it, build with it, donate some of it, and give some of it away. Do something charitable with it. Invest in venture philanthropy. Support the Boy Scouts or another organization for the youth. Start a business that helps others create success like the author did. Back something you feel strongly about. Donate your time and expertise in a passionate pursuit. Go fishing more and take your grandkids. Send a kid to summer camp. Write a check to your former high school for something extraordinary. Set up a family foundation to create a giving legacy.

Leave the World a Better Place Through Charitable Giving

Question: What is the key to happiness in life?

Answer: Knowing exactly what it is that makes you happy!

The eternal quest for lifelong happiness has been the subject of many books, magazines, newspapers, and motion picture films over the years. The search for it has been even compared to finding the Holy Grail. It is also a well-known fact that money alone does not create happiness but arguably can greatly assist in maintaining happiness. It is also an irrefutable fact that we do need some of it to live our lives in a twenty-first-century capitalist American society.

But how much money is enough? What is the ultimate satisfaction level? When do we know when it is time to balance the "taking" and the "giving"? Is there a defined formula for discovering that balance? Is there a budget, ratio, or goal for this? Is it the same amount for everyone, or does it vary greatly among each of us? Does a high level of prosperity equate to a proportionate level of happiness? If not, how is it ultimately achieved? The answers to each of these questions have a lot to do with *what you do* with your newly acquired prosperity results. It admittedly is not the same for everyone based on their unique personal situation, but it is my hope and desire that many of these issues involved in personal prosperity building today have been answered in what you have already read.

Is Money Really a Blessing or Perhaps More of a Curse?

The purpose of a greater abundance in life and in our prosperity is to be able to spread the gospel, feed the needy and the poor, and meet the needs of others who need our help. It is for this specific reason that prosperity building *is to not only become more comfortable in our lives but to also be able to share those personal resources with others to help them achieve their life goals too.* This can be done in many ways and means and is only limited by our imagination.

The ancient adage, *If you learn to give, it will be given to you,* comes to mind as we seek to improve our own lives and that of our fellow man. Indeed, if you will only take your eye off yourself for a moment and look to the needs of others, you become a better and truer giver. There are many, many opportunities to be able to give of ourselves, including our time, our experiences, our talents, our skills, our passions, our strengths, and even our families; yet it requires looking beyond our own wants and considering the needs of those around us who could benefit greatly from our life rewards, wisdom, and experience.

A person can accumulate a vast amount of money in their life and still not be prosperous.

The Very Best Prosperity Gifts

When many people think of gifts, the choice of money or material goods often comes to mind. It hasn't always been this way. To say that money is not a factor in prosperity building would be a lie. However, it is just that in a carefully created personal prosperity plan, it is not the only factor. Prosperity is more of a state of happiness, joy, and well-being than just numbers in an account statement. Doing for others and serving that wants and needs of other people bring happiness to us in an ideal prosperity-building plan. We fulfill our personal success by creating success in others. There are, indeed, many excellent prosperity gifts that are "from the heart" that are perhaps even more valuable than money. Among them are the following:

- **THE GIFT OF LISTENING**. No interruptions. No planning. No response. No advice. Just plain, old-fashioned listening.
- **THE GIFT OF HUMOR**. Sharing funny stories, anecdotes, jokes, and other forms of lighthearted amusement all say that you know how to keep from taking life too seriously and realize that it is important to take things in stride.
- **THE GIFT OF WELL-CREATED WRITTEN EXPRESSION**. The use of a brief, handwritten note, card, or letter that shows genuine appreciation or affection to another person.
- **THE GIFT OF A COMPLIMENT.** A sincere sharing of a kind word at the right time can make someone else's mood change and improve.
- **THE GIFT OF COMMUNICATION.** A well-placed phone call to someone whom you know that could use your support and guidance is a highly effective way of giving.
- **THE GIFT OF AFFECTION**. Being generous with appropriate hugs, kisses, hand holding, and pats on the back say, "I care about you."
- **THE GIFT OF PATIENCE**. In an all-too-hurried world, the ability to slow down and take the time to reflect with others has significant and far-reaching meaning.
- **THE GIFT OF EXPERIENCED WISDOM**. Sharing your commonsense, practical experience and know-how that you have developed over the years can help another person avoid making mistakes that can help improve their lives.

Sharing yourself with other people through each of the above can become the greatest gifts of all. Prosperity isn't about materialism; it is about sharing and creating happiness, joy, and fulfillment using your resources to achieve "giving" in yourself and in others.

Avoiding Prosperity Hubris

- **WHAT IT IS** – Hubris is arrogance caused by excessive pride in accomplishments and personal life achievements.
- **HOW IT IS CREATED** – It is compounded by a string of personal, financial, career, and life successes created over time that allow ego to overcome you.
- **WHY IT IS SO DAMAGING** – It is damaging because it gives you a sense or feeling of invincibility and attitude that your past successes will also dictate your future gains.
- **HOW TO PREVENT IT** – You can prevent hubris from happening by maintaining a sense of humbleness and humility. Remember the

efforts and formula that helped create your personal successes. You should also seek to create value in others by helping them.

- **WHEN IT OCCURS** – Hubris always becomes a factor when everything seems to be going your way and when you appear to be at the "top of your game."

The news media today is filled with many examples of those who started out humbly, worked hard, and developed their skills and careers in sports, business, politics, and entertainment and then lost it all when they chose to make bad decisions based on the ubiquitous hubris factor. This can also be true in your personal prosperity-building plan. If hubris is ignored, remember that you will be meeting many of the same people going down as you met coming up. It just won't be nearly as fun and exciting.

By maintaining your sense of humility and selflessness as you create your desired level of prosperity in your life, you will be able to keep it and enjoy your newfound happiness and contentment—the measure of true prosperity in life.

The Successful "To-Do List" for Prosperity Achievers

A successful winning formula only comes about with hard work, discipline, and commitment. For proof of this, check out the faces of those athletic achievers in life whose grim determination reveals their level of devotion to the task at hand. The successful also understand that you need a blueprint to follow, and they learn to value leadership and strong influence from others who have the tools and drive to succeed. How do you define success? It is not always a championship trophy or a pot of gold at the end of the rainbow. The greatest measure of success is to learn how to do it and then how to deliver on that promise consistently that sets successful achievers apart. They strive to make a positive impact with others and care about helping others achieve their success too.

The Successful To-Do List

1. **STAY HUMBLE** – Work hard to be superior at what you do and always maintain that attitude.
2. **BE PROUD BUT NOT ARROGANT** – Carry yourself with confidence but never brag or boast about your achievements.
3. **REMEMBER THAT IT'S A TEAM GAME** – There is no "I" in team. The individual is never greater than the sum of its parts.
4. **SERVE OTHERS** – Your life and future should be an inviting place to be able to help others achieve their success too.

Second Career Opportunities
"If You're Motivated, Why Stop Working?"

It's never too late to think about creating an encore career opportunity. For many people today, retirement is not the conventional rocking chair variety that our fathers and grandfathers might have experienced but instead one where we can enter a career path or field that includes working in an area that they might have been able to enjoy as a hobby or leisure-time pursuit only. It can include full time, part time, or even volunteering. This is especially true if you make it to retirement and managed to maintain good health and a predictable level of personal income and still have energy left to do it. On the other hand, if you have already made it to retirement and did it by carefully planning, saving, and investing, you eventually made it happen! You did all the right things to be able to live out your remaining days in comfort and style. Your health is good, your kids are on their own and doing well, and you have a bright future ahead of you. Now comes the question: *retirement or rehirement*? All of the sudden, that seemingly utopian world of leisure, travel, fishing, golf, and free time suddenly loses some of that luster after a few months of sitting around, waiting for the phone to ring; and you suddenly realize that life may have lost some of its purpose and that your days are instead filled with more emptiness than you previously imagined. As we discussed in a previous session, work largely defines us. It is the thing that tells others what we are all about. It demonstrates to the world what drives and motivates us, and suddenly, it is gone. The question is are you destined to live out your days watching the grass grow and the paint dry? Like other meaningful periods in your life, a rewarding retirement does *not occur* without a little advanced planning. You have to plan for your retirement period, just like you planned for the other significant periods in your life. Let's look at some options available in the retirement stage of your life.

First, this may well be the *first time* you have the time to be able to engage in anything you choose to do and for as long as you want to do it without interruptions. You have the time to be able to engage in reading, writing, photography, stamp collecting, scrapbooking, coin collecting, or other passionate pursuits, hobbies, or activities of your choice.

Here are some of the other options and activities you may wish to consider:

1. *Sharing your passion with others at the library, church, YMCA, Civic Club or other organization.*
2. *Joining a new group to study, an interest that you never had time to do previously, such as gardening, botany, bird-watching, computers, or others.*
3. *Mentoring others who could use your life wisdom to accelerate their career.*
4. *Creating a small home-based business to supplement your income.*

5. *Volunteering your time and efforts to a museum, park, school, nursing home, or church.*

6. *Working a part-time job to supplement your income and earnings.*

7. *Engaging yourself in more family activities, such as reunions, holiday parties, trips, and retreats.*

8. *Teaching your expertise in a high school, community college, or university class.*

9. *Going back to school to get or finish your degree.*

Some additional considerations in making your giving decision:

- *Since the ultimate goal in retirement isn't merely to accumulate as much money as you can, planning your retirement years is a critical important step in your life. One of the developing opportunities that many Americans are considering today is* second careers. *Unlike original career occupations that were primarily focused on income issues, second careers have less emphasis on earnings and more emphasis on passionate pursuits.*

- *In attempting to determine if this is a good route for you to consider, ask yourself the following key question: "If I hadn't been engaged in the job/career that I worked throughout my life, what* would *I have chosen to do?"*

- *Another consideration when thinking about this option is that unlike your primary occupation that previously existed in your life, this career option will be more on* your terms. *Why? Because you are choosing a passionate pursuit approach rather than merely an income approach. In many cases, second-career people have flexibility in hours of work, types of work, geographic locations, days off, levels of intensity and commitment, as well as compensation that midlifers do not enjoy.*

- *One of the things to remember in choosing a second-career option is* want to *as opposed to* have to, *a key difference in the way of looking at it. Many second-career people whom I have personally known use their second-career incomes to fund schooling for their grandchildren, philanthropic purposes, personal travel, and the extras that their other retirement income does not provide.*

- *It is the* perfect method *to be able to share your expertise, your wisdom and know-how, and your accumulated knowledge that you have developed over the years to motivate, inspire, encourage, and influence others in a paternal or maternal way.*

- *Often, people in the middle of their careers do not have the necessary time or money to be able to accomplish many of the minutiae details that are an essential part of success building. This is where a thoughtful and well-organized mentor can be of significant benefit to one or even more mentees. It is a second-career path that many Americans are choosing today.*

- *A fulfilling life is all about having a purpose. Second-career occupations can give you that sense of purpose and accomplishment that otherwise you may feel is lacking in conventional retirement.*

- *For most people, the ultimate decision to consider a second career if they have planned their finances well isn't about money and income as much as it is about purpose and a way to give back to others at the end of their life. Fortunately, it is not an all-or-nothing decision either. You can tiptoe through the first twelve months and discover whether you even want to engage in this endeavor. Many who have led successful careers have not yet run out of energy. They choose this path to stay mentally sharp, engage with life, and avoid premature old age.*

- *It is also an excellent way to stay in touch with the world and other people since many of our personal friends also have a work connection. It is also a dynamic way to keep working and to do it more on your own terms for a change by exchanging major responsibilities with one of advising and consulting. This is a compelling way to achieve the mutual goals of each party—the giver as well as the receiver.*

- *At the end of the day, it is really all about choices. Some people feel that they have had enough of the "daily grind" and choose a retirement that is more leisure based and laid back. This is, after all, the very definition of conventional retirement. Yet because of many factors involved in health care and life improvements today, the bar is being continuously raised to include the option of second-career opportunities that are increasingly more available than in the past.*

- *Those who have a desire to continue work, perhaps just in a "lower gear," and wish to focus on terms more than incomes are well suited to second-career employment. On the surface, it can provide a suitable supplement to existing income streams; but when more closely examined, it can also provide more of a feel-good feeling that you are helping others discover some of your secrets to success.*

This is the motivation that the author had in establishing The Prosperity Success Institute Learning Center in Arizona. It was a career decision that I made in my late fifties when I realized that I was not ready for full-time retirement. It has enabled me to partly replace my working career income, but more importantly, it allows me to network with those who are seeking improvements in their life in personal finance, business entrepreneurism, success training, and real estate investing, which have defined my personal life and career success. I strongly urge each of you to consider a second-career opportunity!

The eight levels of giving from the twelfth-century philosopher Moses Maimorides is detailed below. When reviewing it, ask yourself what level you are at.

The Three Giving Models

There are but three modes in which surplus wealth can be disposed of:

1. *It can be left to the families of the descendents* (**passed on***).
2. *It can be bequeathed for public purposes* (**philanthropy***).
3. *It can be administered by its processors during their lives* (**spent***).
   —Andrew Carnegie, Author, ***The Gospel of Wealth (1889)***

The Eternal Law of Retribution

"You Get Back What You Give In Life"

Generosity Gives You Greatness

Each of us has the right to do what they wish to do with their income and money—spend, save, or give a portion away. Whether you have the **right** to do this is not the point. It is what is **best** to do with it that separates most people. Many well-to-do people regard themselves as custodians of money for the ultimate benefit of those who need it more than they do. What then is the best approach to charitable giving? Why should one become generous in the first place? Here are some of the reasons that sincere giving is important to each of us:

1. **IT DEFUSES SELF-CENTEREDNESS** – Who enjoys being around selfish people? One the other hand, there is incalculable joy in being around those who actually enjoy giving to others. They experience joy and the true, solid emotions of generosity, having no vanity, greed, or jealousy. It changes their focus from self to others.

2. **IT CREATES VALUE IN OTHERS' LIVES** – It isn't really significant how many people serve you or how much money or talent you achieve in your live. Rather, it is more about how many others you can serve with your talents and resources that is important.

3. **A GIVING ATTITUDE POSITIVELY AFFECTS THE GIVER** – Sincere giving rewards the giver too. It makes your heart and emotions feel good when you do something significant and unexpected for

someone else whether it is a gift of money, resources, or time. It is a feeling that is unequalled in life.

4. **OTHERS MAY TAKE NOTICE AND DUPLICATE YOUR ACTIONS** – One of the far-reaching and intrinsic values of unselfish giving is that others, including children, siblings, friends, family, coworkers, and others, may take notice, imitate the giving cycle, and duplicate it themselves.

It is a fact that one's achievements in life are not defined by what a person **receives** in life but what a person **gives** in life. Generosity is not a result or function of income but of the heart. Adding value to others' lives is a solid way to find significance in your own. Even the Bible has more writings about money and how to use it than even prayer. Generosity is literally created by giving your money away. The investment of time is just as valuable as money. Money can buy possessions or stuff, but a good mentor or teacher can assist by showing how to live a better future through the effective and unselfish use of their time. You are giving the ultimate generosity by this. Recall the special person in your life that gave you the greatest gift of all, their time and talents, to help and assist you in your success. Those people see giving not as a beneficial act of kindness but as an obligation. Adding value to others' lives is a surefired way to be the kind of person others choose to be around.

Dave Thomas, founder of Wendy's and a consummate philanthropic giver of time and money to charitable causes, including adoption, said it best when he stated,

"Give of Wealth – Give of Self"

When giving is involved, there are several things to keep in mind:

- ✓ Do not wait until you are prosperous to start giving.
- ✓ Create an early pattern of sustained giving.
- ✓ Give more. America is the most prosperous nation on earth, yet only 2.5 percent of our income goes to charitable causes. There were 80 percent of U.S. citizens who earn one million or more who leave nothing to charity when they die.
- ✓ Discover more reasons to give. Look for an engaging cause or need.
- ✓ Remember that the ultimate beneficiary of all giving is people who are in need of help. They do not have to be a half-a-world away but can be right in your own community or neighborhood.
- ✓ Keep your eyes open for opportunities to give generously.

Wealth Transfer Philosophy in a Nutshell

"Do your giving while you are living
so you know where it is going."

Quote

"We make a living by what we get,
but we make a life by what we give."

—Winston Churchill

Money and Manure

Money is like manure.
If you spread it around in the right places,
it will cause things to really grow.
Yet if you just pile it up in a corner,
all it will do is begin to smell!

—Old Texas Expression
Heard on National Public Radio (October 6, 2006)

"Blessed are those who can give without remembering and take without forgetting."

*"There is more happiness to be found in creating opportunities than
by going off in search of them."*

What's Your Personal Definition of Giving?

Is this your personal definition of giving?

Or perhaps maybe this?

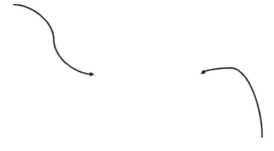

CHAPTER 13

How to Avoid the Common Prosperity Flaws, Pitfalls, Blunders, and Myths

In this chapter, you will learn about the following points:

- *There Is a Lot to Learn*
- *Being Able to Overcome Money Disorders*
- *Fourteen Common Prosperity Flaws, Pitfalls, and Blunders*
- *Details of Each of Them*
- *Your Ability to Offset Prosperity Blunders*
- *The Bottom Line on Failures, Blunders, and Flaws and How to Avoid Them*
- *Eleven Prosperity Myths and Myth Busters*
- *Details of Each of Them*

There Is, Indeed, a Lot to Learn

Just as there are many ways and methods in achieving personal prosperity in life, there are also many failures, pitfalls, and flaws that, if regularly followed, will stall, slow down, or perhaps even unfortunately eliminate your personal prosperity-building program. This chapter discusses a total of fourteen of the most common prosperity-building detractors and fully describes and explains each one of them, how they are formed, their long-term effects on both you and your plan, and how they can be effectively avoided. As you read and study each of them, keep in mind that just like any other worthwhile effort in life, it is always important to "keep your eyes on the proverbial ball," your prosperity plan, so you can avoid experiencing any of these in your personal prosperity-building plan. Take the necessary time to carefully review each of them and understand how each of them can become "prosperity busters" if they are not consciously avoided.

Proper preparation and planning often means knowing what to avoid *as well as* what to follow.

Being Able to Somehow Overcome Money Disorders

Many people have an existing complex, complicated, or perhaps even dysfunctional view and relationship with money and finances, which causes frequent personal hardships. Our troubled attitudes or views often are the result of a lack of knowledge, which has created many incorrect beliefs, behaviors, and habits that can even go back to our childhood and upbringing. In addition, they may also be shaped by some of the financial errors, mistakes, and blunders that we have made in our lives, which resulted in painful personal finance experiences. However, even information is not enough to overcome all the challenges that you may be faced regarding money issues. These beliefs and behaviors are often so deeply imprinted into our subconscious mind that they can shape the way we interact with our money and our relationships with others throughout our entire lives. By taking a close look at our relationship with money and personal finances, we can learn to examine, analyze, and even recognize these negative behaviors that are self-defeating. These behaviors can have the effect of threatening marriage, career, prosperity building, and our ultimate joy, contentment, and even happiness. A few of the more common compulsive money disorders are the following:

- *Compulsive overspending*
- *Using money to influence others*
- *Creating financial enabling*
- *Obsessive money hoarding*

- *Avoiding personal money problems*
- *Using money to buy friendships and love*

The answer to many of these issues is the ability to learn, to recognize many of the symptoms or disorders, and how to better deal with each of them to overcome them. Developing a healthy view or better perspective of your relationship with money or personal finances will help you to be able to enjoy a better, more prosperous life.

Common Prosperity Flaws, Pitfalls, and Blunders

In this chapter, an attempt is made to dispel many of the financial flaws, pitfalls, myths, and blunders that can be the most destructive to your personal prosperity building. These are only a few of the problems; there are many others too numerous to mention that must be identified and overcome. Indeed, there is much in the way of both information and misinformation when it comes to personal finances. According to author Zachary Shore in his book *Blunder: Why Smart People Make Bad Decisions* (2008), infomania is an information-based cognitive trap that is marked by an obsessive relationship to information. Infomaniacs believe that if they can control the knowledge around them, they will profit from it. According to Shore, there are two separate and distinct types: (1) infomisers, who hoard information, believing that sharing their data will undermine their position or situation; and (2) infovoiders, who believe that sealing themselves off from information to keep themselves in an informational void will somehow strangely be to their benefit.

Another term used is "infomindedness," which is defined as an imaginative openness and a skillful exploration of information. It is an eagerness to embrace as much information as you can absorb. Instead of fearing alternative views or foreign customs or worldviews, it is an attitude of embracing and expanding them. It provides a free-flowing, even active, discussion with those of differing minds and opinions and further stretches into what the Germans call *weltoffen*, openness to the world's rich diversity of ideas.

Obviously, the first step is to be aware that misinformation and informaniacs exist while being able to identify them. Once this has been achieved, it is easier to understand and overcome any resistance. The process of becoming aware of misinformation can greatly help your personal prosperity-building program.

In his book *Killing Sacred Cows*, Garrett B. Gunderson has created a unique checklist formula that can help you avoid making an error in your prosperity-building plan, and it consists of six key elements. The use of these questions can assist you in your personal prosperity paradigm. An adaptation of the elements is as follows:

1. *Have a clear definition of your interest. Analyze how or what you are being told and how it aligns with your interests.*
2. *Determine whether following the teaching will help or hinder your efforts to find and live your passionate pursuit in life.*
3. *Make sure to ask the right questions and educate yourself to make sure that you know which questions to ask.*
4. *Understand the value proposition behind what you are being told, particularly with investment advisors, and act accordingly.*
5. *Apply the concept in other areas of your life to see if it holds true in those areas also.*
6. *Compare those opinions with the views of trusted advisors, mentors, or members of your prosperity team.*
7. *Commit to a lifelong process of education.*

The destructive power of each of the flaws, pitfalls, myths, and blunders is that they affect your personal life and prosperity building. Those who don't have good, reliable informational sources do not know where they are going in their planning, become vulnerable to those who come along with a "good proposal," and set themselves up for prosperity setbacks and failures. The resulting blunders can become financially devastating for many years to come in your long-term prosperity-building plan.

Fourteen Common Prosperity Failures, Blunders, and Flaws (FBF)

Definition of a blunder – A blunder is a mistake caused by an individual who gets caught up in a conscious thinking trap that ultimately results in self-defeat.

1. *Failure to Keep Debt Proportionate to Income*
2. *Failure to Create and Live Within a Monthly Budget*
3. *Failure to Regularly Set Money Aside*
4. *Failure to Become Prosperous by Attempting to Only Look Prosperous*
5. *Failure to Have No More Than One Stream of Income*
6. *Failure to Continue Your Life Education*
7. *Failure to Negotiate and Barter Good Deals*
8. *Failure to Purchase Enough Insurance*
9. *Failure to Use Windfalls to Your Advantage*
10. *Failure to Own Your Personal Residence*
11. *Failure to Make Personal Investments*
12. *Failure to Create Retirement Accounts*
13. *Failure to Teach Family Members About Personal Finances*
14. *Failure to Remove Yourself from the "Caste System"*

FBF #1
(Failure, Blunder, Flaw)
Failure to Keep Debt Proportionate to Income

It is a fact. Creating and maintaining too much personal debt is a major prosperity buster and will wreak havoc if allowed to occur on a regular basis. Debt is one of those areas in life that s-l-o-w-l-y slips up on you. You see something you want, you have the available level of credit on your credit card or personal line of equity credit, and you make the emotional decision to buy it. Simple enough. If it were not for the fact that you can afford the payment, it would be the end of the story; but sadly, it isn't. We often continue to charge time after time until our credit cards are maxed out, and our lines of credit are also exhausted. Frequently, some people even go secure more credit cards and take on more consumer loans or even additional credit lines until they are so inundated with personal debt that they cannot afford the payments any longer.

Even worse, by using all this credit, people can no longer produce any discretionary income for savings or investing. Then the inevitable occurs in life—they lose their job, their hours get cut back, or a real emergency of one type or another pops up. Previously, they were in a situation where they could barely meet their obligations and debts. Now they have reached the tipping point where they start to submerge into a pool of indebtedness that reaches insolvency or, even worse . . . Let's hope this scenario does not sound familiar. Where does this cycle of debt begin? How can it be prevented? The solution all starts with having a *proportionate* (key word) level of debt to your income and not an *excessive* one. It comes from avoiding impulse buying or self-gratification. Instead, choosing a strategy that involves self-discipline and willpower that speaks to us, saying, "We cannot afford this now," or "We should save our money before buying this." Finally, self-discipline is a mental attitude that states, "If I buy this, how will it affect my budget, discretionary income, and prosperity-building plan?" It is an attitude that articulates the difference between wants and needs.

It is the first step in prosperity building at work!

FBF #2
Failure to Create and Live Within a Monthly Budget

For many people, the very word "budget" sends shivers down their backside. Their attitude about using a budget creates a feeling that it will restrict or limit their fun and lifestyle. Rather than looking at the positive aspects of how a carefully detailed budget or spending plan can work to their short- and long-term benefit, they instead resist the method to more wisely portion out their money by using one each month. A well thought-out personal household budget plan does not have to be negative. It can instead give the user an ability to take a glimpse at their future expenses and to make a realistic determination of how expenses match up with income. Then expenses can be increased or decreased to create a balance or budget. It is for that reason that the use of a budget is a key part of a fundamental and basic prosperity-building formula.

The failure to use a budget or spending plan can also often result in a lack of discretionary income production (defined as the result of the difference between net monthly incomes less expenses) or only a bare minimum amount of that income. The use of discretionary income is an important part of long-term prosperity-building plan since it will fund your savings and investing fund for your future. The use of an effective monthly budget is important as a planning and preparation tool and as your prosperity plan begins to take shape. The budget can help you continue to keep the ratio of income to expenses proportionate so that you maintain an awareness of keeping balanced and staying on track as you journey down the prosperity superhighway!

FBF #3
Failure to Regularly Set Money Aside

It is easy to justify many of life's indulgences and extravagances. The fact is that our nation has become a debtor and a consumer in the last thirty years rather than an investing and saving government. One of the major flaws to prosperity building in our personal lives is the failure to create the necessary discipline and willpower coupled with the devotion and commitment to set aside even a modest amount of money each payday. Instead, many people spend every income dollar they earn, resulting in no personal funds being set aside for long-term prosperity purposes. Setting aside even a modest $100 to $150 or more if you are committed can be used for each and any of the following areas of your prosperity-building plan:

- *Emergency or rainy day fund*
- *Investment portfolio fund*
- *Real estate investments*
- *Paying down existing debt or credit cards*
- *Adding to retirement account funds*

The secret to overcoming this flaw in your prosperity plan is good, plain, old-fashioned discipline. Once you start setting money aside, it will soon become a habit; and as time goes on, you can increase the amount that you set aside for your long-term benefit. A savings goal is 5 to 10 percent of your net income or take-home pay each month. If done consistently, it will soon start paving the road to your personal prosperity plan.

FBF #4
Failure "To Be" Prosperous by Attempting to Only "Look" Prosperous

The old expression, "If it looks like a duck, quacks like a duck, and moves like a duck, it must be a duck," comes to mind here. Not necessarily so! All things are not necessarily what they seem, and this is especially true when it comes to "visual images" of prosperity. An exterior veneer of prosperity appearance may well belie the reality of paycheck-to-paycheck living and a lifestyle that cannot really be afforded. As a result, it must be supplemented and augmented with credit cards, consumer loans, and equity debt. Many fall into the category of those who give the appearance of living the good life; yet the reality is that it is frequently only that, *an appearance,* and the actuality is something far less than the "good life." Frequently, many marital bickering, disagreements, and discords occur from too much spending and not enough saving because of the fact that we do not want our relatives, friends, neighbors, coworkers, and others to think that we cannot afford something. Unfortunately, this is not prosperity building, only the appearance of prosperity. Learning how and when to make the right financial choice is the very crux of complete and proper prosperity building and can be witnessed by those who have learned to create discretionary incomes with various techniques and methods to achieve their financial objectives.

One thing that they all share in common: they have a disciplined and committed long-term prosperity plan that is carefully scripted to eventually and carefully get there. In the end, *it does not include merely* looking prosperous. *It results in* being prosperous.

FBF #5
Failure to Have No More Than One Stream of Income

The ability to have a good-paying job or career occupation in your life is certainly a powerful tool in your prosperity building but think of the possibilities of having more than one of them. No one is suggesting that you go out and get another full-time job. If you are married, your spouse's efforts to produce regular income could add substantially to your long-term nest egg. You might be able to set aside a modest amount of $100 or more of that income into an IRA, stock portfolio, or other long-term investment instead of applying it completely to your lifestyle. Not only could this conceivably *double* your portfolio building, but it could also proportionately increase the effects of compounding your long-term financial success. If started early enough in life, the results can be absolutely and positively amazing in your prosperity building!

Another good prosperity strategy is to use a hobby or leisure activity to add to your income base also. Some specific examples of this are the following: If you are an avid stamp collector, buying and selling stamps would be a good option, and these profits could be isolated for investing purposes. If you are a good golfer, teaching golf lessons to others could prove to be a viable option, and that income could be used for investing. If you are an avid writer, you could write newspaper articles for your local newspaper as a source of additional investment income. Earmarking these incomes and socking them away in some sort of investment can work wonders for your prosperity building over time. Many get the mistaken opinion that they have to invest huge gobs of money to exponentially grow their investments. A better strategy is to ladder investing into carefully chosen investments over a longer period and then let the powerful effects of compounding do the rest. It is a highly effective strategy that really works for everyone!

FBF #6
Failure to Continue Your Life Education

Some people make the mistake of thinking that once they have left formal education, such as high school, trade school, vocational specialty school, college, or even graduate school, their education is finally (whew!) over. This is a serious mistake. Did you ever consider the word for the service the day of your graduation—commencement—which is used to illustrate how your life is only just *beginning* after graduation? As adults, you should not overlook the opportunities that education provides to continue staying at the "head of your class."

Continuous education takes on many various forms today, including from regularly reading the newspaper or watching the media news to taking an occasional class or course in your chosen career field or other passionate field of interest, to reading books and magazines in different fields of interest, to attending workshops or seminars and other forms of focused education and learning. The long-term result of this continual learning is to experience and be able to use new technology, processes, innovations, techniques, and other useful and meaningful strategies that will significantly assist in keeping you on the cutting edge of job/career/life. Being "in the know" is a fundamental core principle to those who choose to build long-term prosperity plans because they realize that the entire world changes a little bit each and every day. They understand that if they stay in touch with the subtle changes, they are destined to become proactive in their prosperity building and not merely reactive in it. Taking an educational course at your community college once a year or other useful continual education program will produce exceptional results in your personal job/career/life prosperity. A good time to do this is every year in January, February, or March, after the holidays. *It cannot be overstated that education does not end at graduation day for anyone, especially prosperity achievers.*

FBF #7
Failure to Be Able to Negotiate and Barter Good Deals

Many businesses are highly effective at marketing their goods and services. As a result, consumers need to be aware and understand how to buy and purchase goods and services at the very best price to get the best value from their shopping dollars. It is often called getting a bigger bang for your buck. Some of the controversial buying decision issues include the following: Is a rebate better than a discount? Is a tax deduction better than a tax incentive? Is a deferred payment better than a better price? Is the use of an interest free loan a better deal than a cash price? Is a late-model, pre-owned vehicle a better buy than a new one? These and many other negotiating and bartering techniques are highly effective and profitable methods of getting more value from your earnings. Many times, the best deals are not so obvious to the consumer; and often, the most in your face advertising is not a good value, just good marketing. The ability to know and understand good value is an important factor in achieving prosperity building regardless of the size of your savings account, investment portfolio, or net worth. This also underlines the reason that it may be comparatively larger than most other people's. Have you ever noticed how prosperous people just seem to have a "feel" for being able to get a good deal? Instead of simply a sixth sense (arguably a possibility), it can be traced back to their following a well thought-out mental negotiating plan and the discipline to carefully follow it whether it succeeds in purchasing the product. Often, it is not only all about the lowest price too but can also involve an intricately scripted give-and-take strategy that concludes with satisfying both buyer and seller in getting what each wants and needs. Think for a moment how much merchandise, both large and small, you buy in your lifetime. If you can learn to get increasingly better value through negotiating and bartering, think how much more buying potential or more money in your pocket you will have.

FBF #8
Failure to Purchase Enough Insurance to
Adequately Protect Your Assets

Insurance can be defined as one of those expenses in life that you regularly pay for but hope that you never have the occasion to ever use. It is, indeed, one of the most important protectors of your personal prosperity plan. Because there are so many various types and categories of insurance, however, it is always a good idea to spend time comparison shopping, interviewing agents, and even reading the fine print and the policies themselves (yawn, this is sure to put you to sleep but should be done) to know and understand not only what you are covered for (important) but also what your policy *does not cover* (even more important).

Some insurance is more important and needed than others. For example, life insurance is important when your kids are small but less important when they are raised and have left the nest. Homeowners and vehicle insurance coverages are so variable and numerous that you can almost customize a personal policy for your particular and specific needs. Health insurance, on the other hand, is an *absolute requirement* and, as a result, should be at the very top of your insurance list. If you feel that you cannot afford the high premiums, consider a larger deductible or a more generic coverage policy that will become more imperative as you get older. Insurance is all about asset and liability protection that should always be a key consideration of your prosperity-building plan and included in your budget. Without insurance, you risk the possibility that all your prosperity planning, preparation, and investing can come crashing down based on only one incident. You further chance the effects of having to potentially absorb the entire liability and expense by failing to have insurance or not having enough of it. The peace of mind that insurance provides is worth every penny spent on it. Remember too that too much of it or the wrong kind of it will potentially ruin your personal budget.

FBF #9
Failure to Use and Apply Windfalls/Inheritances to Your Advantage

Who does not like a sudden and unexpected gift of money or other assets termed "windfalls"? What is not to like about an inheritance, lottery winning, payoff, bonus, tax or other refund, consumer rebate, cash discount or other financial reward, or outright gift whether it is small or large? We all get them occasionally in life (well, maybe not huge lottery or sweepstakes winnings), yet *how we use them* can say a lot about the successful results of our prosperity planning. These unanticipated treasures can be effectively used to tremendous personal advantage if the recipient has the discipline and willpower not to only simply blow it on a personal indulgence but to also take a large portion of it (60 to 80 percent of it) and add it to your prosperity-building plan. Some possible examples of this can be your investment portfolio, retirement account, and a certain real estate investment or to pay down personal indebtedness. The best strategy to use for small windfalls ($100–$500) is to earmark each of them by putting them into a separate savings account marked "Windfall Money," and when several are collected, place the collective money into an investment.

For larger windfalls (over $500), a good strategy is to *immediately* invest 60–80 percent of it into a good investment while keeping the remainder as a personal bonus for anything you may choose.

Through the magic power of compounding, watch that windfall money, along with your other investment money, and start to go to work for you and your prosperity-building plan. The windfall money will act like steroids in boosting your overall results. Remember that there are *always* more ways to spend money than to earn it; yet when you receive a sudden, unexpected, and unanticipated windfall that arrives out of the blue, seriously consider getting more value out of it by investing the majority of it as opposed to spending it all on your lifestyle. You will thank yourself many times over down the road. It may be perceived as delayed gratification by many, but when you open your statement at the beginning of each month, you will feel good that you saved the money and invested in your future. It is called financial wisdom and is an integral part of a finely tuned prosperity plan.

FBF #10
Failure to Own Your Personal Residence

Homeownership is unquestionably one of the largest single factors in personal prosperity building. When you add the increasing value of numerous tax deductions, equity, appreciation, and long-term investment building, it ranks near the top of a good prosperity plan. In addition, you get to live in it too! It is also why the government has created all sorts of incentives to buy and own your home. Yet the problem in purchasing a house is that people buy too much house for their income level. There are many ratios used in determining affordability in choosing a home. When properly selected, your home can produce a significant asset that eventually gets paid off just before retirement. You are then free to sell it, reinvest the difference, and move to another location; or you can be content to continue living in the house *without* making any more mortgage payments. Planning and preparation are the keys to accomplishing this. Very few things appreciate in value over the years. Real estate ownership is one of them, and you cannot participate in this prosperity builder if you don't start off by owning your own residence. While there are many good reasons to rent for short-term reasons, homeownership is, by far, one of the best long-term personal investments you can make in your life. Another potential pitfall is to continually use the equity built up in your home to pay down credit card and consumer loans, which then results in the possibility that at retirement, your home will not be paid off, a substantial flaw in your prosperity-building plan.

An even further option in real estate investing is investment property that also helps build assets and portfolio equity. It is the traditional favorite prosperity-building tools of many prosperous investors and a solid part of many individuals who have created substantial prosperity plans.

FBF #11
Failure to Make Personal Financial Investments

There are many types of investments to consider in life. Should you invest in your brother-in-law's new business start-up (or maybe you should think about starting your own)? Does a stock or mutual fund account make sense? Should you buy that rental property on the lake that you have been looking at? Is it time to start funding a diverse investment portfolio? The answers to each of these questions are the very heart of any personal prosperity-building plan. Once you realize that your own income, earnings, and efforts will go only so far (your own two hands) in achieving your financial goals, it is time to think about and consider using a more developed and sophisticated investment strategy to help speed up the process a little. What kind of investments? How much should you invest? Where do you get the money? When should you start investing?

Investments come in all sizes, shapes, categories, types, and descriptions. They range all the way from ultraconservative (savings accounts, bonds, certificates of deposits) to moderately priced ones (stocks, mutual funds, ETFs) to wildly speculative types (oil and gas investments, undeveloped land, venture capital). Your choices should be based on a combination of risk tolerance, defined timetable, willingness, self-confidence, knowledge of the market or industry, and other considerations. There have been countless books and articles written about investing in all the financial markets, yet your personal selection of investing is as uniquely individual as the smile on your face. There are numerous ways to make investment decisions, but creating the most successful formula that fits your personal situation is the secret in doing it. *Creating an effective personal investment portfolio is key to your long-term prosperity success, and it all begins with you.*

FBF #12
Failure to Create Sustainable Retirement Accounts

Today there are many creative and innovative retirement building strategies available, and it frequently takes more than just one of them to serve your prosperity-building plan. Although the typical technique is the use of a traditional IRA (individual retirement account), there are others, including the following:

- *401 (k) – This is the most common form of individual retirement planning and is funded by individuals through many employers who may or may not also contribute to your plan. There are many forms of them available.*
- *IRA (individual retirement account) – This is a tax deductible account that allows you to contribute a defined amount of your net earnings each year and results in an additional retirement investment. At receipt, you are taxed as ordinary income and often at a lower tax bracket.*
- *ROTH IRA – a nontaxable account that is funded with taxed earnings, but when received, it is not subject to any tax.*
- *SEP (Simplified Employer Pension) – If you own a small business enterprise, you are entitled to create a SEP account with certain tax advantages.*

There are many other options available to consumers and, in addition, many hybrids also available for each of the above that is being created all the time. This is an area of prosperity planning that should not go untouched, and you should look at your existing retirement plan each year with a competent financial planner or advisor to see if there are any needed improvements that can be made to your plan. This is a key and fundamental part of retirement planning and should be included as soon as you begin your first job. One of the flaws in prosperity planning is to wait until midlife to start funding it. To gain the maximum amount from compounding, it needs to be started early in life.

FBF #13
Failure to Teach Family Members About Personal Finance

Ask yourself where you learned most of your basic, foundational knowledge about personal finances. When it comes down to it, your parents influenced the foundational building blocks that you have used your whole life. We watched how our parents used their money in their life—how it was spent and how it was saved. What happened when your parents used it irresponsibly? What if the lessons that were learned were negative? What effect did these less-than-perfect influences have on us and our money management skills?

The answer to these and other questions underline the fact that we should make a conscious effort to teach and train our family members about personal finances before they even leave the nest. This should be done on a regular and consistent basis and may even include sharing some of your personal finance information with them as well as a few of your major errors and mistakes made. Some families do this by literally making a game out of it using board games like Monopoly, Life, and Money to illustrate the practical and fundamental concepts of everyday money management that will serve to benefit each of them throughout their life. The best and most effective means of teaching and training family members is by the old-fashioned example of doing it correctly yourself. Earning, spending, saving, investing, and risk-taking are some of the fundamental concepts that every adolescent needs to learn at a very early age in life. This education also includes other key principles that they will use for many years in the future. The bonus is that since this learning is not taught in the organized public school system today, it can be effectively taught at home, and it does not have to be experienced as a result of expensive trial-and-error methods and from disappointing financial mistakes. The further bonus is that once it is learned and implemented, your family members will then hopefully teach and train their own children, which will have the effect of becoming a continuing family financial legacy that will serve to benefit your extended family. This could also include setting up a series of individual trusts and even a family foundation to benefit them.

Now *that* is a significant step in anybody's personal prosperity plan!

FBF #14
Failure to Remove Yourself from the "Caste System"

Often, people seem to just be content to remain in their employment, occupation, and comfort zone lifestyle without ever making much of a sincere effort to change or improve it. For some, it is an anxiety-producing event that they are unsure of the final results. Since income is one of the primary ingredients in prosperity building, failing to improve or change it can have a severe impact on your ability to improve your prosperity success in achieving it. These same people may even regret doing something about it later in life; yet perhaps they might not presently have the necessary training, education, or skills to break the shackles of their existing lifestyle. They neither have the contentment with their personal situation nor have the tools to accomplish a higher level of personal financial achievement.

This transition all starts with desire, discipline, and willingness to change. There are countless examples of people in history who came from humble beginnings and origins with minimal resources that carefully and methodically achieved enormous levels of personal financial success through a choreographed method of prosperity building in their lives that focused on their unique talents and skills and that was lavishly layered with a thick coating of *desire* and *determination* that created a successful personal prosperity strategy.

Your Ability to Be Able to Offset Prosperity Blunders

<< *Improving Your Judgment Calls* >>

Many smart, intelligent, well-meaning people are often trapped into making wrong personal finance mistakes that lead into creating prosperity blunders. We have all experienced them in our life at one time or another.

Some examples of these include the following:

* ❖ *You use your large bonus or inheritance to purchase a larger house (that you may not even need), eliminating the opportunity to start a business or invest in a good cash flow real estate investment when one occurs.*
* ❖ *You failed to set aside any of your discretionary income over the years and suddenly wake up one day when you are in your late fifties and realize that you cannot live off Social Security and Medicare benefits.*
* ❖ *You avoid making any financial investments during you life because they sound so complex and complicated and end up with zero supplemental income when you stop working instead of a significantly better one that could have been achieved if you had only learned the investing rules of the game.*
* ❖ *You purchased (or, even worse, leased) expensive new vehicles that wore out long before you paid them off, resulting in lost financial opportunities that could have been achieved by investing only $100 per month in a modest financial investment of some type.*
* ❖ *You live a paycheck-to-paycheck lifestyle complete with maxed-out credit cards, home equity loans, and consumer indebtedness and then lost your job.*
* ❖ *You stopped your personal finance education when you graduated from high school or college and quit learning about new innovations, technology, and other personal improvements.*
* ❖ *You made a large investment in something that you did not research well and knew little about and then relied on someone who just knew it would pay off. When you call the company, they do not return your phone calls.*
* ❖ *You purchased a significant amount of your employer's stock in your 401 (k), and then your company lost several of its largest customers, and they are now experiencing financial difficulties. Worse, they are now teetering on insolvency. As a result, you now stand to lose both your job and your 401 (k) investment.*
* ❖ *You intended to start planning for your post-working retirement over the years and one day woke up to learn that you waited too long to be able to realize any significant gains. The best investing years are now behind you, and the result is that you will have to work a full-time or part-time job for the next ten or more years, while your friends and neighbors are enjoying their retirements, traveling all over the world and playing golf every weekend.*
* ❖ *You tried to keep up with the Joneses throughout your whole life and finally learned that the Joneses' level of prosperity is a charade. You found that they have been struggling with personal finances their entire life.*

Do any of these examples sound familiar? If so, then take heard. Better prosperity decision-making can be accomplished, cultivated, and improved. Instead of shattering your personal prosperity building or ruining your best-laid planning and preparation, you can learn how to skillfully avoid them and develop a deeper understanding of the circumstances or situations that contribute to each of them. By identifying and recognizing the destructive decision patterns, you can learn to escape the results that these blunders often create in your prosperity success. Obviously, it is always easier to look in the past through the rearview mirror and realize how foolish some of your decisions might have been. It is much harder to look in the present or future to avoid these types of errors and mistakes from even occurring.

The Bottom Line on Prosperity Failures, Blunders, and Flaws and How to Successfully Avoid Each of Them

No two individual prosperity plans are exactly alike even though there may be basic similarities in some plans. Just as it is important to know and understand the techniques and strategies that can be used to *build* you plan, it is equally important to do the same with many of the factors that can easily *destroy* or sidestep your preparation and planning. When someone suggests or if you are thinking about making a change to your established personal prosperity plan, then you should carefully consider each of the following points:

>> YOUR PLAN IS UNIQUE TO YOUR SPECIFIC SITUATION <<

It is important to tailor the plan to your personal circumstances, situation, goals, and objectives so those needs must be carefully taken into consideration.

>> NOT ALL STRATEGIES WORK FOR EVERYBODY <<

Some guidelines may be thinly disguised marketing efforts that may create more economic benefits for those who present them than for the investor. Be aware of commissioned salespeople who seek to sell products or services. This is especially true if you do not completely understand and thoroughly know the risk versus reward. Remember that it is always acceptable to say "No, thanks. What you are proposing is not for me."

>> TRUST IS AN IMPORTANT INGREDIENT<<

Building trust in personal financial relationships takes time. It literally does not happen overnight. Good opportunities come and go all the time. It should be emphasized that trust plays a key role in building personal prosperity success and is not easily earned. The process of avoiding failures, flaws, and pitfalls helps you maintain your prosperity-building success and avoids unnecessary "do-overs" and "makeovers" to your plan.

Prosperity Myths and Myth Busters

Many people labor under false ideas and perceptions about the techniques and strategies involved in acquiring prosperity in their lives. There are many myths and misconceptions that distort our thinking about the best methods to use. By being able to learn and apply the fundamental truths that offset these myths and misconceptions, we can learn to achieve higher results and accomplishments. Some of the myths are the result of our family upbringing, where we learned many of our money management habits and behaviors. Yet some of these are fostered by financial institutions, such as banks, insurance companies, securities brokers, and others that benefit from the ignorance and misinformation on behalf of many consumers who do not question financial theories or concepts while simply taking their advice at face value.

As a result, many of our conceptions about prosperity are misguided and unfounded. They are instead directed by marketing and advertising hype, which have an underlying incentive to sell financial products or services on a commission basis. Sadly, we often depend on these specialists and so-called experts instead of learning how to handle our finances ourselves. That is what this book has been about. Another factor that plays a large role in prosperity in the United States is that the school system does not take a more active role in teaching sound personal finance or prosperity principles. Prosperity is such an important part of our lives and future that we should take a proactive role rather than a reactive approach in achieving our goals. Becoming financially empowered can greatly assist you in developing your personal prosperity in life. The fact is that investing in yourself through financial education is a solid personal prosperity-building concept.

Common Prosperity Myths

MYTH – A Fictitious Story, Fantasy, or Fable

There are many myths associated with prosperity building. Each of them is based on fictitious beliefs that people *want to believe* but, in the words of twentieth-century humorist Josh Billings, "just ain't so." As a result, myths can be the cause of much personal, family, emotional, mental, and financial anxiety if they are accepted as financially factual. In the following pages are details of eleven of the most common personal prosperity myths that can and will derail your personal prosperity success if not avoided. Each of these myths reflects the view that the process is either really no big deal, that it is too complicated, that it can be put off until later in life, or that all the planning and preparation is not really all that necessary to achieve prosperity.

This view becomes increasingly more compelling as people reach their fifties and begin to realize that (a) they have not done much to plan and prepare for their future, (b) they have not set much money aside for their nonworking years, (c) they begin to understand that they have lost much of the positive effects of compounding over the years, (d) their retirement is literally around the corner, and (e) they now have to do *something* to make it through the last leg of their life journey. When contrasted with the previous list of "must-dos," in this chapter, each of these prosperity myths takes on new meaning and serves as a useful reminder of many of the strategies that should be avoided at all costs to create your own individual and useful personal prosperity plan.

Eleven Common Prosperity-Building Myths

<u>MYTH #1</u> – Thinking That You Can Wait Until Sometime in the Future to Start Your Plan

<u>MYTH #2</u> – Thinking That Your Future Prosperity Will Somehow Mysteriously Take Care of Itself

<u>MYTH #3</u> – Thinking That Investing Is Too Complicated, and It Is Not Really for You

<u>MYTH #4</u> – Thinking That Your Meager Savings Will Be Enough to Sustain You in Your Nonworking Years

<u>MYTH #5</u> – Thinking That Your Stockbroker Is Your Friend and That They Know Your Investment Strategy Better Than You Do

<u>MYTH #6</u> – Thinking That Social Security and Medicare Will Be Sufficient to Take Care of You in Your Nonworking Years

<u>MYTH #7</u> – Thinking That Your Lifestyle Costs Will Go Down as You Get Closer to Retirement

<u>MYTH #8</u> – Thinking That Your Children and Family Will Take Care of You

<u>MYTH #9</u> – Thinking That Prosperity Plans Are Difficult to Understand and Create

<u>MYTH #10</u> – Thinking That Your Company's Defined Pension Plan Will Be Enough to Sustain You Later in Life

<u>MYTH #11</u> – Thinking That You Can Accomplish Prosperity Without Having a Carefully Created and Documented Plan in Place

Thinking That You Can Wait Until Sometime
in the Future to Start Your Plan

The belief of *someday but not today* is frequently the most significant prosperity challenge. This is arguably and most often the biggest myth in prosperity achievement. It is true that you must plan for many other significant events in your life, such as marriage, a birth, education, and even death. It just makes good sense to realize that the road to lifetime prosperity building starts at an early age—from learning about the proper use of money and income—to later in life, enjoying the wise application of savings, spending, and investing. It is a lifetime process that involves your spouse, family, children, job, or career and significantly affects all these relationships now and in the future. Without the necessary planning and preparation, your financial life is bound to be a series of trial and errors, haphazard wanderings, and financial ups and downs. For those reasons, it is absolutely necessary to avoid putting off the necessary planning and consider documenting your ideas and objectives on paper and beginning the process *now* and not waiting until "life" takes over.

A few dollars investing on a regular basis and in the right areas starting at an early age can produce tremendous results because of the magical effects of compounding over a lifetime.

The best way to offset the effects of procrastination in your long-term plan is to begin setting aside a small amount of money, $50 to $100 per month, into an IRA, Roth, or mutual fund. Doing so at an early stage in life, preferably during your first job, will reap major benefits over your lifetime. Using that approach, you will see the positive effects of the compounding that will be experienced in your investment over your lifetime, especially in the last ten years before you actually retire. The secret in doing this, however, is to *never touch this money for any reason*. By taking money out of it at midlife, you will ruin the effects of the incremental compounding that occurs and will have to start all over again. *Don't do it.*

Thinking That Your Future Prosperity Plan
Will Somehow Take Care of Itself

The view that your future prosperity will be the result of a mysterious, magic, or hocus-pocus process like pulling a rabbit out of a hat is neither a solid financial strategy nor likely to occur. Lady Fortuna does occasionally shine on us in life, such as receiving an unexpected inheritance, getting a large tax refund, securing a substantial insurance settlement, watching an investment escalate in value, or other unanticipated gift; but while each of these are events that can speed up the prosperity-building process, they are not necessarily the type of situation that can easily be counted on or that occur frequently in life. Instead, taking an attitude that starts with setting aside something modest at an early age and increasing it every year into a more sizeable amount will slowly develop into a positive personal financial habit that will be able to compound over a period into a significant long-term investment. This is a far better technique that will improve your personal prosperity building. We all gladly accept the good things that can happen to us in life but also must remember that the accomplishments that are obtained as a result of preparation and planning are the ones that usually bring the desired results and not magic.

Saying that your future prosperity plan will somehow mysteriously take care of itself at some point in your life is like the confidence that you might have thinking that nothing bad will ever happen to you, your spouse, or your family. You are simply kidding yourself that this could ever happen. The offset to feeling that your plan is on autopilot is to take an active role in creating one, especially if you are young enough to be able to enjoy the long-term compounding benefits as you mature. The familiar adage that only you can count on in life is death, and taxes comes to mind here. You must take a proactive role in building your future prosperity plan to see any sustainable effort. There is simply no other way to see any results.

Thinking That Investing Is Far Too Complicated and That It Is Really Not for You

How many things in life are both untroubled and profitable to you? Remember the familiar expression, "If it is so easy, why isn't *everyone* doing it"? Difficulty, it seems, is often what separates the sheep from the goats; and the same is true in building personal prosperity. How does someone get beyond the intricate, complex, detailed world of personal asset building? The answer is simpler than you may think:

E D U C A T I O N Is the Key to Doing This!

Education is the solution and does not require years and years of pouring over textbooks and materials. For many, it can result from focused, specialized training that is found in many formats today, including self-help books, DVDs, computer software applications, and many classes, courses, workshops, and seminars, including the possibility of using a financial investment mentor who has successfully become prosperous themselves. Whichever method you ultimately choose, it will take a degree of effort on your part, but the payoff in the end is certainly worth it in your life. After all, ask yourself what good events happened in your life that are achieved without any effort whatsoever. The secret to substantial prosperity building lies within creating your own personal and unique formula. This will come about as a result of knowing and understanding each of the techniques and strategies that you can use to create your own prosperity. Once created, you will never be sorry that you took the necessary time to learn how to do it.

Creating an effective long-term prosperity plan is a relatively simple exercise. Contrary to popular belief, you do not need an investment advisor (who gets a commission or an hourly rate), a tax planner (although they could provide some benefit), an accountant (even though you should consult one from time to time), an attorney, an estate planner, or other professional. It can easily be a DIY project if you are committed to simply setting aside a little money every month in the early stages of your life and continue to do it throughout your life. Ironically, the sooner that you begin, the less money you have to set aside because of the magic of compounding over your lifetime. Your fund can be of your own choosing based on your objectives, level of risk that you are comfortable with, and timetable you are working with. Once you have determined each of these, the real heavy lifting is just having the discipline to follow through with your decision to do it and not touch the money—ever.

Thinking That Your Meager Savings Will Somehow Be Enough to Sustain You in Your Nonworking Years

In the 1950s, 1960s, and even the 1970s, it did not take a whole lot to sustain you in your nonworking years. Those who were able to set aside some personal savings in addition to Social Security benefits could potentially live a reasonably prosperous lifestyle for many years. Fast forward to the post-millennium period, the cost of living is significantly higher; and a single savings account, which typically earns less than 1 percent APR (in 2009), simply will not generate enough growth or income yield to supplement your lifestyle, even a modest one. In addition, even when coupled with a defined pension or IRA, your income still may fall short. What then is the answer to this problem?

The solution for many is to have several prosperity investment techniques in place, including money market investments, pension, portfolio investments (stocks, bonds, mutual funds), and even passive investments like a small business enterprise, real estate property, and possibly even an annuity investment fund. It does not necessarily need to be an "all or nothing" situation either but instead one that takes into consideration your personal goals, objectives, age, risk tolerance, timetable, and amount of money available and one of the biggest prosperity busters: I-N-F-L-A-T-I-O-N. It is possible to build personal prosperity today. It just takes *education* plus careful planning and preparation.

In this day and age of few defined retirement or pension plans, counting on someone else to fund your comfortable lifestyle when you quit work is more a fairy tale than reality. Even if you are lucky enough to work for somebody (like the federal, state, local government, for example, or a huge company that still offers a retirement plan), you should still consider setting yourself up with your own investments. Examples of a few of the options available are real estate investments and even a small business enterprise that you can morph into an income source at retirement. Those who may consider these type of investments should remember that just a couple of well-chosen real estate investments purchased twenty years before retirement can produce an equivalent amount of monthly income as a retirement pension from a large company. The secret is in doing it now rather than later.

Thinking That Your Stockbroker Is Your Personal Friend and That They Know Your Investment Plan Better Than You Do

Many investors make the mistake of perceiving that their stockbroker or portfolio manager is their friend or, even worse, an advisor. This common misconception leads to many poor investing decisions and strategies. Many of the advisors we use are, after all, merely well-trained salespeople who have been carefully schooled in their craft. The truth is that they do not get paid until you buy or sell something. Although there are many types and degrees of expertise in each of these brokers or managers, the basic premise underlying your relationship with each of them is that of a salesperson (them) and customer (you). For that very reason alone, it pays to be cautious about their advice and even question yourself as to who is benefitting more from the sale and the relationship. What do they really know about other kinds of investments, such as a small business enterprise, real estate, IRAs, annuities, or other investment options? If the answer is "not very much," then why use them?

Admittedly, financial portfolio investments are a recommended strategy to be utilized in your prosperity building but not the only strategy to be used. Remember, when choosing a broker, each of them is primarily a salesperson who is earning a commission on trades, just like any other type of marketer. In the end, they all make money from transactions over the long term even if *you don't.*

What is the true definition of a stockbroker? They are (you might want to hold your breath here for a moment or two) nothing more than *salespeople*! Chances are if you are a reasonably well-read individual, you know as much about the stock market as they do. And when you consider the fact they don't make any money unless you, their client, buys or sells something, you get a dose of the reality that is involved when you work with a stockbroker in person, on the phone, or online. Stock picking isn't rocket science, and their advice is no better or worse than others who work in the business of financial investments. You should limit your funds to six to seven stocks and/or a single mutual fund and take time to research it/them well and then sit back and let the effects of compounding take over. There will be good years, bad years, and so-so years, just like there have been since the start of the stock market many years ago. You cannot outsmart the market, so the best solution is to select your stocks and let 'em ride until something better comes along.

Thinking That Social Security and Medicare Will Be Sufficient to Take Care of You in Your Nonworking Years

It is a compelling myth to think that Social Security and Medicare will become the foundational basis for your prosperity plan since not only are these governmental programs currently underfunded today, but they also do not address any of the prosperity-building issues for those who face retirement in the next few years. Instead of governmental social programs being the entire "cake," prosperity builders need to view each of them as the "frosting" on the retirement cake or even just the sprinkles on the frosting. It is arguably an issue that will continue to play itself out over the next decade because of the fact that increasing pressures on Social Security funds will be impacted since more and more baby boomers will reach retirement age over the next few years.

Again, the answer to personal prosperity building is in creating your own unique formula. This is one that is complete with many of the options that can help you engineer your individual long-term financial plans. The first step is e-d-u-c-a-t-i-n-g yourself with each step of the process and working with a competent professional who will help you achieve your goal. The best strategy is to use governmental programs like Social Security and Medicare merely as *supplements* to your own carefully created program or as dessert and not the "meat and potatoes" of your retirement strategy.

The unfortunate reality is that many Americans have fell into the trap of thinking that the government entitlement programs will fund their post-working life. Over 70 percent of people entering the retirement period today feel that way and are startled to find out that Social Security and Medicare just aren't enough to be able to enjoy any kind of comfortable lifestyle. The problem is that they have waited too long to learn this fact and are now stuck with having to go back to work part time or full time top to supplement their retirement earnings when they could have opted to set aside just a few dollars per month throughout their life and ended up with a sizeable nest egg of $500 to $600 to $700,000 or even more to be able to retire on.

Creating your own retirement plan is the answer, and it doesn't have to be a humongous one either. Instead of flittering away bonuses, inheritances, profits from the sale of personal effects, and home sales, this income can be used to fund a personal retirement account that will produce major income to you if left unchecked in an investment account for years.

Thinking That Your Lifestyle Costs Will Go Down
as You Get Closer to Retirement

It is a serious mistake and myth to believe that your costs of living are going to go down substantially when you quit working at retirement. Admittedly, if you have planned well, your home will probably be paid off. Your children will have left the nest and be on their own, resulting in other proportionate reductions in food, education, clothing, and other expenses. Your tax rate will presumably be lower. These are all examples of expense reductions that you can *reasonably* anticipate experiencing as you begin to enter this stage of life. On the other hand, however, there are several *increases* that you can reasonably anticipate. Trips to the doctor and other health-care providers will increase dramatically as you continue to age. Other health-related expenses will also continue to increase, making health care your *highest cost* during your nonworking, retirement years. In addition, you will still continue to have transportation expenses, vehicle payments, maintenance, repairs, fuel, insurance, and licensing. Then there are food costs and other routine living expenses, such as utilities, real estate taxes, insurance, and related costs.

In summary, your living expenses as you enter retirement will predictably go down *some* (10 to 20 percent), but there will be *other expenses* that will be added to your preretirement expenses. It is important to plan and prepare for the future by creating an effective prosperity-building document formula that details the specific factors of your individual plan. Another good idea is to create a new budget or spending plan that details specifically what your monthly income and expenses will be so that you are not caught short.

Despite the fact that the ideal retirement scenario involves no home or vehicle payments, which can reduce the cost of living during retirement years, there are other increasing expenses that many people do not consider. For example, think of the higher costs of drugs and prescription costs. If inflation averages 3%+- per year, how will this factor alone affect your retirement? This is in addition to the other price increases that negatively affect each of us during our working and nonworking years. The solution during retirement is to have more than one income stream to offset these increasing costs. This can easily be done by creating a retirement cost calculator (one of these is available by e-mailing us at larry.snow@me.com or visiting our website at www.prosperitysuccessinstitite.com) and developing an accurate picture of *exactly* what amount of income you will need at retirement to offset your lifestyle living expenses so that you are not subsisting only on canned soup and grilled cheese (one of my favorite, I might add, but not a steady diet of it).

Thinking That Your Children and Family Will Take Care of You as You Get Older

An attitude that your family is going to take care of you in the nonworking period of your life is more myth than reality. Despite the fact that they may *want to help* and no doubt would even do so in an emergency, you need to remember that they have their own share of expenses and responsibilities in life and in raising their own family. Except in very few cultures today, aging parents are often left to fend for themselves financially when it comes to their nonworking years; and if you have not spent much time planning and preparing, you could potentially be in trouble in your retirement years. We spend a lot of time teaching and training our children to be able to face many of the challenges in life that they will each experience as they grow and mature. The paradox in child-rearing is that this very process will eventually separate parents and children while ultimately preparing them to live on their own. This teaching and training process is duplicated millions of times every year and is the very foundation of human development.

It only makes sense that we not only provide resources to sustain our children in life but we also do the same for ourselves as parents. Given a choice between college funding and retirement funding, you would be wiser to choose retirement funding since it cannot be financed like college loan or other forms of education. This is the reason that prosperity building is a carefully scripted personal design development that deliberately charts your prosperity accumulation formula.

The thought that your kids will take care of you in retirement years is just as erroneous as thinking that they will someday eventually send you a check for their college education costs that you may have even taken out a second mortgage on your home to help finance. It just isn't going to happen anymore than the government is going to make you stop paying taxes at age sixty-five. Instead, you can develop a plan that details and describes exactly what you need to do to fund your retirement lifestyle. As mentioned before, this can be done with a combination of financial investments made over the course of your life, a real estate investment or two, and even the possibility of starting a small business venture just before retirement that will provide needed income.

Thinking That Prosperity Plans Are Somehow Like Hieroglyphics and Likewise Are Difficult to Understand and Create

One of the most challenging and difficult subjects in high school is higher mathematics—algebra, geometry, trigonometry, and calculus. These subjects are arguably cause of much frustration for students unless they are fortunate enough to have an instructor or teacher who can capably take the student by the hand and guide them through the learning concept that is easy to follow. The same is true with calculating your personal prosperity-building plan. Instead of a haphazard approach in understanding the process completely on your own, you can opt to have a guide to take through the proper equation and serve as your resource to define each of the steps along the way with a compelling series of examples to help show you the techniques in getting to the right formula. Without the proper guidance through the process, it would indeed be a daunting and formidable task.

The uniqueness of your result objectives along with the degree of risk tolerance and long-term objectives are just a few of the personal designs and practices that will assist you define your financial destination in life. Once you understand the process, it is then a matter of filling in the blanks to complete the successful prosperity formula, be fully funded, and end up with a big smile on your face.

Creating an effective and useful prosperity plan is not all that difficult. In fact, it can be exciting and even fun, much like planning a cross-country trip. There are a handful of options to consider, however, and should all be part of your *prosperity toolbox*. One of them is to decide a timetable when you really want to start kicking back and even leaving the career work that you have been involved in throughout your life. Next is to make an assessment of how much income and what your expenses will be at that point in your life. Finally, you might also start making a venerable *bucket list* of each of the places that you want to go and things you want to do during those golden years of retirement. It really isn't hard at all. You just have to take paper and pencil and start doing it. There are also all kinds of software and Internet website information available to do this. Start doing this now, not later, for maximum results.

Thinking That Your Company's Defined Pension Plan Will Be Enough to Somehow Sustain You Later in Life

During the industrial boom years of post—World War II America in the 1950s, 1960s, and even into the 1970s, most employers maintained a defined pension benefit program for the benefit of their long-term longevity employees after twenty, twenty-five, or even thirty years of service. These retirement benefits were created to supplement Social Security and Medicare and were quite effective. It was only after the later 1980s and beyond that traditional pension plans gave way to a whole new set of personal retirement options, which placed the onus of retirement planning squarely on the shoulders of the employee. Most employers became aware that they could no longer maintain 100 percent of the contribution in these traditional retirement plans, and the newly created federal tax laws opened the door to numerous opportunities for employers and employees that became known as 401 (k)s, Keoughs, and SEPs.

There were also individual-funded, tax-free plans, such as individual retirement accounts (IRAs) and eventually Roth IRAs as well as other options. Currently, only the very largest and most successful employers, including government workers, transportation companies, utility firms, and Fortune 500 companies, offer defined pensions and even those scarcely cover all retirement living expenses.

The bottom line is this in personal retirement planning: make sure that you have generated your own IRA even if you are planning to receive a defined pension from your employer (if allowed by the IRS rules). A small amount set aside by you ($50–$100 per month) into one of these accounts can provide significant returns when you are ready to stop working. Again, preparation, planning, and having a good personal formula are the keys in accomplishing this.

If you are lucky enough to have a defined pension or retirement from an employer, this doesn't mean that you are off the hook in developing a sustainable retirement prosperity plan. It does mean, however, you may not have to work quite as hard in creating other income streams; but you have to ask yourself this question: what would happen to me/us if, for some reason, you discovered that your pension plan was underfunded, or worse, your employer went out of business and left you high and dry? The answer to this dilemma (and don't think for a moment that it couldn't happen. Just ask the countless number of baby boomers who experienced this very problem in 2006–2011 during the Great Recession) is to create a few of your own retirement income options and a master plan that will supplement your pension. It is not a good idea to stick your head in the sand and think that it won't happen to you. Forewarned is forearmed, especially in this critical area of the post-working period in your life. Remember, there are no second chances when you enter this ubiquitous phase of your prosperity life.

Thinking That You Can Achieve Personal Prosperity Without Having a Carefully Created Plan That Is Documented and in Place

Are you the type of person who reads the instructions *before* putting the "gizmo" together or one who spreads all the parts on the kitchen table and then quickly goes to work, trying to solve the enigmatic "puzzle"? Your style of prosperity building might resemble either one of these two extremes, depending on your personality, aptitude, and objectives. Admittedly, many "assemblies" in life are easier and more efficient when you are given a detailed, easy-to-follow, and understandable set of instructions. In addition, it helps to have many of the "hand tools" to perform the intricate details. It then becomes less "reinventing" and more about following a carefully chosen and predefined list of assembly instructions. Once you have grasped the overall concept in building a personal prosperity plan; added the right individual personal talents, skills, needs, desires, or touches; and documented all the ideas in a carefully written personal prosperity plan, you have then created your own unique, individual formula that tells you and others where you want to go and how you will go about getting there. Your plan will serve as your prosperity instructional directions, assisting you in accomplishing every step of your long-term life.

Ask yourself this question: when you consider taking a cross-country auto trip, what is the first thing that you reach for? The same is true in building a personal prosperity-building formula. It becomes your life's GPS. Your plan is a necessary first step in taking your dreams to reality and serves as a fundamental first step in achieving positive results.

Sadly, today there are many people who enter their sixties and have not taken the time to do much, if anything, with their financial lives. Putting it off, procrastinating, and setting it aside have finally reached the period when reality hits; and they realize that they need to do something, anything, quick before old age sets in. Fortunately, even this group of people has some options, just not as many as those who did their prudent planning and preparations. They can work hard at reducing their monthly expenses, such as paying off their house, credit cards, vehicles, and other large monthly payments. They can immediately start setting money aside for investments. They can begin eliminating some of the nice-to-have but unnecessary expenses, such as entertainment, going out to eat, trips, and vacations they have previously enjoyed; and most of all, they can start changing their mind-set and become more realistic about what they can and cannot afford to do instead of squandering each and every paycheck.

Some Final Thoughts

In the end, the ability to make sound, logical personal prosperity decisions is a learned behavior and can be obtained through education, research, and study. This is available at many classes, courses, workshops, and seminars today and is not something that is, unfortunately, taught in schools or at work. When considering prosperity education, make sure to remember to ask yourself these questions: What is the motivation behind the instruction? Are they trying to sell me something, or are they instead trying to educate me? By thinking more rationally or objectively, you can improve and achieve your level of prosperity-building success now and in the future. It is a process of insight and education that anyone can do with the proper tools and motivation.

All that is needed is willingness, commitment, and desire! After all, who is going to benefit from having a well thought-out personal prosperity plan in the long run, and who will be the one to enjoy the fruits of this labor?

CHAPTER 14

Constructing Your Own
Prosperity Success Story

In this chapter, you will learn about the following points:

- *Going from Prosperity to Posterity*
- *Building Your Foundation for Prosperity*
- *The Peace-of-Mind Factor in Personal Prosperity Planning*
- *A Unique Prosperity Perspective*
- *Documenting Your Success Through Personal Achievement Stories*
- *Why Write One?*
- *How to Write One?*
- *When to Write It?*
- *Other Uses For Your Story*
- *It Can Be a Rewarding Experience*
- *Putting a Face on Your Prosperity Plan*
- *Life Is Not Always Fair*
- *Prosperity Success in a Nutshell*
- *Remember: Prosperity Plans All Start With Goals and Objectives*
- *What Happens When You Miss the Target?*
- *Taking a Peek*
- *Prepare for Liftoff!*
- *What Will You Do Now?*
- *A Recap of the Knowledge Contained in This Book*
- *Some Final Tips*

It's a Wonderful Life
**It Really Is Possible with the Right Planning, Motivation,
Discipline, and Commitment to Do It!**

> *It's hard to somehow get to the top.*
> *It's even harder to be able to stay there.*
> —L. S.

Going from Prosperity to Sustainable Posterity

After developing a plan, applying self-discipline, making a few risks, and starting to apply the techniques and strategies, you've finally made it! You followed all the rules, took the risks, battled the adversaries, paid your taxes, raised your family, slew the dragons, paid the "overhead monster," and finally arrived. You have now reached a level of prosperity that few have imagined, much less achieved. You are at the point in your life when it's possible to kick back a little, take a trip or two, walk the dog more, and take in a round of golf without feeling guilty. Is it the ubiquitous end of the trail now, or is there anything else that you could or perhaps should be doing? What are some of the choices to carefully consider at this stage of your life? What will you do with your newfound time every day? What do you want to do now?

Building Your Foundation for Prosperity Brick By Brick

Your Personal Success Template

"Creating Your Long-Term Personal Financial Freedom Paradigm"

The following are some of the key steps in building a firm foundational prosperity base that will serve to get you off to a good prosperity start. The depth and size of virtually any foundation will determine the strength and height of the structure that it can withstand. Any building that is constructed on a weak or insufficient foundation will soon come tumbling down or might even implode. It takes patience and perseverance to accomplish build prosperity. By following each of the strategies below in priority order, you will be able to survive even the worst personal financial and life difficulties, including "earthquakes," "avalanches," and "tsunamis."

- *Proper choice of job/career/vocational work*
- *Proper selection of a life partner*

- *Develop a Personal Prosperity-Building Success Paradigm*
- *Create and fund a tax-deferred 401 (k)*
- *Decision to buy and not lease your vehicles*
- *Decision to buy and not rent your home*
- *Purchase of necessary insurance for protection*
- *Decision to consistently set aside 10 percent of your take-home earnings**
- *Fund a rainy day account equivalent to 10 percent of your annual earnings*
- *Commitment not to abuse credit cards. In fact, pay them off monthly*
- *Learn to live within your income*
- *Development of a lifelong tax strategy*
- *Establish a will and estate planning documents*
- *Live within your means*

*By doing this alone, you will be able to live off your investments when you retire in twenty-five to thirty years. It will also ensure that you will *never* run out of money and that your earnings will stay ahead of both inflation and deflation.

The Peace-of-Mind Factor in Personal Prosperity Planning

One of the least measureable results of creating an effective long-term prosperity-building plan is the peace-of-mind factor in accomplishing it. On one hand, it is hard to put a price tag on such an undertaking as this; yet it is significant when compared to some of the other, more qualifying aspects in accomplishing it. On the other hand, looking at it another way completely, perhaps the greatest benefit of all is that it provides solid evidence of the likelihood that you will, by carefully creating a master plan, achieve a greater degree of prosperity achievement by building such a preparatory undertaking. By constructing one, you can create a well-placed sense of security, a belief that you have done everything possible to ensure your future prosperity success. It is an especially good solution to many people's success-producing enigma, a reasonably simple method to achieve a worthwhile result with essentially only an investment of a little of your own time, effort, energy, and education in the process of building your plan. What could be more reasonable and affordable than that, particularly knowing the result? Unfortunately, as research shows, many people put such planning at the very bottom of their priority list and not at the top. For the average person, the willingness to develop and plan an effective prosperity plan is often overshadowed by a more compelling desire to get on to the next entertaining event in their life, such as the next golf game, the next vacation or long weekend, the next shopping trip, the next recently released movie, the next party of get-together, the next trend of technology, the next sporting event—the list is endless.

Although it is difficult to run specific experiments with your future prosperity success, the advantages to creating a suitable personal one should be quite obvious to each of you. The risk models for achieving higher levels of prosperity that are available have proven results; however, you must factor in the personal elements of discipline and commitment to accomplish many of them. When viewed in manner, the ultimate cost/benefit analysis appears to be extremely favorable in its undertaking. After all, waiting for prosperity to simply fall into your lap is a strategy, just not a very good one. All that can be said for the "fall in your lap" strategy is *good luck*! Research indicates that when people are not compelled to pay for the cost of their actions (or, in this case, inactions), they have little incentive to change their behaviors. *As it turns out, uncertainty of the future does come at a price.* Isn't it better to be able to accurately predict your personal prosperity future through a little careful planning now? After all, the best and most effective solutions to long-term issues should be both simple and cheap, shouldn't they? As the popular saying goes, "It is also true that an ounce of self-imposed prevention can, indeed, produce a pound (or more) of predictable cure."

Now take a moment to listen to the prosperity gods . . . They are all waiting to hear your response!

A Unique Prosperity Perspective

Each of us has an opportunity to build our version of a unique prosperity formula in our lives. A prosperity perspective can be a change in the way that we look at our personal opportunities for successes and/or failures in our way of doing things. They may often not be nearly as dramatic as lightning bolts or eureka moments, but they can be witnessed in even the smallest things that we do in our lives and careers every day. Many times, the tiniest alteration or change in doing something can have a major impact on the results. It can become a different path that we choose in life and one that can become increasingly more challenging and difficult *because each of us are, unfortunately, creatures of a few bad habits and behaviors that we need to work on and improve to bring us to higher levels of achievement and accomplishment.* Often, the ability to recognize and improve those bad behaviors can result in significant positive results over time.

When you think of the numerous of options and variables you have experienced in life from the time you were born through the many circumstances that you have lived through, you begin to realize how many positive changes there are to be able to improve your "odds in life" once you choose to recognize and accept each of them. Even more compelling is the fact that each of us has control over many of them. When you study many of your successes and failures, it is frequently a repetition of a singular positive habit done time after time that can make a tremendous impact on the eventual outcome of our lives. In the grand scheme of life as we know it, it is something that each of us shares as we journey through our earthly existence. Our pursuit of prosperity is an incentive to make the right decisions and take the right risks and chances and our ultimate personal motivation to do it better and well. It comes down to desire and commitment, and these two factors can often become the difference between *want and have* in our lives.

Documenting Your Successes Through Personal Achievement Stories
"Formalizing Your Prosperity Accomplishments"

Everyone likes rewards. It has been proven that each of us responds better when there is a formal reward system in place. It helps us achieve our goals and objectives and serves to create encouragement to keep moving forward. Even animals respond to rewards of praise and food (Pavlov's dogs were trained to respond to anticipated rewards). It is a fact that we all strive harder when there is a carrot at the end of the proverbial stick. Why then does a reward system that is created through a series of prosperity success stories also make good sense? The answer to this is that it really is effective and does work! By creatively composing individual prosperity success stories that document your individual prosperity successes, you lay the groundwork for establishing a personal bonus system that can become anything that you want it to be, from a long-sought material reward to something more intangible, such as gifting to others. How do you go about creating such a reward system? What is the process that you should use to identify the goals and objectives to calculate your successes and ambitions? What is the motivation that people use to do this?

Why Write One?

Documenting your significant personal prosperity achievement stories makes a lot of rational and emotional sense for the following reasons:

1. *It establishes a formula for future prosperity.*
2. *It documents the realities of your hard-earned efforts in accomplishing your successes.*
3. *It serves as a source for a useful "rewards program."*
4. *It becomes a confidence builder to maintain a successful lifestyle.*
5. *It provides the incentive to create more success.*
6. *It creates a legacy of prosperity achievement that can be used by other family members.*
7. *It is an important foundational document for estate planning purposes.*

The process of identifying personal prosperity success stories can potentially create a benchmark formula for a reasonable reward system for many investors. In accomplishing a fulfilling prosperity achievement, it is possible to set up a reward system that provides a useful method that not only documents your efforts but also serves to establish a "formula" or "template" for future efforts.

How to Write One

Creating your individual prosperity success stories is as simple as documenting the personal financial achievements using a predetermined formula of accomplishment. Often, this is done in a narrative format that is attached to a custom-created spreadsheet format that jointly results in a report that carefully explains the critical information contained. For example, a real estate property investment that was made for $50,000 increases to $100,000 because of improvements, upgrades, and basic appreciation, not to mention that the mortgage is paid off from rental proceeds. This property creates a positive cash flow for the investor and is a perfect instance of an investment success story, complete with many details. By taking 5 to 10 percent of the annual *net* cash flow (after expenses), you have successfully created a prosperity reward system for yourself. You can use this profit money for any personal reason or indulgence while allowing the investment to build in value and while carefully documenting how you did it for future use. Another instance of personal prosperity success stories includes the creation of a small business enterprise that possibly morphs over the years into a full-fledged "cash cow" income producer. In a similar fashion to the real estate example, the investor could take a percentage of the business net (after taxes) profits and use it as a personal reward system. Many entrepreneurs chose this for *exactly* this reason, to reward themselves and their families for the monumental efforts in achieving personal financial success via the business venture.

Still another option is via financial portfolio investing, such as stocks, mutual funds, bonds, notes, money market funds, and others. At the end of a given period, such as year-end, the annual appreciation for the gains or losses could be calculated; and a certain percentage of the gain (5–10 percent) could be rewarded to the investor as a reward bonus (taxable income). By using your prosperity success stories in this way, you carefully document your financial accomplishments and create a self-induced personal reward bonus program that will service to improve even future prosperity performance. You may even create a template that other family members may be interested in duplicating and following, giving you an additional benefit.

When to Write It

Prosperity success stories are one of those undertakings that will take a lot of careful thought, study, and deliberation at first. However, after you have created a useful template, it can easily be duplicated in the future. The best time to update, edit, refine, and add to it is during the year-end to summarize your prosperity achievement over the past year and also to lay the groundwork for the coming year. It is also an ideal time to be able to utilize your "rewards" and to show appreciation to those who have contributed to your prosperity success over the year. Once created, changes only involve a few easy key strokes to update the numbers and create new numbers.

Other Uses for Your Personal Story

Other uses for these prosperity success stories include documentation for lenders in establishing personal lines of credit, accountants and tax planners who can assist you in creating less taxable income, insurance providers who insure your assets, attorneys who defend your legal exposure, and estate planners who will study your "prosperity map" that you have created to improve your prosperity position. In the end, taking the time to create prosperity success stories is an enjoyable, exciting, entertaining, and fun project that should ideally be done over time, usually over a period of several months or more, using the right formula "ingredients."

Examples of some of *these essential ingredients include the following*:

- *Date and name of project or investment*
- *A brief description of the specific goal and objectives of the project*
- *The purpose of the project or investment*
- *A brief description of the project or investment*
- *The amount of start-up or "seed money" used in the project or investment*
- *The timetable or maturity of the project of investment*
- *The annual net returns of the project or investment*
- *A predetermination of the annual percentage rewarded to the investor*
- *Any and all other pertinent data that will define the project or investment*
- *A well-documented narrative for tax and accounting professionals*
- *As a source document for your entire prosperity team*

Once again, a good format to consider is to use descriptive narrative outlines and use all the information that is then attached to a spreadsheet, which will document the specific results. This can then be updated and used for year-to-year comparisons.

Why This Can Be Such a Rewarding Experience

In the end, documenting your prosperity success stories is a rewarding way for you, the investor, and your family to share the results of your prosperity-building and risk-embracing efforts. It also allows you to stay on track, make small adjustments, and create a final result that serves to back up your personal financial statement. Even further, this documentation will become a further source of motivation and encouragement to build higher and higher levels of personal prosperity and will become part of your prosperity legacy.

This will become a pragmatic approach to a highly personal and emotional issue in your personal prosperity while working as a major confidence booster and prosperity map of the future. As a note of caution, do not bemoan every failure as a large one. Don't insist on perfection. You will make mistakes and will err from time to time. When you lose confidence, you lose control of your prosperity. Never let your emotions totally overrule your mind. Finally, in the process of learning how to fish, don't make the mistake of trying to catch all of them. A specific example of such a success story is included for your reference at the end of the manual under Appendix B.

Putting a Face on Your Prosperity Plan
<<*Making It Personal*>>

Many of the readers of this book and educational series have come from a wide variety of backgrounds, occupations, and experiences that include literally everything from A to Z. Yet the goals, ambitions, and objectives are highly personal and uniquely individual for each of you. Your ultimate prosperity success formula is a result of your desire, determination, and discipline, along with your skills, talents, and prosperity education that you have developed by reading and studying this manual. As you have learned from your reading, prosperity is not an event; it is a lifelong process. By applying each one of the steps of your personal prosperity paradigm, you will have created the necessary framework to accomplish a high degree of prosperity in your life.

No two plans are identical. The plan for a schoolteacher will not be that of a farmer, a truck driver's plan will be different from the car salesperson, and a business executive's plan will differ from an assembly line worker's. However, all will have similarities that are included in this book. The common denominator will be the same—*improved prosperity success*. Your personal life contains many opportunities and challenges that are uniquely individual to your personal life situation. No one else has exactly the same situation as you do. As a result, your prosperity plan must include many of the adaptations, calibrations, and modifications that help you create *your personal plan*. In the end, your prosperity-building plan is *your* personal plan. Take ownership of the plan. Even after it is completed, pull it out of the file, drawer, security lockbox, binder, or briefcase or wherever you choose to store it. Continue to fine-tune the plan every once in a while. It is much easier to hit a target if you have it within the crosshairs of your scope.

That is the purpose of a finely tuned and carefully prepared prosperity plan.

It's True: Life Is Not Always Fair but Always Ends the Same

If life was truly fair, there would be a god of prosperity. Everyone would be required to submit their ideas, dreams, goals, and ambitions; and each would be granted an equal share of the "prosperity pie." You would be placed on a list and be notified once it's "your turn" to participate in the bounty. But life is not always fair. You find that you did not get the promotion or raise that you strongly feel that you deserved and needed. Your high-flying investments tanked during the latest recession. One of your adult children went through a bitterly contested divorce and moved back in with you, along with your grandchildren. Then you were the unsuccessful bidder on a big project that your business really needed to get you through the latest downturn.

Even all the efforts that you have made in planning and preparing do not mean that it is always going to somehow magically work out in the end. Sometimes stuff happens in life, and it is not always fair despite all your best efforts. Maybe that even means that it will even stay that way for a while. No matter what, there is no advantage in obsessing over it or even dwelling on it. The best thing that you can do is to get over any setback and go back to your prosperity plan drawing board, which you may have ignored and set aside during better times. It is time to pull out your plan and begin working on it again. It is a much more realistic solution to think that revisiting your prosperity plan will somehow, someway be able to get you over the setbacks, and it will get you eventually back on track. The road to personal financial success and long-term prosperity building is paved with many personal, career, and business tragedies for many people. Those who finally achieve success in the end quickly realize value and appreciate what it took to get them to the destination. Often, the answer to the issue of life being fair is simply put in the words of the fictitious television character Tony Soprano when he says, "Fegetabout it." Get on with things you know you can count on and that you have carefully documented in your prosperity planning.

Prosperity Success in a Nutshell

The true concept of building an effective, long-term, and significant personal prosperity plan can be a daunting experience for many individuals. In truth, there are hundreds of options, techniques, strategies, and formulas that can be used in this process as well as many mistakes that can be made. Here is a translation of the concept reduced to its most abbreviated form in ninety words or less. This is the concentrated version of how it works: *When you earn more than you consume, you create a surplus known as discretionary income. It is really simple arithmetic. This creates and becomes your investment capital. You can use this, along with borrowed money, if needed, to purchase investments, such as real estate and paper assets, or even to start a business enterprise. This investment capital grows and compounds over the years, along with the money that you are setting aside from your earning. At some point in the future, your investment money starts to earn money on its own.* This is how long-term, significant prosperity is created. It is a rather simple formula and the "secret sauce" in creating the right formula based on your own individual and unique situation.

REMEMBER: Prosperity Plans All Start with Goals and Objectives

At the heart of every prosperity plan are your goals, objectives, and ambitions. These are the result of your thoughts, dreams, and ideas. They are also accompanied by the financial numbers that represent the dollar value or cost of each of them. Without writing your goals and objectives down on paper, they only remain mere fantasies. What are the specific things that you value most in your life? Why are they important to you? What is the cost of them both in terms of monetary cost and effort? This may even be the first time that you have given much thought to doing this so take the necessary time to do it completely.

WHAT HAPPENS WHEN YOU *Miss the Target*?

Let's face it; no one hits the target each and every time. Even the best and most successful achievers have their share of misses, and near-misses that bring new reality to their scorecard. So what do you do when this occurs? How do you keep this minimized and keep your "shots" near the bulls-eye more often than not? What can you do to increase the likelihood that your ultimate successes will far outweigh your defeats? It's as important to develop a personal strategy to be able to pick yourself up and dust yourself off as it is to have a long-term set of goals and ambitions. For this reason, I am listing a few effective ways to be able to do this when it happens.

Here are a few tips to remember when you have fallen short of your target goals:

1. **LEARN FROM YOUR MISTAKES** – As the familiar saying goes, "Big achievers know that it is important to learn from your mistakes". This

is especially true today when the costs of failure as high, economically as well as emotionally.

2. **DON'T CONTINUE MAKING THE SAME KIND OF ERRORS** – It's okay to make errors – that's where we all grow and learn – but you should avoid at all costs making the same kinds of errors frequently. This can have disastrous results to your long-term success.

3. **LEARN FROM THE MISTAKES OTHERS MAKE** – You don't have to experience the actual problem to learn from it. The mistakes that others make in your career, business, or profession can serve as useful learning lessons to you.

4. **KEEP THE MISTAKES SMALL** – Try to avoid waiting too long to admit a mistake. This will keep each of your errors small enough to be dealt with at a reasonable cost. The expensive lessons are the ones that hurt you the most.

5. **KNOW WHEN TO SEEK HELP** – One of the signs of success in life is to know when to seek out the advice of someone that has "been there and done that" to be able to minimize the damage.

6. **CREATE BACKUP PLANS** – "Even the best laid plans of mice and men often go astray" so make sure that if there is a lot on the line that you have a good backup plan to put into effect the minute that it's needed.

7. **KNOW WHEN IT'S TIME TO RE-ADJUST** – Even if you have carefully thought out your entire plan and spend hours doing all the 'what-if's' to prevent failure, you should recognize when it's time to huddle and readjust your strategy. This is the single biggest cause of failure among success achievers.

8. **KEEP FOCUSED** – Don't make the further mistake of allowing your temporary set-back to destroy your macro focus. Be smart and learn to maintain your intensity and on the long-term of the success.

9. **THINK: MACRO PICTURE** – It's easy to experience that a failure of some sort will singularly destroy your future. When seen in the grand scheme of things, it will probably only create a short-term hurdle so you need to think about the macro picture more.

10. **FAILURE PRODUCES MORE KNOWLEDGE THAN SUCCESS** – It is a fact that you will learn more from your failures than from any of your successes. Think about it. When you have had a setback, most of us will take the time and examine the reasons why it happened and prepare a better plan for future projects. That's called experience and one of the rewards of failure.

You might as well face it now. There will be failures in your job, career, business, and professional life. There just isn't any way to get around it. It will happen many times in your life so you need to concentrate more on what to do when it happens than on trying to prevent it from occurring. What strategy that you are comfortable in using and that produces the most effective results for you is the one that you should apply in your rebounding to minimize the damages and keep you pointed in the right direction. Mistakes can be minimized but not avoided entirely.

Wisdom is what you get when you have experienced failure.

—L. S.

Taking a Peek

Who among us can ever forget the popular and entertaining television infomercials aired during the eighties and nineties hawking the infamous Ronco kitchen counter appliances featuring the huckster himself, Ron Popele. Popele made a literal fortune for himself and his company by touting every conceivable kitchen electrical appliance imaginable. He would never go to the next step in demonstrating the food preparation process without uttering his highly celebrated expression, "Now all you have to do is," as he was holding his hands up to the audience like an orchestra conductor, prompting them to join him in the famous chorus, "Simply set it and forget it!" We cannot, however, do this when it comes to your prosperity-building planning. Even after your preparations have morphed into a full-fledged prosperity plan, you need to look at it occasionally and even scrutinize it to ensure that it is satisfying your personal goals, objectives, and timetable. Taking a peek at your plan every so often once it is completed is the best method to make sure that you are staying on track.

During that review, you can edit, adjust, alter, change, or even recalibrate your overall plan by making needed modifications based on your continuing life situations, family changes, and environment that required needed improvements. The perfect place to do this is in a computer software program like Excel or Word, where your newly revised plan can be "saved as" with whatever term you want to access the plan later (Revised Prosperity Plan 12.12.10). By saving this plan, it allows you not only to keep the information for future use but also to revise the plan and keep each plan separately for year-to-year comparison. By taking the process a step further, adding charts and graphs, you can create a uniquely personal illustrated prosperity project. This is also the best place to perform many of the "what if" scenarios for those really important life goals and objectives to see what has to be done to accomplish each of them.

Just like when you are on a diet (frequently needed after using Popele's kitchen appliances for an extended period), you do not even need to weigh yourself every single day. The same holds true with your prosperity-building plan. Taking a peek at your results every few months is an effective technique after your plan has been created and in place for a while. It is here that you can apply the prosperity *rules of thumb*: (a) locate your destination, (b) plot your course, (c) maintain your direction, and (d) look at your blueprint from time to time. The next thing you know, you will arrive at your destination on time, intact, and with plenty of prosperity to share and enjoy.

Prepare for Liftoff! Welcome to Your Personal Prosperity Paradigm
<< Being Ready Feels Good >>

Many of us are familiar with the commonly used phrase "A feel-good feeling." Achieving a high level of personal prosperity building is one of those types of experiences. It is the attitude that you have carefully planned and prepared well, which means that you can anticipate a good result in the future. It is a deep down view that despite life's many ups and downs that frequently or unexpectedly appear, you have performed the necessary efforts to develop a secure success in your future life. The anxiety has disappeared, which is a result of not enough or improper preparations. It has instead been replaced with a warm sense of satisfaction in the knowledge and understanding that you have done much of the "right stuff." You and your loved ones will significantly benefit from your hard work in the future. Gone are the anxiousness and the stress of wondering if you have done enough.

You can relax a little now, even reward your efforts with a little personal indulgence. You deserve it because you have worked hard to create and achieve your prosperity.

Congratulations! Now you are ready! It is now time for your plan to take off like a rocket ship!

What Will You Do Now?

Your goal in reading and studying this book and material must always be the *personal application* of its knowledge and principles. It is necessary to put the emphasis on putting teaching and learning into practice because it is far too simple and easy for those who research, read, study, and discuss to follow only an intellectual approach to prosperity building as opposed to one of engaged participation. Frequently, people talk so much about the wonderful concepts and results of prosperity that they forget the reality and how each of the core principles must be exhibited and applied in their lives. It is a mistake to learn the strategies and techniques fail to implement them in your personal situation and to feel that just because you have learned the methods, you are somehow, someway automatically are living them too.

The key issue here is *not* what is *written* or *said* but what is *done*, not what is going to be *said* about it but rather what is going to be *done* about it that is so important. After finishing your study, learning how to apply the knowledge to your own unique personal situation is the only way to experience the positive effects in your life.

A Recap of the Knowledge Contained in This Book

If you paid attention to what I have tried to teach you, then practice what I taught you, then perfected what you learned, and then you are virtually assured of a highly successful personal prosperity in your life. The success traits must be followed in specific order for you to achieve your prosperity, and each of them is equally important since they build on one another. They are ever-evolving and interdependent in a wide variety of ways. Planning and preparation remain the critical ingredients that are consistent throughout the entire prosperity-building process. It is also a good idea to periodically get together with your family and write down your short-term (within one year) and long-term (over one year) goals and ambitions since they form the nucleus of your personal desires, motivations, and objectives. This process works best if you make separate lists and then compare them together to discuss and evaluate your thoughts. Creating an action plan for accomplishing each of the goals is another critical step toward long-term achievements.

Some of the specific issues and events that will help define each of them include family responsibilities, career events, living environment, retirement planning, health issues, and legacy considerations. The ability to take positive action with your life and future has a powerful effect in improving people. It will happen as long as you keep chipping away and developing each of your prosperity traits. Continually fine-tuning each of your goals will help you further achieve a successful result. *We hope that this book has given you the blueprint to make your decision making easier, eliminating problems along the way and making the journey better for you.*

Some Final Tips:

- ➢ *Stay focused at all times.*
- ➢ *Do not let any life events derail your progress.*
- ➢ *Remember that it is a journey, not a destination.*
- ➢ *Understand that the result is highly personal.*
- ➢ *Plan for the unexpected as well as the expected.*
- ➢ *Keep your sense of humor.*
- ➢ *Write your thoughts on paper and refer to them often.*
- ➢ *Do not forget to enjoy yourself along the way.*

What Happens Now?

Are you empowered to experience real prosperity momentum now? Have you got your planning and preparation together to live up to your aspirations? Does your personal prosperity paradigm seem to make sense? Does it create the level of comfort and happiness that you desire? Have you carefully created strategies and preparedness to produce the results you wanted? If so, your options are many. If not, maybe you need to simply tweak your plan a little and keep on plugging away at it. If you are almost there, don't give up! People often see the most results from the last few years of prosperity building, just like compounded investments. The secret is to keep right on doing what you have been doing and to follow your plan right up to the point where you are able to live with the long-term results of your efforts. Whatever the economic level of your results, the reality is that when you have reached this point in your journey, you can begin to start enjoying the fruits of your long-term plan and efforts. It is now time to begin kicking back a little, splurging some, taking that extended trip you have been thinking about, looking for that vacation home, and even supporting your favorite cause. You have finally arrived and have the necessary financial prosperity resources to do whatever you desire. You have now become *officially prosperous*!

In the end, who knows, you might just catch a case of the giggles after arriving at a pause in your journey! This is perhaps the moment in life when it seems that the future of your prosperity is no longer around the corner but at your doorstep!

Good luck and good prosperity to each of you!

By the way, it is okay to smile and pat yourself on the back!

APPENDIX A

**Details and Information About
the Prosperity Success Learning Center™**

Located in Gold Canyon, Arizona

Who We Are – What We Do

The Prosperity Success Institute® and Personal Development Programs® Learning Center is located in beautiful Gold Canyon, Arizona, thirty miles east of Greater Phoenix. It is the result of identifying the needs of many people who want to learn, develop, and create the necessary know-how expertise to be able to improve themselves and their personal prosperity in many areas, including the following:

- **Personal Finance**
- **Business Coaching**
- **Job/Career Success**
- **Real Estate Investing**

At the educational learning center and library, we teach unique yet effective techniques and strategies that are used in personal achievement through a series of weekly and monthly classes, courses, workshops, seminars, and one-on-one counseling. Our education takes place during the week, on weekends, and in the evening throughout the year. It is also available in three different levels of training, including basic, intermediate, and advanced learning levels.

Participants include people from all backgrounds, genders, education, ages, skills, talents, careers, ethnicity, and economic levels. We help them create the necessary life skills and trainings that will have a significant impact on their lives, families, occupations, and professions.

If you or someone you know is looking to improve themselves or are seeking help in any of these areas, please contact us at any of the following addresses and numbers:

(480) 983-3563   E-mail: larry.snow@me.com
Website: www.prosperitysuccessinstitute.com

Mail: 6499 S. King's Ranch Road, Suite #6, PMB 51, Gold Canyon, AZ 85118

Welcome to Prosperity School!

Prosperity Boundaries

Prosperity is bordered on the north by education,

on the east by desire,

on the west by discipline,

and on the south by opportunity.

North - *EDUCATION*

West - *DISCIPLINE*   **PROSPERITY**   **East - *DESIRE***

South - *OPPORTUNITY*

Learning the Four Ps

Passionate Pursuit of Personal Prosperity

***What You Need Is Nothing Short of Prosperity Precision Excellence.
So How Do You Do It? Like Many Things in
Life, Prosperity Success Is a Choice!***

How to Master the Principles of Prosperity Success:

1. **GET INSPIRED** – Discover what really motivates you and why. Explore and develop the passion for your achievements.

2. **CREATE EFFECTIVE GOALS** – Nothing will contribute to your prosperity success more than objectives and a measurement system of accomplishing them.

3. **START PLANNING** – It is going to take a lot of preparation and planning to create your personal formula, so the sooner you start, the sooner you benefit.

4. **FINE-TUNE YOUR FORMULA** – Don't be afraid to tweak your unique and personal formula from time to time based on needs, overall time horizon, and other relevant factors.

5. **JUST DO IT!** – Don't make the mistake of procrastination when it comes to building your prosperity success. The secret to creating it is to start putting it all together **today** instead of waiting until it's convenient.

Prosperity Rules for the Twenty-First Century

<< Your Keys to Hardwired Success >>

RULE #1 – The game of prosperity building is comprised of who is in debt to who and why.

RULE #2 – There is a large difference between risk and risky *(hint: undereducated and uninformed is risky).*

RULE #3 – Creating a short- and long-term prosperity plan is an attitude more than anything.

RULE #4 – An effective prosperity program has three basic components: 1) security, 2) comfort, and 3) results.

APPENDIX B

Examples of Prosperity Success
Stories and Other Templates

Pursuing the Great American Dream
<< *Prosperity Is Both Color and Culture Blind* >>

It is a well-known fact that many immigrants, including Asians, Europeans, Africans, Middle Easterners, Hispanics, Native Americans, and many others, have been able to achieve remarkable prosperity results after arriving in the United States. There is much well-documented research that has been written that reveals that there are indeed a great many reasons for their remarkable prosperity success. Many of them shared one basic theme: they came here because their parents or their grandparents knew that they had great opportunities in the United States of America. If they worked hard and didn't give up, they could do anything they wanted to do. And not only did they do it, but they also left a legacy to their sons and daughters.

Some of their successful traits include the following:

- *They have a high level of family and cultural support.*
- *They have a significant work ethic and often work two jobs when they get here.*
- *They have an overwhelming desire to improve themselves.*
- *They have an overriding entrepreneurial spirit for business building.*
- *They see opportunities everywhere instead of hurdles.*
- *They are emotionally as well as financially disciplined and pour money back into their business instead of wanting large incomes for themselves.*
- *They are highly family-focused and education-oriented.*
- *They have a high level of risk-taking ability and desire.*
- *They recognize the benefits of real estate ownership and small business investment and realize that both are key to long-term personal prosperity building.*
- *They have a hunger to succeed and a determination to better themselves.*
- *They are hard, willing workers who do what it takes to get a business or career off the ground.*
- *They are personal in their dealings with others and are good marketers of themselves when it comes to goods and services.*

Mama Mia Tecla   My family in early fifties   Mom in 1946

I know this firsthand because I came from a lower-middle-class immigrant family. My mother, Tecla Anna Adinolfi (Snow), came to America in 1946 and came across the Atlantic Ocean aboard ship on a thirty-day voyage at the tender age of only sixteen years old from Naples, Italy. This was shortly after World War II had ended, and she married my father, Homer Wesley Snow, whom she had met while working for the American Red Cross in Naples. *The story goes that she was serving coffee and donuts to the GIs stationed in Naples that day, and when he spotted her, he went through the line three times to be able to introduce himself to her!* They started seeing each other, and once he returned to Michigan, he sent for her. Her passage via ship took thirty days, and when she arrived in NYC in January, all her clothes were packed away in her trunk, which left her with only a sundress.

After establishing their home in the small town of Nashville, Michigan, in the south central part of the Lower Peninsula, they eventually sent for her mother, Rosa Roberti, who came to live with us for several years. Sadly, Grandma Roberti returned to Italy, saying that she was too old to adapt to American customs, but not before teaching all her grandchildren, including my brothers and sisters, how to speak Italian, her native tongue, and learn many of the Italian customs.

In addition, my father's high school chum, Frank (Porky) Purchis, who had served in World War II himself in India, married an Indian girl named Peggy. He also brought her to the United States, and together, they started a home plumbing business and raised their family of three children. Not surprisingly, she and my mother were able to become lifelong friends because of their immigrant cultural backgrounds and remained the best of friends until my mother's death in 1991. Peggy still survives, but Porky died in 2005, the same year as my father.

While I was in the marines in Vietnam in 1969, my eldest brother, Bob, who was drafted in the army, was sent to Korea (since the government would not allow two brothers to serve in wartime together and at the same time). While there, he met and married a native Korean, Yung Mi, whom he brought to America; and they settled in the South Central Michigan in the town of Hastings. Soon afterward, they sent for her younger brother, Doug, his American name, who was barely eighteen years old when he came to America, along with his mother. He saved his money by working two jobs for several years, and with my brother's help, he purchased a dry-cleaning business near downtown, and today he is the proud owner of several other entrepreneurial businesses. He enjoys a very comfortable lifestyle with his wife, who also immigrated here from Korea as well as his sister and her husband, also entrepreneurs who own businesses in Grand Rapids. My brother and his wife also started their own entrepreneurial business in Hastings, which is called Snowcraft, and has put all three of their children through college and supplemented their earnings over the years.

In addition, my youngest brother, Randy, and his wife, Darlynn, adopted a daughter from Korea at age two named Eden. She is now a beautiful, young Asian lady and—you guessed it—wants to start her own restaurant when she graduates from culinary school in a few years. In the meantime, she is learning everything she can about food management by working in a local fast-food franchise.

My wife, Kim, also comes from a family of immigrants and entrepreneurs. Her paternal grandparents, the Overmyers, emigrated here from Germany prior to World War II; and her maternal grandparents, the Forniers, emigrated here from France. Kim has related to me many stories of the struggles and hardships they endured in coming to the promised land of opportunity here in America. Kim's father, John, was also a business owner in South Bend, Indiana, who maintained an electrical supply business before successfully retiring.

As a result of this immigrant upbringing, I can testify to the resolve, determination, focus, and tenacity of this select group of people who have learned to call America "home." They all worked hard, paid their fair share of taxes, started businesses, raised their families, and grew their personal prosperity at an arguably higher level than many other domestic Americans who were born and raised here.

There are many other exciting and successful immigrant stories that exist in my immediate and extended family. Many of them own or have owned small businesses, such as convenience stores, retail stores, dry cleaners, supermarkets, manufacturing companies, supply businesses, service businesses, archery equipment, electrical supply, trucking, warehousing, equipment repair, leasing, and commercial real estate businesses. They have made many good investments in their lives, community, and church and provided for their families and sacrificed much to build a level of personal prosperity unmatched by many other Americans.

*This also begs this question: **Exactly why are they so successful?** The answer to that question should not surprise you at all. They each saw opportunities to better themselves and their families and had the wherewithal, the strength, and the courage and were willing to sacrifice temporary short-term pain to make their long-term dreams become a reality for their families and themselves.*

This is the reoccurring and quintessential American dream that occurs time after time with immigrants who see opportunity at every corner here, and they are prepared to take the risk and put forth the effort to achieve it.

A Personal Testimonial Statement from the Founder/Creator of the Prosperity Success Institute, Gold Canyon, Arizona

"I Don't Just Teach It, I Live It Too!"

My name is Larry Snow, and I am sixty-seven years old. For over forty years, I have been personally and actively been involved in developing a prosperity-building program that I call *the Circle of Competence Prosperity Concept®*.

For thirty of those years, I have owned and operated a logistical business operation located in both Elkhart, Indiana, and Phoenix, Arizona, consisting of trucking, warehousing, heavy-duty equipment, and commercial real estate enterprises. In the process of creating and developing each of them, I was able to build a substantial level of personal prosperity; and I was determined to share the method, the ways and the means, of doing it with others to help them in their achievements.

As a result of learning firsthand the processes, techniques, and formulas over the years, I made the decision at retirement in 2005 that my wife and I would create an *encore career* and would design, fund, and build a one-of-a-kind prosperity educational institute that we named *The Prosperity Success Institute™*, which is located at the foot of the beautiful Superstition Mountains in Gold Canyon, Arizona (thirty miles east from Downtown Phoenix). It is there that the subjects of personal finance, business entrepreneurism, job/career success training, and real estate investing are taught through various formats and education, including classes, courses, workshops, seminars, and one-on-one counseling in three levels of education: basic, intermediate, and advanced training.

This is an entirely unique educational prosperity-building program unlike any other available today and was created for the benefit of the participants for the common good and future prosperity for each of them. It has become my personal and passionate pursuit and one that has created a Christian-based formula for prosperity success for each of our participants.

Made in the USA
San Bernardino, CA
28 May 2017